"Whatever [Huang] ends up doing, you can be sure it won't look or sound like anything that's come before. A single, kinetic passage from *Fresh Off the Boat* on the age-old subject of reading Jonathan Swift is all you need to get that straight. . . . I'm pretty sure Shakespeare had the same idea, and Aristotle, too, and a lot of other people between them and Eddie Huang. But none of them set it on a basketball court, and that conceit . . . is his particular genius."
                                                                    —*Bookforum*

"Huang serves up a raw memoir recounting his life as an angry young man chafing under generations of stifling Chinese tradition and all-encompassing American 'whiteness.' Three things inform the multitalented restaurateur's identity: food, basketball and hip-hop. Although not necessarily in that order, each is infused in virtually every sentence, many of which are laugh-out-loud funny. . . . A unique voice with a provocative point of view."
                                                                    —*Kirkus Reviews*

"Brash, leading-edge, and unapologetically hip, Huang reconfigures the popular foodie memoir into something worthwhile and very memorable."
                                                                    —*Publishers Weekly* (starred review)

FRESH OFF THE BOAT

A MEMOIR

FRESH OFF THE BOAT

EDDIE HUANG

SPIEGEL & GRAU TRADE PAPERBACKS
NEW YORK

2015 Spiegel & Grau Trade Paperback Edition

Copyright © 2013 by Eddie Huang

All rights reserved.

Published in the United States by Spiegel & Grau,
an imprint of Random House, a division of
Penguin Random House LLC, New York.

SPIEGEL & GRAU and the HOUSE colophon are
registered trademarks of Penguin Random House LLC.

Originally published in hardcover in the United States by
Spiegel & Grau, an imprint of Random House,
a division of Penguin Random House LLC, in 2013.

LIBRARY OF CONGRESS CATALOGING-IN-PUBLICATION DATA
Huang, Eddie
Fresh off the boat: a memoir/Eddie Huang
p.   cm.
ISBN 978-0-8129-8853-6 (pbk)—
ISBN 978-0-679-64489-7 (eBook)
1. Huang, Eddie, 1982- 2. Restaurateurs—New York (State)—
New York—Biography. 3. Taiwanese Americans—Biography
4. Taiwanese Americans—Ethnic identity. 5. Lawyers—
New York (State)—New York—Biography. 6. New York (N.Y.)—Biography I. Title
TX910.5.H83A3 2013
647.95092—dc23
[B]   201202570

Printed in the United States of America on acid-free paper

www.spiegelandgrau.com

2 4 6 8 9 7 5 3 1

Book design by Barbara M. Bachman

TO EMERY, WHO LIVED IT,

AND EVAN, WHO BUILT IT

"CAN'T GET PAID AND THE EARTH THIS BIG?
YOU WORTHLESS KID."

—*Cam'ron*

"YEAH YEAH, I DESIGN THESE THINGS AND
YOU KNOW I'M IN THE HOOD LIKE CHINESE WINGS."

—*Jadakiss*

"DON'T BE AFRAID, FIGHT FOR IT."

—*Dad*

ONE

MEET THE PARENTS

"The soup dumplings are off today!" Grandpa said.

"Should we tell the waiter? We should send these back."

"No, no, no, no, no, don't lose face over soup dumplings. Just eat them."

My mom always wanted to send food back. Everything on the side, some things hot, some things cold, no MSG, less oil, more chilis, oh, and some vinegar please. Black vinegar with green chilis if you have it, if not, red vinegar with ginger, and if you don't have that, then just white vinegar by itself and a can of Coke, not diet because diet causes cancer.

Microwaves cause cancer, too, so she buys a Foreman grill and wears a SARS mask because "oil fumes can ruin lungs," says the woman who smokes Capri cigarettes and drives an SUV wearing a visor. That's my mom.

I couldn't eat with my mom; she drove me crazy. But she never bothered my grandfather. He was always above the trees. Like 3 Stacks said, "What's cooler than cool? Ice cold." That was Grandpa: a six-foot-tall, long faced, droopy-eyed Chinaman who subsisted on a cocktail of KFC, boiled peanuts, and cigarettes. Thinking back on it, my grandfather created the ultimate recipe for pancreatic cancer. At the time we had that lunch, he'd been battling it for a while, but we tried not to talk about it. That day, we just ate soup dumplings.

"It's the meat, did they not put enough ginger? *Mei you xiang wei dao.*"

"Eh, there's ginger, it's just heavy-handed. Who cares, just eat them! The rest of the food is on the way."

Xiang wei is the character a good dish has when it's robust, flavorful, and balanced but still maintains a certain light quality. That flavor comes, lingers on your tongue, stays long enough to make you crave it, but just when you think you have it figured out, it's gone. Timing is everything. Soup dumplings, sitcoms, one-night stands—good ones leave you wanting more.

The perfect soup dumpling has eighteen folds. Taipei's Din Tai Fung restaurant figured this out in the mid-eighties. While Americans had Pyrex visions, Taiwan was focused on soup dumplings. My grandparents on my father's side lived right on Yong Kang Jie, where Din Tai Fung was founded. To this day, it is the single most famous restaurant in Taipei, the crown jewel of the pound-for-pound greatest eating island in the world. Din Tai Fung started off as an oil retailer, but business took a dive in the early eighties and they did what any Taiwanese-Chinese person does when they need to get buckets. You break out the family recipe and go hammer. Din Tai Fung was like the Genco Olive Oil of Taipei. Undefeated.

The dough is where Din Tai Fung stays the hood champ. It's just strong enough to hold the soup once the gelatin melts, but if you pick it up by the knob and look closely at the skin, it's almost translucent. They create a light, airy texture for the skin that no one else has been able to duplicate. I remember going back to Din Tai Fung when I was twenty-seven and saying to myself, They're off! It's just not as satisfying as I remember it to be! But two hours later, walking around Taipei, all I could think about was their fucking soup dumplings. Across the street from Din Tai Fung was another restaurant that served soup dumplings and made a business of catching the spillover when people didn't want to wait an hour for a table. They were really close to the real deal. Like the first year Reebok had AI and you thought that maybe, just maybe, the Questions with the honeycomb would outsell Jordans. A false alarm.

Grandpa Huang put on for Yong Kang Jie and never cheated on the original. On the other hand, Grandpa Chiao, my mother's father, had money on his mind and really didn't have time for things like soup dumplings. He was the type of guy who would go across the street without thinking twice. He would be fully aware Din Tai Fung was better, but he was a businessman. He had things to do and never lost sight of them. Everything was calculated with my grandfather. On his desk, there was always this gold-plated abacus. Whenever something needed to be calculated, the other employees would use calculators, but Grandpa beat them to the punch every time. With his fingers on the abacus, he looked as slick as a three-card monte hustler. I loved hearing the sound: *tat, tat, tat, rap, tat, tat, tat*. After tapping the beads, he'd always reset them all with one downward stroke, *whap,* and out came the answer. He'd much rather save an hour, eat some perfectly fine soup dumplings, and go on his way.

Mom had other plans. She was my grandpa's youngest and loudest child. Mom claims she was his favorite, and I can't say I don't believe her. Grandpa loved her because she was entertaining and full of energy. As a kid, she took the Taiwanese national academic exam and got into all the best schools in Taipei. After she came to America as a seventeen-year-old, she managed to graduate as the salutatorian of her high school, even though she barely spoke English. On top of that, she's still the best cook in the family. My cousins love talking about things they don't know about and everyone claims their parents are the best, but even the aunts admit my mom goes hard in the paint.

That day, my uncle Joe from my dad's side was with us at Yi Ping Xiao Guan. I think he actually discovered the spot, because it was in Maryland, where he lived. Earlier that day, Grandpa had asked me where I wanted to go for my sixth birthday. He figured I'd say Chuck E. Cheese or McDonald's, but Momma didn't raise no fool. Chuck E. Cheese was for mouth breathers and kids with Velcro shoes. "I want to go where they have the best soup dumplings!"

"Where's that?"

"Even Uncle Joe knows! Yi Ping Xiao Guan."

I really liked Uncle Joe. He built three of the major bridges in D.C. and wore these big, thick black-rimmed glasses. I was into glasses, especially goggles, because Kareem wore them and he had the ill sky hook.

After we ate, I was kinda pissed with the shitty soup dumplings. It was my birthday! Yi Ping Xiao Guan, you can't come harder than this for the kid? Chuck E. Cheese can serve shitty food 'cause you get to smash moles and play Skee-Ball after lunch. But all you have are soup dumplings! How could you fuck this up? Yi Ping Xiao Guan was like Adam Morrison: your job is to slap Kobe's ass when the Lakers call time out. If you can't do that, shoot yourself. As I sat there, pissed off, I saw a waiter pouring off-brand soy sauce into the Wanjashan Soy Sauce bottles. Corner cutting, bootleg, off-brand-soy-pouring Chinamen!

"Mom! Mom!"

"Eddie, stop it, I'm talking to Grandpa. Talk to Uncle Joe!"

If someone was talking to Grandpa, you couldn't interrupt, but apples don't fall far from the tree. My mom was the youngest and never followed rules in the family. She enforced them on everyone else, but she never followed them herself.

"MOOOMMM! Listen!"

"Huang Xiao Wen!"

That was the signal. Black people use the government name when shit hits the fan, and my family would bust out the Chinese. It hurt my ears to hear the Chinese name. Not only did it seem louder and extra crunchy, but it usually meant you were about to get smacked the fuck up. Luckily, Uncle Joe was a nice guy who actually thought it was possible that a child might have something important to say.

"Uncle Joe, I know why the soup dumplings are bad."

"Really? Tell me!"

"Look over there: the waiter is putting the cheap soy sauce in the bottles. They must be using it in the dumplings, too."

"Genius! Genius! *Aya, Rei Hua, Rei Hua, zhu ge Xiao Wen tai cong ming le!*"

Rei Hua was my mother's Chinese name, so Uncle Joe got her attention when he used it.

"Eddie figured it out. They're using that cheap heavy soy sauce now. Look over there, he's putting it in all the bottles!"

"Oh my God! Too smart, too smart, I told you, this one is so smart!"

"Whatever, Mom, you never listen!"

"Shhh, shhh, shhh, don't ruin it for yourself. You did a good thing, just eat your food now."

I think my mom is manic, but Chinese people don't believe in psychologists. We just drink more tea when things go bad. Sometimes I agree; I think we're all overdiagnosed. Maybe that's just how we are, and people should leave us alone. My mom was entertaining! If you met my family, you'd prescribe Xanax for all of them, but then what? We'd be boring.

At any moment, I was around my younger brother, Emery, my aunts, my uncles, my cousins, or my parents. We ate together, went shopping together, and worked together. Sometimes five of them, sometimes twelve of them; on weekends, it was anyone's guess. We'd pick an aunt's house and you'd see a line of Cadillacs, Lincolns, and Toyotas form down the street.

Our family counted all the aunts and uncles from both sides as one team, so even if you were the oldest in your family, you might be second or third in the larger bracket. Got it? Good. So, #1 Aunt lived in Pittsburgh, where that side of the family had a furniture store. She would come down every once in a while with her kids and they were always friendly. We loved that side of the family because we saw them only three or four times a year. #2 Aunt was my mother's oldest sister and she made the best *ti-pang*: red cooked pork shoulder. Her husband, Gong Gong, was a really funny guy. He didn't speak English, so he'd always test my Chinese, check my biceps, shoulders, triceps, and then ask to arm wrestle. Gong Gong was a funny dude, bent over all his nephews, examining them like they were entries in a dog show.

#3 Uncle was my cousin Shupei's dad. I never spoke to him 'cause there were always fifty or sixty people in the house when he came, since it was a big event. He lived in Pittsburgh, had four kids, and they all traveled together in packs. It was awesome when they visited. Shupei and his cousin Schubert, cool dudes who played ice hockey and poker. They were also huge, the first six-foot-three Chinamen I'd ever seen. As a nine-year-old, I'd tell myself I had a chance at going NBA if I grew as tall as they did. Also, Shupei's wife was white, which gave me hope that I didn't have to date someone from Chinese school.

#4 Aunt was my mom's sister. She was crazy and, without any notice, she would say things like "Look how fat you are!" or "You are really stupid, do you know that?" As a kid, I stayed as far away as possible from her and her brother, Uncle Tai, because they were like Boogie Man and Bride of Boogie Man. As I got older though, #4 Aunt became a lot nicer and my brothers and I finally understood: it wasn't her. My mom was the one telling #4 Aunt about how me and my brothers were acting up. As a favor to my mom, she took on the role of enforcer. She was the first person in our family to figure out how to make cheesecake. For some reason, she had more interest in American food than the rest of us did. Ironically, she also made the best American Chinese food: fried rice.

Then came #5 Aunt, also called Aunt Beth; she was my cousin Allen's mom. Then came my cousin Phil's mom, who never took an American name. Next was my Uncle Tai and lastly was my mom, who everyone called "Xiao A-Yi"—Little Aunt. Phil, Allen, and their moms were my closest family.

Aunt Beth put out a good dinner when the family got together at her house on the weekends. It was balanced. Always two vegetables depending on what was in season—it could be *Xiao You Cai* or sautéed *kong-xin cai* (Chinese watercress, literally "hollow heart vegetable"), which is my favorite vegetable. She liked making tomato and eggs, plus some sort of shredded pork stir-fry with either cured tofu or beans, and chicken soup. Aunt Beth was a great host—she served a balanced meal, and let me watch sports before the older people took over the TV to sing karaoke.

I thought my cousin Allen was the coolest dude. He was three years older than me so he knew about everything just before I did. When we went to the mall, he showed me purple Girbaud jeans. He was the first to get a CD player and we always listened to Onyx's *Bacdafucup* together. If his mom had to pick him up from detention at school, I went to go get him, too. Sometimes he'd treat me like a burden, but I looked up to him. I was learning.

My other cousin Phillip was my best friend. He was only a year older than me, but he really took on the role of older cousin. He was the kindest person in the family and smart, too. He knew something about everything, but wasn't afraid of doing dumb shit, either. Our favorite thing to do was to watch WWF together on Saturday mornings at Aunt Beth's house, get hyped, and try out moves in the pool, where they'd body-slam me, causing me to immediately puke the tomato and eggs I'd just eaten into the water.

We fought a lot, made fun of each other constantly, but it was a good time. It was always chaos in the living room when our whole family came over, so Allen, Phillip, and I would retreat downstairs after dinner and play Tecmo Super Bowl or Mike Tyson's Punchout. We'd stay in the basement for hours and every once in a while, they'd send me up to get drinks and snacks. I'd go into the dining room, which was only separated from the living room by one step. A false divider. Although everyone else had gone to the living room for karaoke, one person always remained on the dining room level: Grandma. She'd sit there in her wheelchair and make birds out of Play-Doh. I'd come up to get drinks and see her alone, so I'd hang out with her for a minute. All of us would keep her company at one point or another in the night.

Grandma had bound feet. She couldn't walk, but in the house, she was always present, always watching, an anchor in the middle of the room. No one ever argued around Grandma and we all put on our best faces for her. We revered her, but we also pitied her. The uncles and aunts claimed her feet were "pretty" and that binding was just how things were done in the old days. If you went into Grandma's bedroom, you'd see her little shoes all lined up by her closet, and the Chinese people that visited were always saying nice things about them. Most of the shoes were silk and had intricate patterns or embroidery. Guests gushed over the stitching, but I thought the whole thing was gross. The little shoes ruined Grandma and I hated them.

We weren't supposed to see Grandma's feet, but I snuck into her room once when her nurse was washing them. They were deformed, mangled like potato roots. I was so angry—I couldn't believe they did that to Grandma. But she never complained. I would ask my mom, "Can we fix Grandma's feet?" She said no, but I didn't believe it. My grandma on my dad's side had her feet bound for a while, too, but luckily, her brother went to school outside China in the early 1900s and the first thing he did when he got back was unbind her feet. That grandma lived to 101 years old, did tai chi every morning at six, and got to live her life. I wanted that for this grandma, too. Without ever reading Audre Lorde or Teresa de Lauretis, I understood how shitty it was to be a Chinese woman and really felt bad for them, whether they were my aunts, Mulan, or Grandma. Especially Grandma.

In China during the war, the people had to stand in long lines for food and water. One day, this guy tried to cut the line and my grandpa jumped him. While they fought, Grandma got so nervous she had a brain aneurysm and nearly died. She lived through a lot but somehow always seemed content with the world. Grandpa, Uncle, Mom, Aunt Beth, they all had bad tempers. There was never a dull moment or a plate that lasted longer than three months. But even when people threw plates or staplers or bowls of rice at each other, Grandma stayed calm. She never stopped smiling. One of the best ways to stop the fights between my mom and Aunt Beth was to wheel my grandma into the room. Everyone was too embarrassed to argue in front of her. It was like putting a lid over the hot pot when Grandma came around. She didn't have to say anything. We all knew her story and if she could stay calm, we should, too.

My mother's father had six kids. After the Cultural Revolution, the family fled to Taipei. My grandma was pregnant with my mother at the time so my mother was the only one born there. M.I.T.—Made in Taiwan. My grandpa and grandma were broke and made a living selling mantou on the street, just like Kossar selling bialys or Schimmel selling knishes. The easiest way for Americans to make sense of Chinese history is to compare everything to Jewish history. There's an analogue for everything. Torah: *Analects*. Curly sideburns: long ponytails. Mantou: bagels. My family sold fresh mantou every morning. People would buy them on the way to work and eat them with hot soy milk. Back then, most didn't have money for meat so you just ate the bread alone.

Grandpa would bring the whole family out to do business together every day. The youngest daughters were charged with selling the mantou because pretty girls represented the best chance to close. There was a man from Hunan that would come by like clockwork. One day, he lingered and asked to speak to my grandpa. Turned out that he owned the only textile factory in Taipei at the time and he really liked our family. They were there on time, rain or shine, and the mantou were always hot. He respected the family hustle.

The family that was working for him at the textile factory hadn't shown up for an entire week. He needed new workers, so he offered to have my grandpa bring over the whole family and get to work. This was one call my grandpa didn't need the abacus for. As my family likes to tell it, they dropped the mantou on the street and went straight to the factory. They busted ass, learned the trade, and a few years later my grandpa opened his own factory. Eventually, he became one of the first Taiwanese millionaires. They ended up staying in Taiwan about seventeen years, then came to America and opened a furniture store, Better Homes, in northern Virginia. Why leave a country when you're on top? Whether it was another communist scare or the even greener pastures in America, no one ever gives me a straight answer. (The only thing anyone can agree on is that they still miss the island.)

WHEN I WASN'T in school, I was at Better Homes, in the office where all the aunts worked. Better Homes was a quintessential eighties mini-mall white box with a square glass front. Built to sell. I spent the first five years of my life handcuffed to a playpen in the middle of this mini-mall furniture-store office. Before I even knew about guns, I was trying to shoot myself.

Outside the office was the showroom, which is where the action was. I liked it. My mom was the only one of her sisters to go to college, where she trained as an interior designer. She had a big part in laying out the store and I thought she did a pretty good job as I toddled through the aisles.

When business was slow, I'd go around and test out the couches, poke the mattresses, and shake hands with customers. I was working. My mom would lose track of me most days so she'd come out to the showroom and shout my name.

"Eddie! Where are you?"

"Mom, I'm over here! Come sit in this chair."

"What are you talking about?"

"Please, relax, sit in this chair."

"Eddie, I'm busy, why do you want me to sit in this chair?"

"Just sit in the chair, Mom! I want to sell you something."

"You're crazy!" she'd say, laughing. "Why do you want to sell me something?"

"Because I'm a businessman!"

All day, I saw my dad or my grandpa sit with customers on couches or chairs, and within twenty minutes, cash was exchanging hands and furniture started moving. I wanted to be like them. They got to wear suits, customers loved them, and they didn't have to work in the white box. Grandpa had a big office separate from the aunts and so did my dad. I figured, if I could sell, I could escape.

I was too young to be a businessman, but Uncle Tai had a way out for me. One day, I was wandering around the sales floor looking for my dad, when I ran into Uncle Tai.

"Hey! What are you doing on the floor!"

Uncle Tai was always yelling at the kids.

"Looking for my dad."

"He's busy! Go back to the office."

"I don't want to go to the office, it's boring."

Most of the cousins didn't talk back to Uncle Tai. He was notorious for disciplining kids, but he knew not to touch my brother, Emery, and me. We were Louis Huang's kids, not his.

"Hmmm. Do me a favor, then. I need a pack of cigarettes, Marlboro Red."

I'd seen people get cigarettes before at the Sunoco next to Better Homes, and thought nothing about it.

MEET THE PARENTS   13

"Cool. Can I get a grape soda, too?"

"Yeah, if you get me the cigarettes, you can get a grape soda."

I was dumb excited. Grape soda was my shit! My favorite part was that you got Grimace lips after drinking a can of it. It was a sunny day outside and it must have been the summer. As soon as I opened the door, DMV* humidity just hit me in the face. I walked the 150 feet to Sunoco, got on my tippy-toes, knocked on the window, and waited for the attendant to get on the microphone.

Brrr. "Can I help you?"

I was barely tall enough to talk into the microphone, but I reached up, pressed the button, and just leaned toward it as I spoke.

"One pack of Marlboro Reds and a grape soda, please!"

Usually, the attendant would just grab your stuff and put it through the window, but he opened the door and came outside.

"Who asked you to get them cigarettes?"

I could tell something was wrong.

"No one. I like Marlboro Reds."

"You don't like Marlboro Reds. Who told you to get them?"

"No one."

He looked away and thought to himself. After a few seconds, he went back in the Sunoco, grabbed me a grape soda, held my hand, and walked me back to Better Homes. It didn't take a rocket scientist to deduce that the seven-year-old Chinese kid had wandered over from Better Homes and that it was Uncle Tai, the pack-a-day smoker, who sent me. We walked in the main doors of Better Homes hand in hand. I was nervous. I started drinking the soda. I knew I'd done something wrong, but he gave me a grape soda so I was a bit confused. Was it my last meal? Was I being poisoned? I stopped drinking the soda.

That's when he found Uncle Tai.

"You sent this kid to buy you fucking cigarettes!"

I remembered that word. My parents said it all the time right before someone would start throwing chopsticks.

* D.C., Maryland, Virginia

"So what? It's right next door, no big deal!"

"No big deal? This kid can't be seven years old and you want him buying cigarettes? The hell is wrong with you!"

After that, I stayed away from Uncle Tai. My dad never got along with him anyway. He was Grandpa's only son, but there was always an uneasiness because Pops worked more closely with Grandpa. In a lot of ways, Uncle Tai was Sonny to my father's Michael. (Still trying to figure out who Fredo was.)

One day at Better Homes, Grandma was coming to eat with us after work. I was really excited: we were going to this Vietnamese shack down the road. We rarely ate anything besides Chinese, Mexican, and Chesapeake Bay seafood. When we craved it, my mom would take us to Roy Rogers, but Grandpa had high cholesterol, so we tried to keep him away. This Vietnamese place was unstoppable. They did a lot of things well: spring rolls, summer rolls, pork chops, and crab patties.

From the outside, it looked like a crane literally had picked up this wooden shack from Hanoi and dropped it into the DMV. The front door was hanging by one hinge and the wood was weathered and cracking. As soon as you opened the door, you got hit by the smell of caramelized meat sizzling on the grill. Even at seven years old, I was obsessed with Vietnamese pork chops and quail. The combination of white meat, sugar, and fish sauce on the grill gave me the screw face every time. It was just fuckin' mean. Good food makes me want to hit a punching bag like, Dat's right motherfucker. You done did it there.

I liked this place because, even if I couldn't exactly describe it at the time, they clearly brined their meat. It was juicy, bursting, and flavorful, without being overly salty.

The temperature of the grill is also important. Some people think you should barbecue slow and low on a grill. I disagree. If you're going to do slow and low, do it with indirect heat in a smoker. The only time I like a grill is for high heat searing with brined meat: half-inch pork chop, get a nice seared crust, three minutes on each side, and serve it ready to burst. As soon as your fork touches the meat, it just gives.

Not only did this place have amazing pork chops, but they did quail, which most restaurants don't bother with anymore. It's not easy to do. Quail is a small, tender cut of meat and if not done right, it can get dry and sinewy very quickly. There's also a slight gaminess, but that's what I really loved about it. That, and picking the meat out of the bone crevices. Their quail had a very light marinade; they let the meat speak. Of course, there was lemongrass, sugar, and fish sauce, but little else. Maybe some garlic, but not enough to overpower anything. The flavor really came from the sugar caramelizing on the grill, the hint of lemongrass, and the essence of the fish sauce. I wish I could remember the name of the joint. Best Vietnamese I ever had.

My brothers liked the place, too. I have two brothers: Evan and Emery. Emery was born three years, six days after I was and Evan was born two years and seven months after Emery. Until the age of eight or nine, I really saw my brothers as having a single purpose: ordering things I'd like to try but didn't want to order for my main dish. They hated me at dinnertime. I'd tell them what to order, eat their food before I ate mine, and if I liked theirs better, I'd try to trade. My mom was the one who always complained.

"You are always eating Evan's food! Eat your own, Eddie."

"Yeah, he eats mine, too, Mom!"

"I know, Emery, everyone can see he's eating everyone else's food! His knees look like grapefruits."

"Whatever! You are cheap and don't order enough food, so I have to eat everyone else's."

My brothers both developed techniques to prevent me from bumming off their plates. Emery would poke me when I was trying to eat, or he would touch all his food with his hands so that I wouldn't want to eat it anymore. Evan, on the other hand, was a fucking momma's boy. He'd cry to my mom.

"Mooommm, this is my favorite food and Eddie keeps eating it!"

"Eddie! Stop eating his food, pi par tofu is his favorite!"

It worked every time. This asshole had so many favorites we lost track: pi par tofu, radish cake at dim sum, Yan Yan chocolate sticks. He was a genius and a snitch. But we still got him back.

One time my mom bought us Nickelodeon Gack and then left us alone for five hours. Bad idea. Gack was this nasty, goopy, dense, sticky green slime that had a consistency like warm Laffy Taffy. Emery and I would put little pieces of it in the carpet just to see if we could get it out, but we were left with polka-dot green carpet. After realizing the power of Gack, we decided to fuck Evan up. We wrestled him to the ground and put all the Gack in his hair. He started crying hysterically trying to get it out and pulled out mad hair in the process. This was before cellphones, so he couldn't call my mom. He thought he was going to die. It was great. But Mom did eventually come home.

"WHAT ARE YOU BOYS DOING?"

"Mom, they said they were going to 'fuck me up'!"

"No, we didn't, he fucked himself up."

"No one is fucking anyone! Who taught you to fuck people up? Did you put all this Gack in his hair?"

"YES, they did it, Mom!"

Emery and I were loving it. We knew we were going to get our asses kicked, but watching the snitch cry was the best. And as long as Evan had a headful of Gack, we knew Mom would be preoccupied.

We weren't happy for long.

Mom poked around at the Gack for a few minutes, went to the kitchen, and came back with a bottle of Heinz white vinegar. She took Evan to a bathtub and poured the vinegar over his head. Instantly the Gack started to bubble and dissolve.

"Oh, shit."

"Run."

Without even waiting for my mom, Emery and I took off up the stairs to his room. We always hid in his room. Even though I was the oldest, we liked hanging in Emery's room best. His room had more light, action figures, and goofy patterned furniture. We drew our master plans to escape on his desk, made forts on the floor, and went out on the roof through his window.

In those days, we were all about getting away. My parents got married young, after knowing each other for only three months and Mom had me when she was twenty. You know the deal. Mom likes to say we grew up together. When she had problems with Dad, we'd ride around in the car and she'd tell me all about it, even though I wanted nothing to do with it. I was seven; how was I supposed to play Dr. Phil?

"We're running away, Eddie!"

"To where, Mom?"

"Away from your dad! He's crazy."

"You always say that and we always go back home."

"This time is different. I'm not going back anymore."

"Emery and Evan are still there."

"Shut up!"

She knew she was going back.

My dad was a tough dude. Didn't waste a word. He was firm, smart, and pretty damn funny, too. The worst part for my mom was that when she wilded and tried to make fun of my dad, he had all the jokes. She was from the more suburban and sheltered part of Taipei so he called her *shambala* (country bumpkin) or a *fan tong* (rice bucket). He was a hilarious dick.

When they fought, we'd all lock ourselves in Emery's room. Evan would get scared, so we'd make forts and read comics. My mom only ever bought us three comics (*Uncanny X-Men #1, Punisher,* and *X-Factor*) so we just took turns reading them over and over. From those three comics we created our own characters, gave them special abilities, and then played out scenes from the worlds we created ourselves. The Punisher was my favorite, a bad dude with good intentions. Any means necessary to do the right thing. I liked that blurring of good and evil. At an early age I realized, like Black Star said, "Things ain't always what they may seem."

When I was only five, my mom got in a fight with my dad at dinner.

"You told me you'd take me to the mall!" she yelled at him. "You promised! You always break your promise!"

"I'm too fucking tired, OK! It's six o'clock. I don't want to go on the Beltway and fight traffic."

"Loser! You're a loser! Never keep a promise!"

Then he flipped the table. Food went flying everywhere. Plates broke. That's when Mom went Connie Corleone.

"Yeah, break all the plates! We have tons of money, just break the plates!" Dad screamed.

As Mom started kicking plates and Dad walked away, I picked up a pair of chopsticks. Held the shits tight.

"Mom . . ."

"What!?"

I showed her the chopsticks.

"I'll go fight traffic with you, Mom."

To this day, that's her favorite story. I was always ready.

SHORTLY AFTER THAT birthday dinner at Yi Ping Xiao Guan, my grandfather passed away. We knew it was a matter of time, but you're still never ready. My parents loaded us up in the car and we all had to wear suits. No one said a word. The limousines met at Grandma's house on a cold fall day. Gray skies, no breeze, just kind of frozen. It wasn't the cancer that killed Grandpa. He ended it in the basement. The illness was terminal; the pain was too much. My mother told me what happened, but none of the other cousins knew. I don't know why she told me, but there's no reason not to. I dealt with it. Quietly. And didn't speak a word of it to anyone, not even my brothers. I had a feeling my family would never be the same without Grandpa at the top. I remember when my grandma died years later, everyone was hysterical, crying, loudly mourning. With Grandpa, it was silence. I can't say why; maybe it had to do with the suicide. Or perhaps we knew he didn't want anyone to cry for him. He never really needed our sympathy. Or maybe everyone was worried about themselves. Mind on the money.

What happened after is "adult business." Suffice to say, primogeniture was alive and well in 1980s Chinese families. My father decided not to work for Uncle Tai managing the furniture store after Grandpa passed. My dad had loved Grandpa and he always says that Grandpa was his best friend. But Dad was a grown-ass man; he never would have taken orders from anybody but my grandpa. So when my grandpa passed, he went solo. Mom loved her family, but she understood why my dad struck out on his own. My dad opened up his own store in the Fair Oaks Mall. He became the first Thomasville furniture dealer in Virginia.

Coming over as a broke Taiwanese immigrant, he was really proud of himself and I was, too. He somehow saved up enough to get the shop going, but things went south quick. Within two years, the store folded and my dad left home. My parents were constantly fighting, because we had lost everything and the court froze our bank account. For a while, it looked like my parents might even get separated. It was one of the worst times in my life. Even as a seven-year-old, I knew exactly what was going on.

The winter of 1989 was the worst. My father decided to take a new chance to make it happen for himself in America. He left the DMV and went down south to Orlando with his friend Lao Zhou, where he got a job as a line cook at Steak 'n Ale and L&N Seafood. He wasn't really trying to kick off a career as a line cook. What he wanted to do was get into the restaurant business. He knew some people who would help him get on his feet, and restaurants were going up all over the place in Orlando. Landlords would give you a restaurant with no key money and three months free rent if you'd sign a lease. It was a theme-park and sunshine-fueled boomtown. After working a few weeks as a line cook, taking notes and watching how they set up the operation, my dad signed on his own spot: Atlantic Bay Seafood.

I couldn't believe it. One second we had a frozen bank account and no furniture store; the next, my dad had gone down south and he and Lao Zhou had a restaurant. Mom wasn't convinced by Dad's reports. She kept us back in Virginia while she went to go visit Dad, to make sure he really was a success. It was Thanksgiving weekend. #4 Aunt moved in to babysit us for the week and all we ate was Domino's Pizza every single day. For years after that, I didn't want to see another fucking Domino's Pizza box ever again. She wouldn't let us play video games and we weren't allowed to go outside or stay up past 9 P.M.

One night, I crept out of my room. I usually never did that, because we lived in a one-story house with a long hallway that looked like it had no end and I was scared of the dark. There was one night-light on the right side so I put one hand against the wall, held my breath, and walked toward the light. I got to the living room, turned on the television, and put it on mute so #4 Aunt wouldn't wake up. Surrounded by Domino's boxes, I watched the news and they kept talking about this wall coming down. On either side, people were going nuts. Some were banging on the wall, they were holding signs, others climbed on top of the wall. I saw families. I knew they were families, because they were embracing, hugging, crying. I figured they hadn't seen each other for a really long time and I started crying, too. I just wanted to see my dad.

2.

GOD HAS ASSHOLES
FOR CHILDREN

That spring, Dad came home and we were reunited. But before we could enjoy it, they dropped a bomb on us: we were moving to Florida. How could I be so dumb? Of course we were moving to Florida! Dad wasn't going to live there by himself forever, but it just never registered in my mind that I'd be going, too. It caught me and Emery totally by surprise. My mom might have told us that it was happening, but we still weren't ready for it. With two weeks left in the school year, we packed up the house over one weekend, and prepared to leave on Monday. I didn't want to go.

I still remember sitting in the back of our Starcraft van, parked at the top of Phil's driveway.

"We'll still be friends, Xiao Wen."*

"Yeah . . . but I'll be in Florida!"

"So what, we're cousins! My mom says we'll come visit."

* Xiao Wen was my original Chinese name. When I started getting in trouble around third grade, my parents went to a fortuneteller, who named me Xiao Tsen, and when it got really bad in middle school, I was reborn for the third time as Xiao Ming. But to this day, Phil calls me by my first name: Xiao Wen.

"I may get eaten by alligators by the time you come! Gators are everywhere in Florida."

"Hmmm, that's true. Remember to run in zigzags if you see one!"

Phil was smart and knew everything about animals. He told me that if an alligator had its mouth closed, you could put your hands around it and it wouldn't be strong enough to open again. Shortly after, my parents, aunts, brothers, and Allen came outside as well. The whole family was on the driveway to say goodbye. I really didn't want to leave, but then the van started to move. . . . Getting farther and farther, the people got smaller but I could still see Phil in the front waving me goodbye. I remember thinking their hands would stop waving, but they never did. All the way until they disappeared, you saw their hands waving in the air and then poof! They were gone . . . and there we were, just the five of us going down to Florida in a Starcraft van like the "Definition" video. "Hold your head when the beat drop, Y-O."

Two days later, we got to Florida late at night, groggy, and stinkin' from the ride. We pulled into the parking lot of this place called Homewood Suites; I liked it 'cause their logo was a duck. We usually stayed at Red Roof Inns, so I was pretty impressed with this place they called an extended-stay hotel. Emery and I walked around touching everything in the room, but my parents were tired so they made us shower and go to sleep.

We all woke up super-late the next day. It felt like we slept a year! Dad was already at work. The best part about Homewood Suites was that you could look outside and see the sign for Atlantic Bay Seafood and Grill. It was a monstrous neon sign you could see from the highway and follow all the way from the exit.

"Mom! Why does Dad do American food and not what you make at home?"

"Because nobody want to pay for REAL Chinese food."

"Why not?"

"Because they not Chinese! Stupid question! Your dad is smart, he has white chef so people don't know Chinese own Atlantic Bay and we can sell seafood for more!"

"Is Atlantic Bay like Chesapeake Bay?"

"Hmm, kind of!"

"Yeah? Do they have hush puppies?" I asked.

Before she could answer, Emery chimed in, too: "We can eat all we want since we own it, right? We don't have to have more aunts for more free kids meals anymore!"

"Yeaaahhh! I want fried cod and hush puppies with Tabasco!"

"OK, OK, you guys can eat all you want. Let's go see Dad."

"We don't need aunts anymore! We OWN the restaurant!"

Emery and I were dumb excited to see Atlantic Bay. It was huge! Three times bigger than our old house and they had cool uniforms: polo shirts with big blue and white stripes. But my dad wore a suit! We found him in the kitchen and it smelled so bad. It was the first time I'd been in a restaurant kitchen. The food smelled great, but there was this funky old mildewy smell that I'd never smelled before.

"Dad, why's it smell so bad? Isn't it supposed to smell good in a kitchen?"

"This is a restaurant! It smells like a . . . factory or industrial place because we have strong cleaning chemicals."

"It smells like a dirty dishwasher!"

"Well, the dishwasher is always going so you'll smell that, but this is just how restaurants are."

"Mom said it's like Chesapeake Bay. Do you have hush puppies?"

"No, but we have homemade biscuits! You'll like them."

Dad pulled a hot biscuit off a speed rack and handed it to me steaming hot. It had a good hard crust. It wasn't a super-flaky biscuit, but I broke it open and it was really moist on the inside. I took a bite and remember how distinct the flavor was. It had a sweetness that most biscuits didn't have. I wasn't going to forget about hush puppies anytime soon, but it wasn't bad. I found Emery hanging out by the fish tank at the front of the restaurant.

"Hey! We don't have hush puppies."

"Really?"

"Yeah, but we got biscuits!"

"Biscuits? Are they good?"

"Yeah, not bad. Kinda sweet, but good."

"OK, I guess that's cool."

"We don't own a Chesapeake Bay, but I think we have a Red Lobster . . . 'cause they have biscuits, too."

THAT SUMMER WE had no friends because school was over, but Mom dropped us off every morning at the Aquatic Center for swim camp, while she worked with my dad during the day. All the swim groups were named after Florida college teams so I was a Hurricane and Emery was a Gator. It was 1990, so I was pretty happy to be a 'Cane.* All summer, all we did was swim and wait for my mom to pick us up—and she was always late. We'd end up sitting outside the Aquatic Center in lawn chairs for at least an hour after camp was over every day. Luckily, there were lots of lizards around so we tried to catch them while Mom took her sweet-ass time. The months blended into each other and in August, they enrolled me at Bay Meadows Elementary.

The first day I got there, I recognized all the books. They were using the same books for third grade that we had for second grade in Virginia. These Florida kids were kinda slow, too. No one really asked questions in class and recess was pretty boring. We used to wrestle during recess and lunch at Oakton Elementary, but no one wrestled at Bay Meadows. This one kid with a birthmark played tetherball with himself every day, so I went to hang out with him. He was pretty good; every time he hit the ball, it wrapped around the pole at least three times. His name was Jared. I guess he was my friend, but he didn't talk much.

Unlike D.C., there weren't many Chinese kids around. The only one was a girl that spoke Chinese, who got moved to our class because she couldn't speak English. I was the only other person at school who spoke Chinese so I helped translate for her every day. My Chinese wasn't great, but I guess it was good enough because I won Student of the Month for helping her out. I never won anything before, but my parents ruined everything.

* Five words: RANDALL HILL SHOOT 'EM UP.

"Louis, we need to put him in private school."

"Ahhh, it's so expensive!"

"Eh! Don't be cheap, school is important! He never wins award in D.C. then all of a sudden he wins Student of the Month here! I don't want him to be like you with bad grades!"

"So? I own my own restaurant now! And he doesn't have bad grades. He's winning things here!"

My parents always insulted each other. Mom was a good student and thought school was important. Dad agreed even though he had a chip on his shoulder because he never got good grades. He learned most things from running around on the street, but in a funny way, my dad was smarter. He'd always tell me stories of old generals, emperors, and philosophers. My mom never remembered what she learned in school because she just memorized stuff for tests; it was my dad, who had bad grades, that actually remembered everything he learned. After arguing for a few weeks, my dad gave in and they pulled me out of Bay Meadows. That's when it all went down the shitter.

We rolled up to this joint and it looked like a compound—huge white buildings that looked like Decepticons, a skyscraper-sized cross on the front lawn, and minivans everywhere. This was my new school, Baptist soccer mom heaven. Pinks and pastels, ribbon sandals and croakies, oh my. First Academy went from kindergarten to twelfth grade but when I scanned the crowds streaming through the front doors, somehow Emery and I were the only Asian kids. I'm even counting Eurasia. Up north, even if you're the only chino in a working town, at least you got some Eastern Bloc homies from Poland or Russia, but down south it was you, yourself, and I.

Since kindergarten my parents had been sending me to Christian schools, where the teachers would feed me soap and made me use my right hand even though I'm a lefty, because we supposedly got a better education at parochial schools even if we weren't actually Christians. If you asked my parents, they'd say they were Buddhist. Buddhists that ate meat, never went to temple, but did say *A-mi-tuo-fuo* seven times if they saw roadkill. Religion wasn't a big deal in our house. I don't think it was a big deal in most Chinese households. We always had photos of ancestors, oranges, and incense in bowls, but the family unit was bigger than any religion, or government for that matter. Besides education, there weren't any social issues I remember my parents getting down for. I remember watching TV or listening to the radio; anytime there was crime, you could hear my parents in the background screaming "Where are the parents?" It was never about what you could do for your country or your country could do for you, but what were you going to do for your parents?

What we did do was go to Chinese school. Whether you lived in D.C., Ann Arbor, New York, or Orlando, if there were Chinese people, there were Chinese schools where you went every Sunday to take Chinese language and culture classes. Chinese people would drive hours from every direction to take their kids to school. All teachers were volunteers and the parents chipped in to keep it going. While the rest of America went to church, we learned how to read right to left.

WHEN I ENTERED the classroom at First Academy that first day, instead of math, science, or English books under my chair, I found *The Storybook Bible*. That blue one with photos of Joseph, Mary, and Big Baby Jesus* on the cover. I'd seen this version before; they ran commercials for it in the afternoons during *Wonder Woman* and *The Dukes of Hazzard*. For the first few days of school, all we did was read out of this book, starting from the beginning. The teacher was Ms. Truex, this tall white brunette that a lot of the kids and parents thought was cute, but I didn't get it—she was pasty, cold, and vanilla, a good look for ice cream, I guess. She kept telling us Adam and Eve were our "parents," so by Thursday, I had to say something.

"If Adam and Eve are my parents, then why does Cole have blond hair and I have straight black?"

"Eddie, that's a good question and the Tower of Babel will answer your questions about that."

* R.I.P. ODB.

"What happens in the tower?"

"We're not there yet, Eddie, so you'll just have to wait."

That was the end of the exchange. It all seemed pretty mild to me, but the whole class was shook. Thirty sets of eyeballs turned and ice-grilled me as if I'd just taken my book to the front of the class and set it on fire. Three days in and no one wanted to hang with me. We kept reading the Bible, but from then on every time I challenged a story that didn't make sense to me—how the universe was created in six days, why Cain killed Abel, how fucking big was that ark?—Ms. Truex put me in time-out. By the time Christmas came around, while all the other kids made cards, she had me sit in a corner and face the wall because I wasn't a "believer."

The time-outs were worse than that time Optimus Prime died in the first twenty minutes of *Transformers,* so I gave up. I waved the white flag and asked Ms. Truex what I needed to do to be like everyone else. She told me that if I wanted to participate in class and go to Heaven, I had to "let Jesus into my heart." So for the first time in my life, I sold out. One winter day, just after Christmas break, Ms. Truex asked me to stay late. The classroom emptied out until it was just me and her. I didn't know what to expect, but I didn't care. I just wanted to be down.

Ms. Truex walked behind her desk and broke out her Bible. I remember that Bible. Black, leather-bound, King James Version. She asked me to come to the front of the class and sit in one of those Kentucky-Taco-Hut school chairs. You know the joints with the desk, chair, and basket in one? Then she told me to repeat after her, "God almighty, I let you into my heart and believe that you sent your only son to forgive me of my sins."

She looked down at me with a smile and prompted me with a nod to repeat it. I was ready to sell out but was stuck between wanting to laugh and wanting to run screaming for my mom. It was creepy, like playing "Bloody Mary." I don't think people realize how fucking weird Christianity is if you're not raised around it. But, hey, it got me off time-out. And, who knows, maybe a billion white people can't be wrong and it's all really true.

When I told Emery what I did, he laughed.

"Ha, ha, you 'let God into your heart'?"

"Yeah, man, it's a good deal! You gotta do it, too, or we can't hang out after we die."

"But you don't believe it!"

"So? If God is real, you should let him in just in case. If it's real and you didn't, then you go to Hell. It only takes two minutes!"

"But if God is real, then doesn't he know you don't reaaaallllyyy believe?"

"Well, I'll convince myself."

"You can't convince yourself! You either believe or you don't believe."

"People can be convinced of anything! We're stupid. Plus, this is like those lottery tickets Mom buys. We know she's not gonna win but just in case, naw mean?"

"You and Mom . . . crazy ideas all the time."

My conversion only got me so far with these Christians. Months into the school year I made one friend: Chris Nostro. Peep the last name, you already know. His pops owned a pizza shop and he had the biggest schnoz you've ever seen. We became friends betting on sports, specifically the 1991 NBA All-Star Game. I remember coming to school the day after the game.

"Man, did you see the end of that game?" Chris said.

The other kids didn't know what he was talking about, but I did.

"The All-Star Game?"

"Yeah! I bet on the West but Karl Malone ruined it!"

"You should have won; Kevin Johnson's shot was going in!"

"I know! I lost five bucks! Stupid Karl Malone!"

I mean, come on, who *does* like Karl Malone? Karl Malone doesn't like Karl Malone!

Even though I made a friend in Chris, the other kids avoided me like spinach. When we'd get together to ball after school the kids, led by this older boy named Blake, elbowed me whenever I tried to get rebounds or pushed me to the ground when I tried to drive the lane. I'm not going to say it's just because I'm Chinese, but it didn't happen to anyone else. I didn't fight it—I was outnumbered. My mom would pick me up after school and see the bruises on my face from the elbows or cuts on my arms from the hard fouls and trips. Soon she'd seen enough.

"What is going on? Why you have the bruise?"

"It's just basketball, Mom."

"No, not basketball! Michael Qiao dan* does not have bruise like this."

"That's 'cause he's black, Mom. It doesn't show up."

"You lie to me, who hit you?"

"Mom, no one hit me, this is just what happens."

"If you don't tell me, you don't play basketball!"

I had to tell the truth. I was getting picked on, but I didn't know what to do. When Mom told Dad, he told me he wouldn't be mad if I got in trouble for fighting, but no one in our family ever went down without a fight and I wasn't going to be the first. The dude didn't give me no blueprint; he just told me not to lose! What my parents didn't understand was that it wasn't just basketball. I was miserable every hour outside the house.

I kept coming home with infractions, for asking questions or drinking milk through my nose, so she had to have a parent-teacher conference with Ms. Truex. Mom came to school one Friday afternoon to pick me up and spoke to Ms. Truex alone while I sat outside. I couldn't hear what they talked about, but I could hear my mom raise her voice every few minutes to defend me, saying things like "He comes home with bruise every day! You complain but who protects him?" I remember watching other Asian parents in D.C., whether it was at the grocery store, school, or the mall, get yelled at and picked on by white people, but my mom always spoke up. She wasn't scared. She would haggle, honk her horn in traffic, push people out of the way if they tried to cut us in line. It was really funny. Mom wasn't even five feet tall but she was tough. Even when she had parent-teacher conferences, I wasn't scared if my grades were good, because that's all she cared about.

"This bitch is an idiot."

"I told you, Mom! Everyone thinks she's pretty, too."

* That's how you spell "Jordan" in Chinglish. His nickname was Kong Zhong Fei Ren = Mid-Air Flying Man.

"Pretty? Boring and so slooooow. Take forever to talk to her, talk, talk, talk, all garbage. I tell her get to the point!"

"What'd she say?"

"She say you ask weird questions, but I say you're student, you supposed to ask! Her job to answer! I say you're lazy, if student ask, you answer!"

"Yeah! She told me my real great-grandparents are these white people named Adam and Eve!"

"Bullshit! But hey, Xiao Wen, be smart. Why you argue with her about that? You know they believe this stuff, just let them believe."

"But she told me I was going to Hell if I didn't believe and told me to ask God into my heart!"

"Ha, ha, yeah, she told me, too, think she do something sooo good to help you. Whatever. You know it's lies, let those idiots believe. Just focus on *real* school. Don't be stupid and fight them, you'll lose."

Mom was smart. I stopped questioning Ms. Truex about God—but lunch was still a problem. Every day, I got sent to school with Chinese lunch. Some days it was tomato and eggs over fried rice, others it was braised beef and carrots with Chinese broccoli, but every day it smelled like shit. I'd open up the Igloo lunchbox and a stale moist air would waft up with weak traces of soy sauce, peanut oil, and scallions. I didn't care about the smell, since it was all I knew, but no one wanted to sit with the stinky kid. Even if they didn't sit with me, they'd stand across the room pointing at me with their noses pinched, eyes pulled back, telling ching-chong jokes. It was embarrassing so I asked Mom to start packing me some white people food.

"What do white people bring to lunch?"

"Like sandwiches, chips, and juice boxes. Everyone likes Capri Sun, Mom!"

"Ohhh, the foil drink? That's expensive!"

"Mom, it's worth it! Everyone says it's really good."

"What's wrong with your soy milk? You always like soy milk."

"It's different at school, people laugh at you! My stomach hurts when I eat 'cause I get mad."

It was true, my stomach would cramp into angry knots when those kids clowned me. It got extra shitty when show-and-tell came around. My parents didn't want to spend money on show-and-tell, so Mom's idea was to bring something exotic for lunch and kill two birds with one stone. That day, I walked to the front of the room knowing I was about to give the wackest presentation any third grader had ever seen. I opened my lunchbox and took out a plastic container of seaweed salad.

"For show-and-tell today, I brought seaweed salad."

"Eeeewww! What's seaweed!"

"It's like spinach but from the bottom of the ocean."

"Gross! I would never eat that."

"If it's on the bottom that means sharks poop on it!"

"Sharks don't poop on seaweed! It's really good for you and tasty."

"No, it's not, you eat shark poop!"

The teacher jumped in to stop the other kids, but I had no comebacks. I just went back to my chair and ate my seaweed salad. My mom saw that the relentless food shaming was getting to me and gave in. I loved my mom. We didn't have much back then, but she always did everything she could to get us what we wanted. I remember being at Chinese school hearing all the kids complain that their parents wouldn't buy them toys, new clothes, or McDonald's. Some kids really wanted to be white. I joined in and told jokes about my parents, but I knew they tried hard and that was enough for me. OK, I'd admit that it seemed a lot nicer to be white, but I liked my parents! I was OK without Ninja Turtles and McRibs; I just didn't want any more stinky Chinese lunch. That night, instead of going to Dong-a Trading or Hong Kong Supermarket for groceries, she took me to Gooding's and Publix. We walked the polished, halogen-lighted, air-conditioned aisles looking for lunch stuff. She really cared that I ate well and didn't want to just pack me sandwiches and sugary drinks.

"I like this penguin, Mom!"

"Ha, ha, you always like penguins or pandas."

"Yeah, they have cool colors and waddle around. They're friendly."

"OK, let's see, what is in this meal? Chicken nuggets, peas, mashed potatoes. What is this called?"

"Kid Cuisine!"

After the nutritional information panel met with her approval, Mom loaded up the cart with Kid Cuisines and Juicy Juices.

The next day at school I couldn't wait to break for lunch. There was a microwave oven in our classroom and every day a few kids would take their lunches and get in line. I proudly pulled out my Kid Cuisine, still cold in my hand, penguins grinning, and got in line. I was third in line so I wouldn't have to wait too long.

There was one black kid in our class, Edgar. He had the same trouble I did: he was a loner without many friends. But he was Christian, so at least that was going for him. I was still the buffer between him and the bottom. He lined up behind me.

The two people in front of us were taking too long. Why were they taking so long? What are they doing up there? I stood waiting as our lunch period ticked away; I felt Edgar's mouth-breathing ass creeping behind me. By the time I finally got up to the microwave, there were only fifteen or twenty minutes left for lunch. I was getting ready to pop open the oven door when Edgar grabbed me by my shirt and threw me to the ground.

"Chinks get to the back!"

I looked up from the ground, dumbfounded.

My dad had told me about the word, and what it meant, but you're never ready for your first time. It just fucking happens. I waited for Ms. Truex to get involved but she just sat on her fat ass eating lunch like David Stern watching the Malice at the Palace.

Finally, something went off in me. I was nine years old, and I called 'nuff. I jumped up from the floor and went right at Edgar. The boy was bird-chested. I grabbed his arm and threw it in the microwave. With my other hand I grabbed the door and slammed it on his arm as hard as I could. I wanted to kill him. I don't know if I broke his arm, but he slumped to the floor crying. I stood over him like Ali and wouldn't back off. I went to kick him and that's when Ms. Truex finally got involved. She shouted over to another one of the students, the kid named Cole.

"Cole! Help!"

"Yes, Ms. Truex!"

"Cole, you take Eddie to the principal's office. Take Chris with you to be safe! I'll take Edgar to the nurse."

"He hit me first and called me a chink!"

"Eddie, you are in enough trouble! You go straight to the office with Cole and Chris."

"Eddie, just go to the office, man . . ."

I walked down the hallway with Cole and Chris flanking me; I was shaking the whole time. I didn't know why. I wasn't scared of the principal or Edgar, but something was wrong. I was shaking like crazy and couldn't even keep my hand still. We got to the principal and I started crying. Cole told him what happened and I was so shook I couldn't speak. The principal took away my lunch, locked me in a walk-in closet, and wouldn't even let me out to go to the bathroom. When my mom came to pick me up, they pried open the closet door to find a kid drenched in piss. Mom bugged the fuck out.

"You stupid ass! How do you do this to my son! He was hit first!"

"Mrs. Huang, your son was out of control today and severely injured another student."

"He called him a chink! You think that's OK? Words hurt, too. I hear you people say that words hurt like sticks! Look at him!"

My mom would always get sayings wrong, but they knew what she meant. I was never happier to see her. Every day I went to this bullshit school alone and no one ever had my back besides my mom. But despite her best efforts, I was never the same. She always talks about how I was a happy kid, deep-thinking, liked to read books, and didn't bother with drama. Even when other kids in the neighborhood got caught up, I'd just shoot hoops, ride my bike, or listen to music. I tried to fit in and get along, but people weren't havin' it. Edgar forced me into my William Wallace moment. From that day forward, I promised that I would be the trouble in my life. I wouldn't wait for people to pick on me or back me into a corner. Whether it was race, height, weight, or my personality that people didn't like, it was now their fucking problem. If anyone said anything to me, I'd go back at them harder, and if that didn't work, too bad for them: I'd catch them outside after school.

WHEN MY DAD got home, he took the whole family out for dinner as if he'd been waiting for this day. I couldn't believe it. He was prepared. We all piled in his Lincoln Town Car and went for a ride over to Chinese Choo-Choo's fast food on Orange Blossom Trail. My dad told me a story about when he was a bartender at my uncle's restaurant. These customers ordered a martini straight up so he went to pick it up at the bar. There wasn't a garnish on the drink, though, and he couldn't remember whether it was supposed to get an olive or a cherry so he just put a cherry in, figuring it wasn't a big deal. When he finally got to the table, these assholes clowned him for being an FOB, so he came back and threw olives on the table, but he never forgot it. We weren't Americans like everyone else. We'd always be the other in this bullshit country. From that point on, he put me in kung fu classes, started sparring with me, and gave me a belt to wear to school. If anyone fucked with me, he said to use the belt. It was the most important thing my father ever gave me: A License to Ill. Things started to change.

When I played ball now, I emulated Charles Barkley. I was short, but I boxed people out, posted them on the block, and stuck my elbows out on pick-and-rolls. I went to five schools in seven years because I stayed in trouble: knocked a dude out in a parking lot, fought kids at the JCC playing ball, and hit a twenty-three-year-old dude at McDonald's with a bat when he broke my friend's hand in a fight.* Anyone who had something to say, I dealt with it. I was never proud of it. My psyche just clocked out that day and gave up. No more diplomacy. It's not OK for people to say "Ching Chong Eddie Huang" or squint their eyes at me. It was the most important decision I made in my life. China went through the Cultural Revolution and a lot of bad decisions by Mao, but you know what? That man expelled the barbarians and so did I: everybody out.

---

* When I was fifteen, we were hanging out at this McDonald's parking lot when these two guys in a Camaro rolled through. Both were twenty-three years old but liked the girls we were with so they started a fight with my boy, Lil' Cra. Cra got the first punch: cracked it on the guy's head and broke his hand. I had seen it happen from inside McDonald's so I ran out with a tee-ball bat and handled that. Readers, pay attention, if you tryin' to fuck people up, leave the baseball bat, bring the tee-ball stick, you'll always beat them to the kneecaps.

One interesting thing happened that year. A man called Master Wu came to Orlando, Florida, as part of a global tour. He was a chi gong master who also practiced Taoist face reading. I didn't understand the concepts, but he was revered. After Chinese school one night, the parents threw a big potluck dinner in his honor and everyone was invited. I remember wandering around with a party plate of food, huddling with Emery and Evan to avoid parents, when all of a sudden, he pointed toward me.

"This one! He has the face of an emperor! *Ta hwai jwo gwan!*" (He will be a public servant.)

I certainly didn't look like an emperor with half-chewed Taiwanese *mei fun* hanging out the side of my mouth.

"Hi."

"What is your name? Whose son is this?"

"Huang Xiao Ming. That's my mom."

I pointed toward my mom, and she'd never been that happy to claim me.

"He is my son!"

A few weeks later, Master Wu came to Atlantic Bay because he wanted to meet me. I'd never seen my parents that proud, and the best part was I didn't have to do anything for this guy to pick me out of a crowd like I was Kung-Fu Panda. He read my palms, checked out my face, talked to me about *chi,* and declared I surely had the face of an emperor. I was confused, but Emery had a great time with it.

"Ohhhhh, my brudder the emperor! Please, Huang Di, give me *Teenage Mutant Ninja Turtles* for SNES!"

"You will have all the Ninja Turtle games, my brother! I also give you Tibet!"

"Ha, ha, yes, Tibet is mine!"

"Hey, Mom, don't you think you should get us some more stuff? I'm going to be an emperor one day."

"Oh, shut up."

That year Louis Huang took the child emperor to his first NBA game. The Orlando Magic sucked. I thought their name was wack and there were mad cornballs on the team like Scott Skiles and Jeff Turner. They used to play this song on the radio making fun of the squad:

"Orlando Magic, they are so tragic, ooooohhhh watch out beware . . ."

But it was still fun to be at a game. My first game was Magic versus Warriors. The Warriors had Chris Mullin and Tim Hardaway and I loved Hardaway, but my dad was a sucker for the Magic. It was part of his "we're Orlandoans" campaign. The rest of the family hated Orlando. It was full of ass-backward transplants, bad food, and doo-doo basketball players. It was everything that sucked about the South with none of the benefits. People drove ride-on lawn mowers through their neighborhoods wearing Home Depot hats, but you couldn't find any decent barbecue within five counties. No Southern hospitality, just hot asphalt and suburban phoniness. All the ignorance, none of the sense.

We sat down for the game and every time Hardaway crossed someone over, fans would scream "double dribble" or something equally embarrassing. These fans had no basketball IQ; they didn't know about that UTEP Two-Step. Hardaway was breakin' fools off left and right; it was dope. But my dad insisted I cheer for the Magic. He came up with his own "cheer" and slick-talked me into doing it with him.

"Next time Chris Mullin gets the ball, yell, 'al-co-holic' and then stomp your feet."

"What's an alcoholic?"

"Chris Mullin is an alcoholic."

"OK, cool!"

He had the whole section screaming "al-co-holic." He was officially a brain-damaged Orlando resident, but at least he was having fun. My dad and I always watched *Married with Children* together and this was my Bud Bundy moment. Instead of beer and strippers, we had nachos and Run TMC. I really liked this Mullin guy: the man's jumper was wet and he had a flat top like me. I thought to myself, "I wouldn't mind being an alcoholic . . ."

When I changed schools the next year, to Park Maitland, another private school, this time ninety minutes from home, it was basketball that helped me make friends. A bunch of us collected basketball cards and read *Sports Illustrated for Kids* so we'd stay after school and trade cards and play ball. That year, the Magic were supposed to get the number-one pick and Shaq was coming out of LSU. We couldn't wait. Every day, we sat around after school thinking about what would happen if Shaq came to Orlando.

"Dude, we could beat the Bulls!"

"We'll never beat the Bulls!"

"We can beat anyone with Shaq! He breaks backboards, man!"

"We should get Shaq and then trade him for Charles Barkley. He's even better than Jordan."

"No way, man, Barkley stinks. He's so fat!"

My best friend was Jeff Miller. We both read the Encyclopedia Brown books and made up fake crimes to solve at school. We all loved Kris Kross and Hammer so we tried to rap. But all roads led back to Shaq and we bugged when we found out he rapped, too. We were obsessed. Teachers would try to ask us questions about science or math and we would answer back with news about Shaq coming to Orlando. It was an exciting time.

One day, Jeff invited me over to his house for a sleepover. I had never been to one before, but I always saw other kids going home with their friends at car pool and I was curious. He told me he had a Super Nintendo and tons of board games. I couldn't wait, because we didn't have shit at my house. My brothers and I shared three comics, two dinosaurs, and one copy of *Coming to America* between the three of us. There was one blue dinosaur that Emery and I both liked, and this big shitty orange dinosaur that neither of us wanted to play with. My kindest act as a brother was to let Emery play with the blue one. That was the apex of my accomplishments as a good older brother. I mean, damn, I ate all the kid's food, he should at least get the blue dinosaur.

Of course, I had to ask my mom for permission to go over to Jeff's house.

"What do his parents do?"

"Doctors."

"What kind?"

"Uhhh, anesthetic?"

"Anesthetic? I have not heard of this."

"Yeah, Jeff says he gives shots to people so they fall asleep before surgery."

"Hmm, let me call your aunt, she will know . . ."

After calling several of her sisters and friends, she figured it was a good job and approved.

"OK, you can go to Jeff's house. Me and Dad will drive you Saturday. Good job. You make a good friend."

My mom was pretty proud of herself. Her plan to have me rub elbows with the children of rich kids was working. From a young age, Mom made sure I was aware of money and how important it was. Everything revolved around money for her. School was important, but it was only a means to some ends. If you asked her why we came to America, she'd tell you straight up: cold hard motherfucking cash. Why else? We didn't like the food, people, culture, anything here. My dad "believed" in America, but my mom didn't. She just wanted the eggs.* I wasn't mad, though—I couldn't wait to play Super Nintendo and watch wrestling with Jeff. Every Saturday, WWF came on TV and my favorite wrestler was this big greasy Latino dude named Razor Ramon, who threw toothpicks, kicked sand in people's faces, and did the Razor's Edge. He'd put someone on his shoulders like a reverse cowgirl (pause) and then slam them down on their backs for the pin. I liked Jake the Snake, too—I did his signature move, the DDT, on Emery all the time—but Razor Ramon was my favorite. As a bonus, Jeff said we could practice the Razor's Edge on his little brother.

When the day finally came, my mom dropped me off.

"Hi! I'm Jessica. Are you Jeff's mom?"

"Yes, I'm Mrs. Miller. And you must be Eddie! It's so nice to meet you. Jeff talks about you every day."

"Yeah, hey, Jeff."

"Hey, man."

"Well, Jeff, go on ahead and take Eddie upstairs; you boys can play video games."

---

* What up, Woody? *Annie Hall* . . . you already know B.

We were so excited we ran upstairs to play games, but I could hear my mom from downstairs.

"Thank you so much for having Eddie over! We brought this for you."

My mom had brought a gift. She always brought gifts everywhere we went, usually some sort of dessert or a bottle of wine from the restaurant.

"Oh, thank you! Yes, we're very happy to have him over."

"He says your husband is a . . . uh, anesthetics?"

"Oh, you must mean anesthesiologist?"

"Yes, yes, he gives the shot, right?"

"Well, yeah, he gives people shots or treatment before they go into surgery."

"Ahhh, like the novocaine."

"Yeah, sort of like that."

"Oh, great! I know the novocaine! I get it all the time at the dentist."

"Well, that's, that's . . . fantastic."

"OK! Great. Well, I will see you tomorrow. We pick up Eddie around three?"

I mean, people loved my mom and all the parents said nice things, but I would just laugh my ass off inside listening to her try to show people she knew what was up. That novocaine shit had me rolling.

I walked up to Jeff's room—they called it a loft because it was upstairs and had a low ceiling; I couldn't believe my eyes. Everywhere you walked: toys, games, huge television, stuffed animals, it was like living in a Toys 'R' Us. I remember thinking to myself that if I died, I wanted to come back a white man. These fuckers had EVERYTHING. I didn't know what to play first, I was so confused. I literally rolled around in video games, read the instructions, looked at all the *GamePro* magazines, and then went to the bathroom and wiped my ass with their fancy toilet paper just to see how it felt. When you washed your hands, they had hand towels so you didn't have to wipe your face with the towel your brother wiped his balls with ten minutes ago. For real, if you are a broke-ass kid, you are wiping your face with your brother's balls. I felt like some wild gremlin child living in Chinese hell after going to their house.

By that point, I was ready to convert. I wanted to be white so fucking bad. But then dinner happened. All of us sat down. I had never eaten at a white person's house, but I just figured they ate pizza, hot dogs, or something like that. After a few minutes, Jeff's mom came out of the kitchen with two bowls. One bowl was filled with goopy orange stuff. For a second, I thought they might be little boiled intestines in an orange sauce, which I could get down with, but on closer inspection they were unlike any intestines I'd ever seen. The other bowl was gray and filled with a fibrous material mixed with bits of celery. I thought to myself, These white people like really mushy food.

She also gave us each two pieces of bread, the same plain Wonder Bread I saw at school. Jeff started wiping the gray stuff on the bread. I didn't want to come off like an idiot so I did the same thing. I put the other slice on top, lifted up, and went to take a bite, but holy shit, that smell. *What the fuck was in this?* Jeff and his brothers couldn't get enough but I was scared. I took a deep breath, clutched my orange juice, and forced myself to take a bite. Right on cue, gag reflex, boom went the orange juice. I couldn't hide it anymore. I had to ask.

"What is that, man?"

"You've never had tuna fish sandwiches?"

"No, never. Where do you get it?"

"At the grocery store, you want to see the can?"

"OK, but what's the orange stuff?"

"Macaroni and cheese."

"What's macaroni?"

"It's pasta."

I didn't know what pasta was, but was really starting to feel like a dumb-ass so I didn't ask. The shit was so nasty. We never ate cheese and it stunk like feet. A lot of Chinese people are lactose intolerant, so it's just not something we eat normally. We drink soy milk instead of cow's milk and stir-fry our noodles instead of covering them with cheese. I suddenly realized that converting to white wouldn't be easy, but still, that toilet paper was like silk. I tried to force myself to eat the macaroni and cheese but literally barfed it through my nose. Jeff and his brothers couldn't believe it. I realized no matter how many toys they had, I couldn't cross over. I'd much rather eat Chinese food and split the one good dinosaur with my brother. Macaroni is to Chinamen as water is to gremlins, teeth are to blow jobs, and Asian is to American. It just didn't fit.

3.

ROSETTA STONE

always liked sneakers. You had to look fresh playing ball, but I didn't have to have the illest pair. That is, until I saw what Chaz Crowfoot had on his feet that day. . . . I still remember creeping through the basketball court, and BAM! There they were and I could never go back to life without the knowledge that they existed: fire-red Jordan Vs with the lace locks. It was the first time I remember ever wanting to jack someone. The shits were so fresh, it was like having cars on your feet. That silver 3M tongue was dancing, light just bouncing off all angles, calling my name with the Jumpman in the middle. I had to have them.

Of course, my parents never bought us anything, but I thought maybe, just maybe, this one time, things would change. I went home that day on a mission. When I walked into the house, my mother was waiting and I seized the moment.

"Mom, I never ever ask for shoes," I started, figuring I should remind her of my silent sacrifices to date. "But I gotta get the Jordan Vs."

"Eh! I like Michael Qiao dan, how much are they?"

"I don't know, but everyone says they have them at Belz Outlet Mall."

"OK, we go after dinner."

"Really?"

"Yeah, after dinner!"

I thought to myself, I can't believe this, but I'll take it! The truth is, I probably should have started the "Please Buy Me Jordan Vs" tour about two months earlier, but I blocked out those thoughts and tried to run the two-minute drill. Whatever mind games I could play, I tried. I opened doors for everyone, I took out the garbage, I let Emery out of the car first. I swore to the god I didn't believe in that if I got those damn shoes I would do this forever.*

We pulled up to City Sports at the Belz Outlet Mall and didn't even have to look for them: there they were, visible from twenty feet away, in the right front window on a five-foot pedestal with two platforms. The white ones on top, black ones on bottom. 3M tongue *dancin'*. Even Emery and Evan were in awe. They were the hardest sneakers I'd ever seen. Hands down, all time, O.G. Jordan V Fire Reds no doubt, no question, illest pair of shoes ever made. The reason you love sneakers changes as you grow. Some people follow players and cop the signature shoe. In high school, it's a style thing. And when you get your first job, you buy every Jordan in sight just to make up for lost time or cheap parents. But when you're a ten-year-old, there's one reason you buy J's: to jump higher.

I hated Michael Jordan with a passion. I was a Barkley and Ewing and later on Chris Webber or AI fan, all day. But Jordan could jump over a backboard and was on his way to six rings, so it went without saying that he had the best technology in his shoes. The Jordans were packaged with these cards that would tell you about the materials with a level of seriousness that matched the Manhattan Project. Whether it was Spike's, Mars's, Phil's (Knight), or Jordan's fault I can't say, but we swore we could jump higher with J's. They were a rite of passage. I remember when my friends got Jordans we'd lower the hoop to seven feet and try to dunk. Every ten-year-old back then thought you needed the Jordans if you were gonna yam it someday. The shoes were literally your hopes and dreams in a box. My mom took one look at the shoes and she knew, too.

* Or at least until the VI's came out. Can I live?

"Hmm, that's a pretty shoe."

"It looks expensive," my father said.

"Dad, it's an investment! I can go to the NBA if you buy me these!"

"Ha, ha, man, you suck at basketball!"

"That's because you buy me shitty shoes!"

"No, it's because you're fat!"

I saw a sales rep standing around in the store so I asked him for a pair of size 7 Jordan Vs, but before he went off to the back, my dad had a question.

"How much are these shoes?"

Before it even started, it was over.

"A hundred dollars! No, no, no, no, no, that's too expensive."

"Dad, just let me try them on, you'll see, they're worth it!"

Of course, Emery had to chime in.

"A hundred dollars is crazy! We never buy anything for a hundred dollars!"

"Shut up, Emery!"

"Hey! Don't yell at your brother, now you definitely aren't getting those shoes!"

The sales rep didn't move. There would be no Jordan Vs that day. I didn't even get to try them on. But my dad walked over to the wall of shoes and found a pair of orange and white Air Force high-tops.

"Who wears these shoes?"

"Charles Barkley! They're only sixty-five dollars, too," said the sales rep.

"Hey, you love Charles Barkley, why don't you try these shoes."

"Dad, they're heavy! You can't jump in those shoes."

"Eh, these commercials are lies. No shoe is going to make you jump higher when you're this fat anyway."

This is how it always went. Before we even had a chance to believe in Santa Claus, my dad told us he was fake. Santa Claus, Jesus, the Tooth Fairy, and Jordan Vs never existed in our house. When I ran in after a touch football triumph and told them I'd play quarterback for the Redskins, they laughed at me. When they beat that dream out of me, I said I'd be a sportscaster on ESPN and I'll never forget what my father said:

"They'll never let someone with a face like you on television."

To this day, I wake up at times, look in the mirror, and just stare, obsessed with the idea that the person I am in my head is something entirely different than what everyone else sees. That the way I look will prevent me from doing the things I want; that there really are sneetches with stars and I'm not one of them. I touch my face, I feel my skin, I check my color every day, and I swear it all feels right. But then someone says something and that sense of security and identity is gone before I know it.

THAT SUMMER, MY cousin Allen came to visit from Virginia and he had on the new Bo Jacksons. I didn't understand. We were all the same family, we were all Chinese, why did he have stuff and we didn't? I don't think it was money, 'cause at the time, things were starting to come around at Atlantic Bay; Dad always wore nice suits to work but Emery and I wore his old hand-me-downs or Allen's old stuff that Aunt Beth gave us. Allen was three years older than me so he knew just about everything before I did, *and* he even had a white girlfriend. I really looked up to Allen, but he didn't like me because when we went to Taco Bell, Aunt Beth would get the family pack of tacos that had half soft tacos and half hard shell. We both liked the hard shells, but I was younger so Aunt Beth made Allen eat the soft ones.

I got to hang out with Allen a lot that summer. He had tons of jokes, made fun of everyone, and had the best cut-downs. Most of the time, he made fun of Emery, Phil, or me, but I didn't care—he was funny! He showed me my first *Sports Illustrated* Swimsuit Issue with Kathy Ireland in the artificial grass skirt by the artificial pool. One day toward the end of summer, he gave me something. A cassette tape. I put it in my deck, pressed play, and I'll never forget what came out the speakers.

"This is dedicated to the n!gg@s that was down since day one . . . [click clack] Welcome to Death Row."

It was *The Chronic* and, just like when I first spotted the Jordans, life would never be the same again. These rappers on the record talked like my parents when they were fighting, dropping words like "fuck," "bitch," and "shit," but they had new slang, too, like "eat a dick." I was all about this Chronic shit and didn't even know what it was.

"Yo, what is this, man?!?!"

"The Chronic."

"It sounds like rap, but not rap."

"It's rap, but it's hip-hop."

"What's the difference?"

"Hip-hop is that real shit. Rap is just . . . rap."

"Word . . . I like this hip-hop! You got more of it?"

"Yeah, *Doggystyle* comes out soon and I'll send it to you."

When I got *Doggystyle,* my dad took it away.

"What is this stuff? These dogs are having sex on the back! Who is this Doggy Dog?"

YOU'RE PROBABLY IMAGINING my dad as this maladjusted, socially inept FOB who didn't know what he was saying to me. He was just the opposite. At home, he'd walk around in his underwear and house sandals, but if he had a meeting out came the Jheri curl, gator shoes, and Cartier sunglasses. Dude was a smooth-talkin' motherfucker, who chose to come with the hammer. I didn't understand why he had to be such a dick. I didn't even really have to do anything serious. If I talked back to him, he'd step to me. I never backed down. I'd stand my ground, defend myself. But whether he was wrong or right, it usually ended in an ass-beating.

One time, we went to Busch Gardens. For half the day it was one of the best trips we'd ever been on as a family. We never liked going to Disney because the rides sucked, but Busch Gardens was like Six Flags in Tampa Bay—less about creating worlds around licensed properties and more about riding big-ass roller coasters. I was still crazy high and giddy from riding the Kumba and if there was ever a day I loved my dad, love in the form of sixty-dollar day passes, this was it. But, before that feeling stuck, he took us all into this medieval souvenir shop he found. The shop sold the most fucked-up souvenirs: they had replicas of weapons and torture items. I can't remember the names of everything, but the one that I'd end up seeing a lot was a three-foot-long leather whip. My dad saw the shit in a bin, picked it up, and turned to me and Emery:

"This is for the next time you cause trouble!"

It didn't end there. He kept walking around the store with a wild grin on his face and stopped in front of this hard, heavy, three-foot rubber alligator with skin dotted by sharp points on the scales. The rubber was hard, cold, and flexible. You could hold the head, whip the body back, and just come with it. He copped both. The whip wasn't so bad. He could get us from a distance with it, but it was light. Nothing more than a belt, really. But that alligator . . .

To Americans, this may seem sick, but to first- or second-generation Chinese, Korean, Jamaican, Dominican, Puerto Rican immigrants, whatever, if your parents are FOBs, this is just how it is. You don't talk about it, you can't escape it, and in a way it humbles you the rest of your life. There's something about crawling on the floor with your pops tracking you down by whip that grounds you as a human being. The bruises and puncture wounds from the scales of the alligator were clearly excessive, but I didn't think anything was wrong with my dad hitting us. Emery and I were troublemakers. Just like he was.

The thing my dad's employees, American friends, and associates didn't know is that my dad was a motherfucking G in Taiwan. His mother, my grandmother, was the daughter of a county mayor of Hunan in the last dynasty. She lived with us in Florida for a while and ended up hanging on until she was 101 years old. The last memory I have with her is hanging out in the hospital watching George Mason play Florida in the 2006 Final Four. At that point, she couldn't talk, and had bedsores, but my dad's family wasn't the type to be overly somber or pretentious. They were strong, sharp, independent thinkers, especially in comparison to the bougie Taiwanese women on my mom's side. My grandmother was already over 100. We knew she was old, we knew she wouldn't be here forever. So we watched the game.

My grandfather was in the Internal Ministry of Taiwan when Chiang Kai-shek first fled China. He spoke seven languages and was from Hunan, just like my grandmother. For those that don't know, Hunan produces revolutionaries out of proportion to its size. Mao and General Tso are both Hunan natives, which leads a lot of people to say it's the food that gives men from Hunan their "fiery" disposition. In Chinese culture, you are what your father is. My mother's family is from Shandong, but my father's from Hunan, so I am Hunanese.

Once when I was a kid, I had a meal of Wu Gin Tsang Wan, a spicy pig intestine casserole, with Uncle James, the second brother in my dad's family. On the lazy Susan on the dining room table, there was this metal bowl sitting on top of a Sterno keeping it hot. Inside the bowl were pig intestines, green onions, garlic, lots of chili oil, and pig's blood. Wu Gin Tsang Wan is one of my favorite dishes to eat over rice because the flavors—the spice, the herbs, the blood—seep into the rice really well.

"Hey, this little guy really likes the pig intestines, huh?"

"He eats anything. Look how fat he is!"

"Ha, ha, that's not nice, he's your son."

"Like he doesn't know. When he walks, it looks like he has an air conditioner for an ass."

I wasn't fat, they were just dicks. But my dad just loved telling the air conditioner joke and this time I didn't give a shit, I just kept eating pig intestines. But the Sterno was a little too hot and some pieces weren't coming loose from the casserole bowl. When I pulled at one piece with my chopsticks, I upset the bowl and a splash of hot chili oil flew into my eye. While I screamed in pain, my uncle pointed at me and laughed.

"Ha, ha, hey, Soosin, xiao Shandong ren yong yan jing ci la jiao!"

Translation: "Hey, Louis, look at the little Shandong kid eating chili with his eye!"

"Ha, ha, wan ba dan."

Translation: "Son of a bitch."

ANY TIME WE had trouble with chilis or hot sauce, they made fun of my mom's side of the family for being from Shandong. Whenever we lost our tempers, it was attributed to Hunan. I was proud to be a Hunan Ren because my grandfather is one of the most honorable people I've ever known.

I met him only once, as a month-old baby, but walked by his portrait and a scroll with his name on it every day on my way to my bedroom. That's what I love about Chinese homes: you're never allowed to forget where you came from. My grandfather had a highly respected position with the Internal Ministry involved with distributing land and resources when Chiang first installed his government in Taiwan, but he saw a lot of corruption. These days, many Wai Sheng Ren hold Chiang up high. My mom says that when Chiang died she cried for days, and that for the Chinese people of Taiwan it was like the Kennedy assassination. My dad's family was very liberal and saw another side. In his mid-thirties, with a promising political career ahead of him, my grandfather retired. He didn't agree with what was being done to the Taiwanese natives and, with corruption rampant, he felt isolated in the government. When he resigned, of course, it left the whole family broke. There aren't pensions in developing countries and my grandmother had a gambling problem, so what money they did have was lost over mah-jongg. This is probably the one time I'll ask you not to laugh at the fact that my family is a walking stereotype.

They all struggled after he retired, but it was worth it to maintain our family honor. Grandma might have liked the tiles a little too much, but she held it down, too. For a woman that came from royalty in Hunan, she stuck it out for my grandfather and took full advantage of the fact that her feet were unbound, courtesy of her foreign-educated brother. From a young age, that single event, my grandmother's unbinding, taught me to appreciate education and challenge conventions—just because everyone else is doing it, doesn't mean you shouldn't flip it over, look around, poke at its flaws, and see it for what it is yourself. I mean, damn, if my great-uncle wasn't a curious motherfucker, my grandma wouldn't have had feet.

My father was the youngest of the family and although he respected the family, he hated being broke. His older brothers had seen money, had been there when Grandpa was in the government, and understood the transition. Pops, on the other hand, was born into a small-ass house on Yong Kang Jie right by the original Din Tai Fung, which used to sell oil. He didn't pay attention in school, had horrible grades, and ran his neighborhood with one of the largest Taiwanese gangs. No one in his neighborhood fucked with him. I remember when I was thirteen, one Christmas Uncle Xiao Hei came to the crib and brought a gift.

"Soosin, it's been too long."

"I know, and you're still dark as hell."

Xiao Hei means "Little Black." My dad used to tell us stories about running his crew in Taiwan, but we never understood the full extent until Uncle Xiao Hei came to America. This dude had an ill scar on his face and was as dark as a Samoan. He most likely had to run the streets because Taiwanese look down on people with dark skin. I asked Uncle Xiao Hei how he knew my dad and he turned to me with a crooked smile: "Your dad? I carried his knife."

Uncle Xiao Hei finished his drink and got up to go to his car. Five minutes later, he came back with a big black bag that looked like a guitar case. He put it on the table for my pops and announced, "Merry Christmas." My dad tried to hide it, but I could see his eyes widen into a smile. He sent Evan and my mom into the next room, but Emery and I stayed. When Evan and my mom were gone, he closed the door and walked back to the table, rubbing his hands. He unzipped the bag and flipped it open and *pow*: an all-black gun, the biggest one I'd ever seen. Dad used to fuck around while we were watching cartoons and just cock the shit on Emery and me.

"Click, clack, GOT YOU!"

Pops was fucking crazy. He never did it when his white friends were around, but when his old homies from Taiwan came, they were all checking out each other's ratchets and knives. Just like my friends collected basketball cards, these dudes were laying out .45 semiautos, twelve-gauge double-barrel shotguns, and other guns, showing them off, comparing them.

WHEN I WAS twelve, we went back to Taiwan because my pops wanted the family to *ke-tou* (kneel, bow, and pay respects—*kowtow* in English) to my grandpa's ashes.

My most distinct memory is running around Taipei looking for bootleg video games and Jordan 8s—the Aqua 8s with cross-over Velcro. Taiwan was going nuts for the joints. My dad and I walked around for a minute trying to find a pair for cheap and ended up on Yong Kang Jie. The streets of Taipei were nothing like central Florida; they were like walking into the future and into the distant past and into a dream. One moment, we were walking down dark, dingy alleyways looking at bootleg merchandise and all of a sudden, we were at the alley's end, where there was only a canopy of laundry hanging, cloth blankets, one food cart, and a big bright light from a single streetlamp. Shining under the streetlamp was an old man and his cart of noodles. Just one stainless steel metal cart that you could tell was well worn but still shining. There was a stack of colorful melamine bowls in the front left corner. That's the style in East Asian street food, melamine bowls and chopsticks.

We walked up to the cart and I didn't say a word. I knew where we were. My dad had told me about this man for years. Every few months or so at home, Pops had to have Taiwanese 'Mian. Not the Dan-Dan Mian you get at Szechuan restaurants or in Fuchsia Dunlop's book, but Taiwanese Dan-Dan. The trademark of ours is the use of clear pork bone stock, sesame paste, and crushed peanuts on top. You can add chili oil if you want, but I take it clean because when done right, you taste the essence of pork and the bitterness of sesame paste; the texture is somewhere between soup and ragout. Creamy, smooth, and still soupy. A little *za cai* (pickled radish) on top, chopped scallions, and you're done. I realized that day, it's the simple things in life. It's not about a twelve-course tasting of unfamiliar ingredients or mass-produced water-added rib-chicken genetically modified monstrosity of meat that makes me feel alive. It's getting a bowl of food that doesn't have an agenda. The ingredients are the ingredients because they work and nothing more. These noodles were transcendent not because he used the best produce or protein or because it was locally sourced, but because he worked his dish. You can't buy a championship.

Did this old man invent Dan-Dan Mian? No. But did he perfect it with techniques and standards never before seen? Absolutely. He took a dish people were making in homes, made it better than anyone else, put it on front street, and established a standard. That's professional cooking. To take something that already speaks to us, do it at the highest level, and force everyone else to step up, too. Food at its best uplifts the whole community, makes everyone rise to its standard. That's what that Dan-Dan Mian did. If I had the honor of cooking my father's last meal, I wouldn't think twice. Dan-Dan Mian with a bullet, no question.

My pops stood in front of the cart waiting for the old man to look up. He hadn't been back in that spot in front of the cart for a decade, the last time he took me to Taiwan. The old man rose and looked straight at my dad, with no surprise, no shock, just acknowledgment. Not even a word, he just grunted.

"*Hggghhh.*"

"*Hai hao ma?*"

"*Hai hao.*"

That was it. How are you? Good. Pops had only told me about the noodles and the old man, but I had no idea they were that close. It was as if they were each carrying something for the other. A secret, a burden, a past, but I knew better than to ask. Within minutes, two bowls of noodles appeared for us. Huge melamine bowls with khaki noodles, steaming soup, and a gremolata-like mixture of crushed peanuts, pickled radish, and chopped scallions. Of course, my pops put chili oil in it immediately, but I wanted to taste the broth: intense, deep, and mind-numbing. It was one of those bites that make you think maybe, just maybe, your taste buds carry a cognitive key that can open something in your mind. Like the first time I heard Lauryn Hill's voice scratch over "Killing Me Softly," I felt that I just had a mental breakthrough via sound; there has to be something like that with taste. It was then and there that I realized, you can tell a story without words, just soup.

Pops told me that the old man's noodles were so popular that he would sell them until he ran out of bowls. If people wanted noodles after he ran out, they'd have to either wash the bowls or bring a bowl of their own, and they did. After a few minutes the old man asked my pops:

"*Lao Da ma?*"

"*Dui.*"

The old man assumed I was the oldest of my dad's kids and he was right. He was flattered to understand that this visit was a rite of passage. There was silence again and then the old man turned and spoke to me in Chinese.

"Your pops used to protect me from the other punks in this neighborhood. Every day. This was his neighborhood."

"But you had me that one day!"

"Ha, ha, ahhh, we're even."

One day, apparently my dad got caught wide open on the street without Uncle Xiao Hei, his other homies, or a weapon. People from a rival gang chased him and he had to come through that alley with the quickness. Of course, the first thing out of the alleyway is the noodle cart. Twenty-five years ago, the noodle man was young, too, like Taipei's own Artie Bucco. So, the old man sees my pops on the run and reaches into his cart for his cleaver. Pops grabs another one of his knives and they have it out on the street right there, slashing away with cleavers and cooking knives until the other gang runs away. I looked up at my dad after the old man finished the story, watched him empty the last bit of broth from that bowl of Dan-Dan Mian, the rough fingers of one hand still delicately clutching his chopsticks. My pops was a gangster. And suddenly, shockingly, I was proud to be who I was.

THOSE FIRST FEW years in Orlando, I hated being Chinese. All the fucking kids I saw at Chinese school were herbs and I didn't fit what their parents thought a Chinese kid my age should be. I called everyone's parents "Auntie" and "Uncle," said "Please" and "Thank you," but I threw my tennis racket when I was pissed, took hard fouls playing ball, and if I didn't study, I'd copy other people's homework. I knew I wasn't built like them.

After I went back to my dad's neighborhood, everything started to make a little bit of sense. The whole neighborhood loved him. He hadn't been back for twelve years and it was like he never left. He wasn't just some old fucker kicking my ass, he was a neighborhood legend trying to make me a man, just like him. For the first time, I saw him and Taiwan as part of me. It wasn't a country full of kids with salad bowl haircuts and TI-82s. There were bosses in stretch Benzes, bad bitches selling betel nut, and master chefs making Dan-Dan Mian. It was a country with characters, characters that I related to and found interesting. I wanted to know more about Taiwan and what it meant to be Taiwanese. Why did we come to this country where I can't even be on ESPN, if we could have stayed in Taiwan and been anyone we wanted to be? I didn't understand! My parents told me it was for money and, yes, the houses, the neighborhoods, and the cars were nicer in America, but it didn't matter to me. They didn't have to grow up in America. I did.

My dad sat me down and told me that even though it seemed like he was respected growing up in Taiwan and had what he wanted, coming to America was necessary. To him and his generation, this was the land of opportunity, free love, and the Bee Gees.* I'll never forget the talk he gave Emery, Evan, and me that year. I was barely twelve years old at the time, when he sat us down for breakfast.

"Boys, I know you like Taiwan, but America is beautiful. You know what the best part is?"

"Yeah, we know . . . land of opportunity, make money, blah, blah, blah."

"No. Your mom doesn't want me to talk about this, but one day you will understand. In America, you can do anything you want. I couldn't grow my hair long in Taiwan; in America, no problem! I had a band in America, we're free in America!"

"Man, you ran around shanking people with Uncle Xiao Hei in Taiwan and you're telling me you can't grow your hair out?"

"Look, difficult to explain, but I tell you this way. In America, you can 'sports fuck.'"

Emery couldn't help himself. This type of shit was his wheelhouse.

"Sports fuck? That sounds awesome, what's that?"

"You're too young. Eddie, you're too young, too. Evan, this guy definitely too young, but keep in your memory. In Taiwan, girls only 'make

* The Bee Gees are clearly a British group, but my dad equated rock and roll with America.

love.' You have to take them out, lie to them, tell them you love them, etc. But in America, it's like sports! They'll fuck you for fun . . . or practice! When you guys are old enough, you gotta take advantage. Sports fuck, don't forget it."

That was my dad. The one man besides Al Bundy who could take me on a magical trip to Taiwan, a trip that set me on to a huge soul search, set me up for what I expected to be the Rosetta Stone talk, and then tell me about sports fucking. I had to come to grips with the reality that my dad didn't come to this country for freedom or opportunity or any special way of life. He came to America, knocked up my mom at a house party in college, married her three months later, and there he was that day, sitting in our kitchen, blowing up in his early forties, still figuring out how to be a dad. I realized that day that anyone can be a parent; you just need live bullets. My dad was always proud that he quit smoking cigarettes the day Mom had me. I believe it, but I don't believe cigarettes were his only vice.

4

ROTTEN BANANAS

I remember my grandma always asking, "Are your parents still fighting?" I hated when she asked me that shit. If I could keep it quiet and pretend ain't shit going on, she should, too! You're almost a hundred years old and you don't know the rules to this game? Everyone knew they were fighting. The whole neighborhood could hear it like LT breaking Joe Theismann's leg. People throwing woks at each other is some pretty loud shit. And if you missed that, you definitely didn't miss my mom driving our van through your bushes.

The only person that held me down was Emery. Every week, I'd still say or do something my parents didn't like and they'd make me kneel on the kitchen floor for a few hours. Emery would see it, laugh, say something else crazy, and get stuck kneeling next to me, too. We were a unit. If one of us got stuck, the other would be there. If he was the one in trouble, I'd get him water or food or just talk to him. I wasn't dumb enough to say some shit in front of my parents and get punished, too, but I'd check on him.

One day, Emery didn't want to play piano, so my mom went to hit him with a steel brush. Both parents would hit us, but my mom was under control. It would hurt, but she'd never black out on us or get flagrantly creative, like it was her hobby. She'd use kitchen utensils or beauty products while my dad would use all kinds of joints: belts, whips, bo staffs, kala sticks, whatever he could get his hands on that would walk the line between really hurting and disabling us. He was smart. He never hit us in the face, he never hit us on the arms, and when he hit us on the legs it was above the knees. Smooth criminal. That day, my mom told Emery to hold his hand out to get hit but Emery wasn't having it.

He was different than me. As the oldest son, I always felt like I could argue with my parents, but I couldn't hit them back or disobey. But Emery would run, push my dad, and fight back. That day, Emery tried to run. He darted up the stairs and Mom reared back and threw the steel brush at him like a spear. It scraped him across his face like bear claws. She felt bad immediately, but it was done. He had pretty bad cuts on his face the next morning. Not knowing any better, my mom dropped us all off at school and when the teachers saw my brother's mauled face, they went a little apeshit. Within the hour we were in the principal's office, split up. I saw administrators and police talking to Emery and I was placed in another area. I could tell Emery was shook, but any chance I could make eye contact—when they'd walk me to the bathroom or the water fountain—I gave him a look like "everything's OK." Whatever I had to do or say to hide what was going on in our house, I did.

There was an unspoken understanding that Emery and I had. I would never, ever tell him how I felt about Mom and Dad, but he could read my face. He'd say what I was thinking before I said it.

"You don't like Dad, do you?"

"No, I do. He's your dad, you have to like him."

"Mom's crazy, huh?"

"No, she's just excited. If your mom is crazy, then you are crazy. Are you crazy?"

"Maybe?"

"No, you're not crazy. Trust me, I'm older."

"Why do you always get stomachaches?"

"Because I'm upset."

"About Mom and Dad?"

"No. Just eat your food, Emery."

Emery wouldn't go talk to my parents about the things he really cared about or about how he really felt; he'd talk to me. When he talked to them, they just yelled at him. When he came to me, I'd always get stomachaches because I didn't know what to do most of the time. I just told him what they'd taught me about how we should behave: respect your parents, respect your family, speak Chinese at home, take off your shoes at home, be polite at other people's homes, don't borrow money from people, but if other people need it from you lend it to them, as long as it's inconsequential. Don't fight, but if someone calls you a chink, fight.

I don't think my parents know how much I defended them to Emery and to my aunts, uncles, cousins, and grandparents. That day, I defended my parents to the police. After speaking to each of us individually at school, the Department of Health and Rehabilitative Services (HRS) drove us home. I kept thinking, Please don't snitch. I couldn't talk to him without the cops hearing so we just spoke with our eyes. Emery knew. He was in full Bojangles mode, shucking and jiving, but almost over-the-top. With a big gap-toothed smile, he told a story about how he fell down the stairs. In a genius move, Emery talked about it so loudly in the car that I knew what his story was. No snitching.

We got home and my mom answered the door. Pure shock on her face. I had never seen her like that, but she adapted quickly, just like us. After the initial five seconds of shock, she got her game face on. Smiling, measured surprise, gracious, *oh, I could never have done that* routine. They kept us off to the side with one of the officers and my mom wasn't allowed to speak to us. We didn't get to hear the conversation from outside but we could see inside the house. My initial reaction all day was worry. I didn't want my mom to get in trouble, I didn't want to be a foster kid, but after a few hours, I gave up. I quit worrying. I realized the truth: they fucking deserved it.

I was glad they got caught. There's a difference between hitting your kids to discipline them and kicking the living shit out of them. I could be a man like my dad without all this extra shit. On top of the physical abuse, the mental attacks were worse. Constantly being told I was a *fan tong* (rice bucket), fat-ass, or waste of space. The worst happened twice a year, as predictable as summer and winter. It was the only time I'd break down. My mom and dad had a cycle of fights, culminating in an epic, semiannual battle that would end with my mother screaming that she wanted a divorce. She'd then turn to me and say, "I wasted my life for you! *Dao le ba bei zi mei.*" Translation: I wasted eight lifetimes for this. What she meant was having me in college and giving her life up to be a mother. Whenever my mom got frustrated over money, not being able to work, being married to my dad, or her own health, this was her refrain. I knew she loved me, but twice a year she was really fucking convincing when she railed me for being born. When Emery saw it, he'd cry sometimes, too. I'd just be there in the kitchen or my room minding my business when she'd run out of her room after fighting with my dad. She'd grab her purse, the car keys, knock something over, and just let me have it. Same thing every time: *Ba bei zi mei!*

It was those two days every year that I cried, but then said to myself, Whoever you are, whatever you've done, wherever you are . . . if someone is doing something to make you feel that way, it's probably not right. It's the same feeling my grandfather had when he left the Internal Ministry. Everyone needs those moments. The times that something forces you to step outside of yourself and realize, yes, I'm sure there's a reason for what you're doing and I want to respect your idea of morality, but in my eyes, at this moment, that shit you're doing over there? THAT shit, son? That shit ain't right.

I read everything I could about Charles Barkley during those years. I saw him on television getting made fun of for being short, fat, and unable to beat Jordan. I saw people hammer him for marrying a white woman, spitting on a girl, throwing someone through a plate-glass window, and not being a role model. But he was for me. I'd read about Charles and how he persevered. I figured, if this guy is being made fun of every day on national television and can throw it back at people, never forgetting to smile, I could, too.

I read *Thank You, Jackie Robinson*. I read Hank Aaron's biography and all the hate he faced breaking the home-run record. Without anyone to talk to, I just read books about sports heroes and the racial barrier. There wasn't a section in the library titled "Books for Abused Kids" but there was black history and somehow, some way, it made sense to me. I listened to 2Pac. I remember when "Me Against the World" came out, Emery and I would just sit by the radio reading comics listening to that song over and over. People in Orlando never understood why two Asian kids were rocking Polo, Girbauds, and listening to hip-hop. We didn't do it because it was cool. At private school, teachers, parents, and other kids looked down on us for listening to hip-hop. It was a "black thing," downward assimilation. They didn't understand why we had flattops and racing stripes in our heads, but we did.

And when you get stranded
And things don't go the way you planned it
Dreamin' of riches, in a position of makin' a difference

Pac made sense to us. We lived in a world that treated us like deviants and we were outcast. There was always some counselor or administrator pulling us out of class to talk. We stayed in detention and we were surrounded by kids who had no idea what we were going through. We listened to hip-hop because there wasn't anything else that welcomed us in, made us feel at home. I could see why Milli wanted to pull a pistol on Santa or why B.I.G. was ready to die. Our parents, Confucius, the model-minority bullshit, and kung fu–style discipline are what set us off. But Pac held us down.

After an hour or so, the cops brought me inside. My mom was in the living room. They spoke to me in the foyer.

"Eddie, we need you to be very honest with us right now."

"Of course, I have been the whole time."

"Good. We spoke to your mother and your brothers, but we still have questions."

"Sure, come with me, let's go somewhere my mom can't hear us."

I remember thinking to myself, These cops probably don't think I'm old enough or smart enough to use a red herring. I figured if I make them feel like I'm going to ask for privacy from my mom that I'd give them the real story. I told them to come with me to the dining room, where we sat down, and they took my mom outside. Realizing they were hungry for something, I told them, "Look, I really don't like my parents . . ." I waited for them to process that, read their faces, and then proceeded. "But, really, who does like their parents?" I looked for laughs, but none. I remember almost to the word what I said to them.

"I'm sure you guys can tell, Emery is a bit goofy and last night he fell down the stairs. I told my mom not to let him go to school, but she sent him anyway because she never thought anyone would think it was from anything but a fall. I mean, I thought it was pretty obvious she should have kept him at home, but she's clueless. Look around, I hate them, but they're good parents. We have food, clothes, a nice house, we're clean, we have a dog, there's really nothing a kid needs that we don't have. Do you see anything wrong?"

I baited them with exactly what my dad had been using as a cover for years. Show good face, always put your best foot forward in public, don't show any cracks in the family unit, stick together. All our values still derived from the mind of Shihuangdi, the man who built the Great Wall and unified China.

After deliberating for a half hour, they brought me back in with my brothers to see my mom.

"Mrs. Huang, we are going to keep an eye on you guys, but this one here . . . You've done a good job. There's an old man hiding in that kid."

From that point on, my mom kept calling me *Lao Erzi*: old son. She was proud of me and once the cops left she was apologetic. Evan forgave her. He was just happy to be home. Emery felt guilty because in his mind, he had brought the trouble, but me? I was fucking pissed. I didn't want to defend them, but I did because it was the right thing to do for my brothers. Evan and Emery still needed parents. I remember thinking to myself, Motherfuckers owe me a pair of Vs for this one . . .

———

THE HOME SITUATION made it extra difficult to stomach the kids at private school. These kids had parents picking them up in Benzes, blessin' them with kicks, throwing them birthday parties, surprising them with cupcakes and shit. Not only did they have all that good shit, but they had to stunt on me, too. They couldn't just leave me, my chinky eyes, and my hand-me-down clothes alone. There's nothing worse than someone who got shit and can't recognize other people don't. I just wanted to dance on their motherfucking cupcakes. So around this time, I started to scrap with these kids. I remember kicking a kid into a bush and throwing him into the air conditioner when he laughed at my lunch. Another kid was taunting me because my parents wouldn't buy me Mad Libs so I put him in the Rick Flair Figure Four Leg Lock and stole his Mad Libs. One kid was talking shit saying he had a Batmobile and I didn't so I put his toy on the ground and DDT'd his face on the joint. I saw these kids just livin' the cupcake life while I was limping around because my dad went opposite field on my right leg. I didn't feel bad because they stepped to me first. They should have just let wounded dogs lie.

By the time I hit seventh grade, I wasn't the same anymore. My mom noticed, too. The complaints from teachers went from "Eddie needs to stop telling jokes" to "Eddie purposely threw a basketball in another student's face when he wouldn't let him play." I didn't take shit from anyone at this point. I only had one rule: don't pick on people who were already being picked on.

One school got so sick of Emery and me that they demanded we get psychological counseling before we could go back. We had good grades, but we disrupted class telling jokes or arguing with teachers. I didn't need Howard Zinn to know Christopher Columbus was a punk-ass stealing from colored people and I let it be known. Emery was a beast, too. I started lifting weights and he did it with me. He wasn't even eleven years old when he started. I think it stunted his growth, but by the time the boy hit eighth grade he was Megatron just stompin' out the other kids that fucked with him.

When we went to see the psychologist she asked us questions, we did the Rorschach blot shit, we took IQ tests, and just talked. We went for like three weeks and afterward she announced her diagnosis.

"Mrs. Huang, I am pleased to say there is absolutely nothing 'wrong' with your boys. The school is concerned, but they're just a couple of really bored kids."

"Bored? What do you mean? They have lots of activities! I take them to piano, swimming, karate, they are busy!"

"No, by bored, I mean, intellectually. They aren't being challenged."

"I buy them homeworks all year round. I pay for Kumon! Even in summer, I give them more homeworks, there is no way they are bored."

The psychologist could tell there was a cultural gap trying to explain this concept to my mom.

"OK, take a look at these tests. Emery has a very high IQ on this timed test. He tested off the charts."

"Oh! He is genius!"

"Technically, he's 'gifted.' Now, Eddie is interesting. He doesn't score high or do well on the timed test, but on the IQ test without time constraints, he scored exceptionally high."

"What about Evan?"

"Evan actually scored the highest."

"So all three boys, no problem!"

"It's not that simple."

No, no it wasn't. On my thirteenth birthday, I won the 740 AM Final Four Pick 'Em, which was open to all of Greater Orlando. I remember the radio station calling my house and not believing it was a thirteen-year-old kid's entry. I was also running NCAA pools at school, taking bets on NFL games, and selling porno. Emery and I figured out how to download Internet porn before the other kids so we put GIFs on 3.5-inch diskettes and sold them to other kids in school. Mind you, this was when everyone was still reading magazines, before USB drives or CD burners.

The porno hustle was ill. We'd break up more popular photos into different sets and sell them for more like greatest-hits mixtapes. For people who wanted the physical magazines, Emery found my dad's stash of *Pent-*

house magazines and would tear out individual photos and sell them that way to the highest bidder. Ten years before I ever heard the Clipse talking about breaking down keys and sellin' 'em like gobstoppers, we were doing the same thing with porno in middle school. I liked selling things or taking bets on sports because it was a challenge. School was easy for me, but no one, not teachers, not parents, not friends, taught me how to hustle but myself. Every time I sold something I felt a sense of pride like a kid taking his first shit. "Look, Mom, I made this myself!" What did we buy with all this money? Video games, trading cards, snap-back hats, and Starter jackets.* All the things our parents wouldn't get us, and we really fell in love with the paper because to us, money was synonymous with freedom and all we wanted to do was get free from our crazy-ass family.

One day, we were eating breakfast and my mom comes running out of Emery's room with pages ripped out of *Penthouse* magazine. Fuck . . .

"Soosin! Soosin! Emery wants to be a serial killer!"

"What are you talking about?"

"Look! He cut out these girls from a dirty magazine!"

"Hey! That's my magazine!"

"Who cares whose magazine? He is sick!"

"Mom, Emery's not a serial killer. He sells the photos to kids at school."

"Wait . . . people buy this?"

"Yeah, people love it!"

"Ahhh, almost heart attack . . ."

When my mom found out what we were doing she wasn't upset. She respected the hustle. Whether it was in school, piano, or porno, her entire American experience was about the paper.

AFTER THE COPS came to our house, my mom changed a bit. She would try to temper my dad when he hit us. She also realized how close she was to losing her kids. Emery had to go to the nurse's office and take off his clothes every Friday at school to show he wasn't being hit. We had to go

---

* It was the nineties, dun.

to counseling sessions and the school kept a close eye on us. We felt like criminals, but we hadn't done anything wrong. Around this time, we also stopped most of our Asian after-school activities. We stopped going to Chinese school and I didn't want to play piano, tennis, or any of that shit anymore. I think my parents gave up. They could see it was a struggle and a fight they weren't going to win. For years they'd tried to beat us into doing those things and we refused. With HRS checking on them constantly, they threw in the towel. I just played basketball in the neighborhood, listened to hip-hop, and in a way, tried to distance myself from Asian family bullshit.

Around this time, my cousin Allen started to change. I'd see him in the summers, in D.C. during holidays, weddings, etc. Something was different. He looked tired. Aunt Beth was always hard on him, comparing Allen to other cousins or his sister, and even at his house she'd yell at him for joking around with me or not getting better grades. I didn't understand. He was the coolest dude I knew, played on the football team, always beat me at Tecmo Super Bowl, or this board game Hotels. To me, Allen was invincible, but as with all great Asian men, his moms was like fucking kryptonite. I saw this woman literally suck the marrow out of his life. Aunt Beth didn't mean wrong, she was just doing what Asian moms think they're supposed to do: ride their kids, make sure they do their homework, stay out of trouble, go to an Ivy, and be either a doctor, lawyer, or engineer. When we were kids, she'd throw Allen's crayons on the floor and make him pick them up. As we got older, the crayons became board games, then video games, then CDs, but the process was the same. Anything Allen liked besides school was thrown to the ground. Well, except for the *Sports Illustrated* Swimsuit Issue. Aunt Beth was so out of the loop in Allen's life that she didn't even know he was into girls. When she found the issue, she was so happy and told people, "I'm so glad he's not gay!"

A few years later, my cousin Angela, Allen's sister, started dating this guy Tom. He was Chinese, too, and from California. Aunt Beth kept talking about how great Tom was because his parents owned a burger stand in California, saved their money, and sent Tom to Northwestern, where he was going to study to be a doctor. During winter break one year, Tom and Angela came to stay with us. Tom was the first Uncle Chan I ever met. He was so proud about starting the Asian frat at his school, being pre-med, and basically everything that Asian parents wanted us to be. The first night, we all went out to dinner at Atlantic Bay Seafood. I remember Angela ordered a Midori sour. I wasn't drinking yet at this age, but even I knew it was some bullshit. She took one sip and turned bright red. By that time, I had snuck off to the bar to watch Monday Night Football with the bartender and we just laughed at her.

I didn't want to eat with my parents anymore. I'd take my food and go watch whatever was on ESPN during dinnertime. My parents said it was rude and I'd get my ass kicked for it, but I didn't care. Dinner had become the time for everyone to be picked on in roundtable fashion and I hated it. I knew what they were going to say before they were going to say it, and I quit. We went back to the house that night and I hung out with Emery in his room. I remember we had just gotten 2Pac's *All Eyez on Me* album and we were listening to the shit when Tom came in.

"You know, guys, this is garbage."

"Say what?"

"This hip-hop stuff. It's garbage."

"Man, you, your parents, your burger stand is straight garbage, son!"

"You know, I'm going to let that go because this is a phase. You'll grow out of this."

Tom was wrong. It wasn't a phase; I never stopped listening to hip-hop. From the day my mom bought me the Fresh Prince and DJ Jazzy Jeff's "Nightmare on My Street" to the moment Allen put *The Chronic* in my tape deck to the day the next Nas descends upon planet Earth and blesses us with another perfect hip-hop album, it will never stop. That was all I knew. I was a Chinese-American kid raised by hip-hop and basketball with screaming, yelling, abusive parents in the background. If that makes me a rotten banana, well, tell it like it is.

5

THIS AMERICAN LIFE

Dave had no shoes. This was something I noticed was very common with white people down south. They went everywhere with no shoes. Their parents would drive barefoot, then throw a pair of sandals on the asphalt as they walked out of the car and into Publix. I didn't get it. The bottoms of their feet were all red, there were little pieces of gravel between their toes, and somehow they didn't care. I mean, Dominicans hate socks and love Aventura, but at least they still got Jordan 7s on.

"Hey! I'm Dave."

"Wassup, I'm Eddie."

"You guys just moving in, huh?"

"Yeah, we moved in yesterday so unpacking now."

"Welcome, dude! You play football?"

"Nah. I'm a big Skins fan but I never got to play."

"Oh, you'll love it, good ol' American fun!"

"You play basketball?"

"Nope, just football and roller hockey."

Then Dave invited himself and his stank-ass feet into our house. I liked the guy, but I knew that as soon as my mom saw him walking around on the carpet with his dirty-ass bare feet, she would bug. Everyone knows to take their shoes off in an Asian home, but the fuck you supposed to tell Huckleberry Finn when he rolls in barefoot? There's no answer for that. It's unprecedented behavior on our continent, unless you're a wounded samurai that got his wooden *chancletas* stolen.

Dave came in and started wandering around, touching things, and didn't notice the footprints he was leaving everywhere. It was nasty, but I thought he was hilarious. I actually couldn't wait for my mom to notice. Watching Dave explore the house felt like watching some prehistoric Encino Man that just came out of a block of ice. He was curious about everything, the way I was at Jeff Miller's. Compared to other white people, he wasn't the least bit judgmental. He just kept picking stuff up, turning it over in his hands, and then putting it back down again, covered in fingerprints. There was a genuine curiosity I appreciated. When he wasn't picking stuff up, he tossed his football in the air over and over like an old Chinaman with his Baoding balls. He was looking at the house, but I was watching him. Then Mom came home.

"*Xiao Ming! Ta de jiao zang si le!*"

(Translation: EDWYN HUANG, his feet are disgusting.)

"What'd your mom just say?"

"Uhh, she just said hello."

"Hmm, that's a lot of words for hello!"

"Let's just play football, dude."

My mom had this habit of speaking Chinese in front of Americans. She didn't give a fuck that they probably thought it was rude. I was caught in the middle. There's a part of me that loves immigrants who throw niceties to the wind and just speak their tongue all day, every day. The older generation never felt integrated in society anyway so they don't care if you see them as "rude." I mean, cot damn, "rude" is probably a compliment compared to the shit people used to say to them. This is our language and it's your problem if you don't speak it, right? But another part of me feels, "What's Dave got to do with it?" He's just a nice kid that wants to see what a Chinese home is like. More than that, he just wants to see if the new kid plays football.

Dave was two years older than me and we didn't talk much about anything besides football, but for the next three years he was my best friend and every day after school, we played. Football took over my life. I got John Madden Football for Super Nintendo and started copying the plays from the game—literally diagramming them on a piece of paper—so Dave and I could practice them with our brothers. It was always Dave and me versus Billie G. and Billie F. plus whoever else wanted to play in the neighborhood. There were a bunch of other kids who would play, but in four years, never once did Dave and I get split up.

The Billies were a couple of douche bag Zack Morrises. Pretty-boy cheap-shot artists. Crunchy in the face types. Billie G. is a pro wakeboarder now and he's still the biggest cock and balls you'll ever meet. I was the smallest and slowest out of the four, but Dave and I won most of the time because we were smart and nasty when we had to be. Billie G. was the most athletic—fast, tall, jumped high, all that good shit. But he had no plays, and Billie F., while also athletic, was a huge pussy with alligator arms.

Dave used hustle and worked to play Billie G. to a draw every time. Billie G. was like Randy Moss, the callous but supreme athlete, and Dave was Darrell Green, all heart. I played quarterback and covered Billie F., who was faster than me, but he'd hear footsteps and get shook. I bumped him a lot, ran him off his routes, and hit him hard when he did catch the ball. Dave had trouble getting open against Billie G. so we ran a lot of play-action, screens, flea-flickers, all that crazy shit. Anything to get Dave matched up against Billie F. The funny thing is the Billies were dumb as rocks. Their only play was for Billie F. to fade back into the end zone and throw it as far as he could to Billie G.

Our little brothers and the Atkins kids played, too, so we usually had eight- or ten-man games. It usually ended up as the Huangs and Williamses versus the Atkinses and Billie G.'s and Billie F.'s clans. Our ace in the hole was Emery, clearly bigger, faster, and tougher than all the other kids his age. He also hated Billie G. and Billie F., because their moms would make fun of our mom for being an FOB. Billie G. was the boogie man, though. He'd hit you late, chip you with his elbows, and tell mad Chinaman jokes. He terrorized us for years.

In seventh grade, my parents enrolled me at Trinity Prep. I was dumb excited because Dave went there, too. We couldn't wait to go to school together and he told me about the football team. I registered late for the team because it was my first year at the school, but the coach, Mr. Rock, let me start practicing in early August. They didn't have enough helmets so I was the only kid without one for the first week.

"Huang, what position do you play?"

"Quarterback."

"No, really, what position do you play?"

"I play quarterback. I got plays and stuff."

"Let's start you at wide receiver, see how that goes."

Organized football was a lot different than street ball. I always played quarterback in the yard, but standing five foot four in seventh grade, I wasn't about to start at quarterback. I'm kind of glad there weren't smartphones back then because a midget Chinaman telling his coach to start him at quarterback would be viral video gold. Almost like Eli Porter* freestyles. Yet, no matter what, in my own head, I was a quarterback.

Playing wide receiver really didn't start off very well. I always rocked my pants with a sag so I wasn't very comfortable in football tights. I asked for a size big and when I ran routes, the shits would start falling and my hip pads would flop all over the place. I was too small to run the crossing routes I was good at and I was too slow to run the go routes guys my size needed to. It was a constant struggle in my life, a big man trapped in a little man's body. Charles Barkley shit. The coaches laughed and the other players gave me a hard time, but I just kept working.

After our first game, it became clear I would never see the light of day at receiver. Coach Rock switched me to defensive tackle and right guard. It made no sense. When they lined us up at offensive line, it looked like Niagara Falls. Tall guy, tall guy, tall guy, Eddie Huang? The fuck you doing here, son? I honestly think Coach Rock thought I was helpless and put me at line so that I'd quit. The first rep I ever took on the line, he put me at left tackle and had Kwame line up across from me. Kwame was the

---

* The hardest MC in the game: "I'm the best mang, I deed it."

biggest dude on the team, played defensive end, and was a straight terror on the edge. I started talking to myself.

"Yo, you got this, son. Ain't nothin', just get low, get leverage, and send this boy packin'."

"Blue nine, blue nine, yellow, yellow, hut!"

Kwame fired off the line and I started to shuffle back. Before I could even set my feet, BOOM. He just chucked me with two hands on a bull rush and I went flying. Literally, two feet off the ground, whiplash on my neck, and I tumbled over twice before coming to a stop. Dead fucking meat.

"Huang! Get up, Huang!"

"Whuuuh?"

"Huang, can you hear me?"

"Kwame?"

"No, this isn't Kwame! It's Coach Rock. Get up, Huang!"

Coach Rock was stumped. He had no idea what to do with me. I absolutely sucked at organized football. But I never once thought about quitting. In some crazy, sadistic, twisted way, I was having the time of my life. I was part of something. It wasn't Chinese school. It wasn't family. It was good ol' American Fun and I loved it. When the helmets and pads were on, for sixty minutes, I wasn't Chinese anymore. I was part of the team. Instead of being singled out and laughed at for being Chinese, I was being laughed at for totally sucking at football. It was a relief.

Mom kept trying to get me to stop playing because I came home injured in some form or other every single day. She used to watch me get tossed around by Billie G. in the backyard or wait on the sidelines to play at practice. She would be crying when I came home, but she never told me why until I got older. I had no idea she was watching, because she always hid from view, but my mom was always there. Without ever asking me, she understood that I needed it but wished I didn't. I wasn't built for this American life. I was like a lil' shih tzu tryin' to run with the pit bulls. That was Dave and me. You see it a lot. There's the toy dog barking and leading the big goofy dog around. Isiah and Rodman, AI and Dikembe, Eddie and Dave. Life doesn't always make sense.

Three weeks into the season, Coach Rock introduced new drills into practice. The first one was the Indian Run. The entire team, fifty-plus kids, all ran around the football field. You had to stay in line and the last guy in line had to sprint to get to the front until everyone did it twice. The first time we did it, the team thought to slow down a little bit when it was my turn. Everyone figured I was the slowest and it was to their benefit for me to get it over with as soon as possible since another forty-nine guys had to do it, too. Coach Rock was a wily motherfucker, though, and made the team run even faster when it was my turn. He was on to it. I understood why the guys wanted to slow down and I understood why Coach Rock wouldn't allow it. It was a pivotal moment.

I looked at the ground, clenched my teeth, pumped my arms, and ran as fast as I fucking could. Couldn't nobody help me but myself this time . . . I just kept chopping my feet. Up, down, up, down, up, down. My pads, helmet, pants, were all too big. Shit looked like a yard sale. By the time I looked up, I was a good bit in front of the first guy and snot was coming out of my damn ears. Twenty minutes later, the drill was over and I was over by the fence puking my guts out.

"BRRR, break it down!"

At the end of practice, we'd all get in a big circle and break it down. Coach Rock would yell some random shit and we'd yell back, but I was so tired, I literally passed out on the ground.

"Look at Huang! This guy left it all on the field today, y'all!"

"WHOOP!"

I couldn't believe it. Coach Rock said something nice about me and the team was cheering.

"Good shit, Huang!"

"Listen up, team! Huang is the smallest guy on the team, but he gave it up today. If we practice like this, we'll win some damn games this year! So, player of the day today, Eddie Huang, let's hear it."

To that point in life, I'd never been more proud of myself. For twelve years, I really never once did anything that made me proud. There were things that made my mom or dad happy, but this was mine. It wasn't much to most kids. I mean, I was basically getting recognized for being straight dogshit, ignoring that I was straight dogshit, and doing anything in my power just to maintain my dogshittiness. I think on Urban Dictionary that's the definition for insanity—or a Michael Bay film. It was just one good day of practice, yet it meant everything to me. There was hope.

The next day, we had another new drill, the Circle. Coach had the whole team form a circle and inside the circle, he'd put a football in between two guys in a three-point stance. When Coach blew the whistle, the two guys would fight as hard as they could to push across the football. It was my favorite drill, all heart. Kwame dominated the defensive line, Dave worked the receivers, and there was this one guy, Friedman, the biggest seventh grader and the only one who had a chance to start. He played offensive line. Friedman should have been the best lineman, but he didn't always give it his all. In the circle, he'd win, but not as easily as he should.

"Friedman! Huang! In the circle!"

I couldn't believe it. Coach never let me match up against Friedman. Usually I just went up against the sled or this other kid who sucked so bad I forgot his name. All I remember was that he was so fat his head didn't fit in the helmet so it looked like he always had bitter-beer face. But Friedman actually started and played in games. I strapped on my helmet and ran to the middle. The whole team was screaming. I had a good day with the Indian Run, but this was different. I was nervous in my stance. As soon as Coach Rock blew the whistle, I clenched my teeth, closed my eyes, dug my feet in the ground, and kept 'em moving. That was a theme with football. I closed my eyes when tackling. I don't know why but I tried to mentally block everything out and hit the other player as hard as I fucking could.

I COULDN'T BELIEVE it. "Wooo! That's how you do it, Huang! Friedman, get your ass up! Let's go again."

This time Friedman put up a fight. He got me with a good punch first, but I stayed low and just chopped my feet back and forth. My height became an asset once I learned to move my feet. I won again. I probably got a little overexcited so Coach brought me back down to earth. Later that day, he had me go against Kwame in a simulation and of course, he crushed me, but not like before. I got pushed back, but I didn't go flying.

For the next three weeks, literally every day, Coach Rock named me player of the practice. I was an animal. I got my confidence and just kept pushing back furiously with my eyes closed. Other people couldn't compete. They were playing a game but I treated it like life and death. The zenith was about six weeks into the season. We always played simulated games on Wednesdays, Offense versus Defense, and that day I was lined up against this new kid, Jason, who had transferred from Apopka. He was at least five inches taller than me, with long arms, but he didn't know how to use them. He had an awkward chicken wing and sucked at setting his feet. I was playing left guard and we usually ran belly right. At that point Coach Rock used me as the rallying cry, but he didn't actually believe I could play.

Instead of blocking Jason right like the play was supposed to go, I wanted to see if I could blow him off the ball. I faked right, planted, set left, and started pushing him into the linebackers.

"Huang! What are you doing?"

"Coach, we're not going anywhere right. I can blow this guy off the ball, let's run left!"

"Hey! You hear this kid?" yelled Coach Rock to his assistant coach.

"What'd that boy say now?"

"He says he can blow your boy Jason off the ball."

"Oh, yeah? Run that ball left!"

"All right, Huang, belly left, let's go."

Coach Rock thought he had me. I was out of line, but we'd developed a rapport and he knew I meant well. But football is a hierarchy. The players don't change the plays. So Coach Rock figured that he'd play along, tell the defense we're running left, and I'd get smacked.

"Blue, blue . . . blue, blue, thirty-two, hut!"

Jason knew we were going left, so I couldn't fake right. I got as low as I could, gave him a good punch under the shoulder pads before he could set, and just drove him into the strong-side linebacker. My center did his

job and pushed his guy right and Rosado, the running back, came screaming through the hole.

Put your two arms up / touchdown. *

"Wooo, Huang! You son of a bitch! That's a hole! That is a cot damn
hole! You heard this kid call the play in the huddle?"

"You told me, I told them. Still couldn't stop the play! God damn
Huang . . ."

"I told you, Coach!"

"Shut up, Huang."

That was the first practice in three weeks where I didn't get recognized
as player of the practice, and I understood why.

I HAD STOPPED doing homework. I just didn't care. Football was my life.
I didn't even pay attention to what my mom was cooking. I honestly can't
remember any single item of food that stood out. Every other phase of my
life is littered with food memories, but during this time, the only thing I
can muster is sesame fried chicken from this takeout spot, Forbidden City.
It's literally American Chinese sesame fried chicken, but these guys figured something out. There wasn't anything else worth eating there. Even
their General Tso's, which had a similar technique, was nasty. Yet this
sesame chicken was ethereal.

It was on the way home from school, so we'd stop by all the time and
pick up three orders. One day we went to Forbidden City and I had first-
quarter grades in my backpack. My mom was all excited to go so I figured
I'd wait till we were in the car and finished eating before showing her my
report card. Man, that fucking chicken was good. Evan sat in the front a lot
of the time because he was the youngest and my mom wanted to watch
him. He was always the last one to finish eating. He didn't really seem to
like food like Emery and me unless we went to Wong's for pi par tofu.

* It's killa, dog. (Cam'ron, "Dipset Anthem")

That was his favorite. Silken tofu mixed with shrimp paste, steamed in soup spoons, fried into golden ovals, and served with brown sauce over rice. Shit was unstoppable.

But then it had to happen.

"Mom, here's my report card."

"How'd you do?"

"Good."

"Evan, read me the report card."

"I don't know this word, Mom."

"What word?"

"The one at the top."

"Let me see . . ."

My mom took the report card from Evan.

"That says 'Progress' . . . *WAN BA DAN!*" (Translation: You piece of shit!)

Mom flipped. I got a C in pre-trigonometry.

"Evan, hit him with this brush!"

My mom gave Evan the big metal hairbrush with copper bristles and told him to hit me with it, but I just kept ducking.

"Ha, ha, Eddie's scared of the brush."

"Emery! No one is talking to you. Where's your report card?"

"I don't have one, Mom, my class just has stickers."

"Well, stop talking, then, Emery! Eddie, hit yourself in the face!"

"Mom, what's progress?"

"Evan, shut up! You think this is funny, huh? I'll kill us all!"

My mom drove this ridiculous Starcraft van that couldn't turn without looking like a club sandwich falling apart. When we fucked up, she'd purposely swerve the car in and out of lanes to make it feel like we were going to get in an accident. I honestly don't know how we survived this three times a year, but we did. Evan always started crying, I would go quiet and get really annoyed, and Emery would laugh 'cause that's what Emery does.

While this was going on, she'd lower the window so other people could see, and I'd have to slap myself in the face the whole ride home. It was the most embarrassing shit I had to do as a kid. If I didn't hit myself hard enough, she'd have Emery slap me, too. But that motherfucker had way too much fun doing it and my mom would end up smacking him when we got home, too.

Of course, there was Emery, as always next to me getting hit, with no front teeth,* smiling the whole time. My parents always wanted things to be serious and the kids to be remorseful, but Emery loved drama, fights, jokes, etc. Anything irregular, that kid was all about it. If anyone in the family had off-kilter romances, strange habits, or skeletons in their closet, Emery was most excited to recount them. Things like supermodels with athlete's foot interest Emery. He wasn't a gossip; he just saw everyone for the weirdos they were and not the normal people they pretended to be. So when the fucked-up shit came to the surface, he rejoiced. Eddie vs. Pre-Trig, Tyson vs. Holyfield, Tiger vs. Ambient? He loves that shit.

"You think this is funny, huh? I'm taking you off the football team!"

"You can't take me off the team!"

"Oh, yeah? Who's going to pick you up from school?"

"I'll get a ride from Dave!"

My mom called Dave's mom and Coach Rock; I was off the team, just like that. I didn't think anyone would care. Despite all of Coach Rock's cheering during practice, I never played in a game. Yet, when I told my friends Peter and Andrew, they reacted differently.

"What? You can't quit!"

"I'm not quitting, man, my mom told Coach not to let me play."

"Dude, Coach is gonna flip."

"He never even lets me play in the game, man. You guys will be fine."

"Who do you think he's been talking about all season? Every day he tells us to practice like you."

"So practice like me, ha, ha. Just run until you puke."

For two weeks, I didn't get to play. I just sat around at home doing math homework and hung out with Dave when he got home. That Thursday, around 8 P.M., the phone rang.

---

* Our last year in D.C., Emery tripped in the parking lot of Better Homes and slammed his teeth on the curb. It took years for them to grow back, so all through middle school I have this memory of Emery with no front teeth, looking like one of the Red Wings.

"Hello?"

"Is Mrs. Huang available?"

"Coach Rock? Hey, man!"

"Eddie, put your mom on the damn phone."

"Mom! It's Coach Rock!"

"What the hell does he want? He ruined your life!"

My mom took math pretty seriously and was sick of football, but Coach Rock had a way. He was actually the advanced math teacher for eighth and ninth graders so he talked to the seventh grade teachers about my troubles. I wasn't even doing that badly. I mean, I got C's. He really respected my mom. Most parents put sports before academics, so it was refreshing.

"Mom! What'd Coach say?"

"He say you work hard at football. But you don't work hard at math."

"I *can* work hard at math, though!"

"He says he guarantee you work hard at math so I let you play football."

That Friday, I came back to the team. I walked into the classroom where we usually had the pregame meeting and it was all dark. They had just finished screening *Rudy*.

"Eddie's back, guys!"

It was insane. Motion picture shit. We never watched movies before games, but Coach always talked about *Rudy*. I don't remember much about that moment or what was said because I was just so fucking happy to be back and wanted to get to the game. We strapped on our helmets and ran onto the field. That game, even my dad was in the stands. I don't know what Coach Rock told my parents or the team, but something was in the Gatorade. It was my first game Pops ever came to and the whole team seemed to be in on something. With one minute left in the fourth quarter, Coach Rock called my name.

"Huang! Get in there! Right defensive tackle, let's go!"

The offensive and defensive linemen all lost their shit. We were a unit and I was the little guy. Kwame, Dave, and this other big guy who played left tackle started the cheer.

"Eddie, Eddie, Eddie . . ."

That shit was craze. Coach Rock basically recreated *Rudy* with a short, fat defensive tackle that should have been in *Karate Kid*. I was so excited, I lined up over the wrong guy. I was supposed to be lined up over the guard and I lined up over the center. They saw I was out of position so they ran the ball my direction, but, somehow, some way, I came off the ball faster than I'd ever fired in my whole life. There I was in the backfield, past the whole line, staring at the quarterback. I should have just tackled the fucker, but I was so used to tackling running backs that I waited for him to hand the ball off so I could hit the running back. He saw me in the hole so he cut right and our defensive end gang tackled him with me.

"Ahhh! We got him, Huang!"

By this time, the whole stadium was screaming my name and we just went nuts. I stayed in for two more plays, until the game ended. We ran straight toward the locker room, but there was my dad at the side of the field.

"Ha, ha, you suck, man!"

"What do you mean I suck! Everyone was cheering for me, Dad!"

"You should have tackled the quarterback! You let him hand the ball off, ha, ha."

I always believed him when he said I sucked . . . but this time, just this once, I knew he was wrong. He had to be. I played a logic game in my head. Like that shit teachers told you about philosophers and snub noses; I took my dad's assumption. If I tried my best, puked my guts out, did my math homework, and fired off the line as fast as I possibly could and STILL sucked, I should probably die on the spot right there. But I didn't want to drop dead. I mean come on! I was having the best ten minutes of my life. Even if I sucked, who cares?! We lost the game, but the whole stadium was cheering my name. Shit, our whole team stunk, but we went out there every week and had a really good fucking time. I didn't have an abacus like Grandpa, but I was pretty confident in my calculation. Either my dad was wrong or he didn't matter. For the first time, I thought to myself, Even Dad can't ruin this for me, and then I ran to the locker room where my teammates were waiting for me.

———

THE FUN WASN'T over after football season. My birthday is March 1. That year my parents threw me a party in the backyard. It was the best birthday party I ever had. All my friends from school, Dave, his friends, and some guys from the team came. My mom went so far as to buy us water guns, balloons, all that good shit. Halfway through, in came the boogie man.

"What, I'm not invited to this party?"

Billie G. and Billie F. Before I could say anything, they started stomping out my balloons and kicking around our chairs, my presents, the tables.

I'd had enough. I wanted to tear Billie G.'s fucking eyes out, but I knew I couldn't fight him one-on-one without getting my ass kicked, which, even in my rage, I knew was not going to be a good look. So I cleared my head and did what any Zen master would. I waited for them to finish. My friends were all smaller than Billie G., and two years younger so they just stood around, too. Dave was the biggest one, but he'd already left the party. My mom saw the whole thing, but in classic Jessica Huang fashion, she didn't bail me out. She wanted to see me fight through it. The boys finished laying waste to my party, streamers wrapped around their legs, hands smeared with cupcake icing.

"This shit sucks, man. Happy birthday, Huang, ha, ha."

The Billies left. Their dumb asses thought it was over, so they just walked next door and stood around on Billie F.'s driveway, laughing about what they'd done. But it wasn't over.

I took all the water guns and put bleach in them. We didn't want to permanently disable them—none of us wanted to end up in juvie—so we diluted the bleach but kept just enough so that it'd burn. I gave my friends the water guns and drew up a plan like Joe Gibbs. We ran up on the Billies on that driveway and as soon as they turned and saw us, we shot bleach right into their faces.

"Oh my God, dude, it burns, it burns! There's something in the water!"

The assholes tried to run, but we had them circled. While they were distracted, Emery opened one of the windows to Billie F.'s bedroom and put our hose through it and flooded his whole room. Dave saw it going down and joined in with his brother. Kids from the whole neighborhood came out because we all hated the Billies. Even Ryan Sistar, who lived three streets down, heard about what was going on and ran over with his water gun late, waving the loaded Super Soaker around, looking for trouble.

All of a sudden Billie F.'s mom came out of their house and confronted my mom.

"What is going on! Your kids are fucking flooding my house! What kind of parenting is this!"

As this happened, one of my friends started spray painting Billie F.'s driveway with smiley faces. My mother looked at Billie F.'s mom for a second and started sputtering.

"You, you have a shitty nose job!"

I couldn't believe it: my mom felt no remorse and just blurted out some shit about this woman's nose job. The Billies were running in circles with their faces on fire, but I wasn't done. I wanted something they'd taken from me. People say kids always tease and that it's an innocent rite of passage, but it's not. Every time an Edgar or Billie called me "chink" or "Chinaman" or "ching chong" it took a piece of me. I didn't want to talk about it, and kept it to myself. I clenched my teeth waiting to get even. Unlike others who let it eat them up and took it to their graves, I refused to be that Chinese kid walking everywhere with his head down. I wanted my dignity, my identity, and my pride back; I wanted them to know there were repercussions to the things they said. There were no free passes on my soul and everything they stole from me I decided I'd take back double.

I had a Russian wolfhound named Nick, who hated the Billies. Nick was a funny dog. If he saw people hit me playing ball or just fighting in the neighborhood, he'd go after them. My dad kept him on a leash because neighbors complained and tried to put him in the pound. But that day, I let Nick out on the Billies and he chased Billie G. around the whole neighborhood. Kid never came around again. Justice was served. Welcome to America.

6.

MO MONEY,
MO PROBLEMS

When I was in seventh grade, I met my first Asian homie, Joey Vano. We'd hang out at his house almost every weekend, which was perfect because mine was an embarrassing shitshow, but sometimes my parents would insist he come to the crib because they were worried that I was a burden on his family.

Every time Joey came, I'd tell myself it would be different. But no matter what I did, how good I was, or how hard I tried to keep Emery under wraps, my mom went apeshit like clockwork. Every Saturday morning before we even woke up for cartoons, Moms would be acting a fool. She'd come busting out of her room yelling, throwing pots, calling my dad an asshole, telling everyone she was going to crash the car into a tree. We never got to sleep in past eight or nine because that's when the Mom Show came on.

Mom acted out even more when guests were at the crib 'cause she knew it'd embarrass Dad even more. Who was my mom? A Chinese-American woman in the nineties with no career, three kids, and a husband that didn't pay attention. I felt her pain. It pissed all of us off how much my dad would cater to guests, outsiders, and Chinese uncles with five rings and a perm, but break out the bullwhip for his own fam. After all their brawls, there was nothing Moms could say that would hurt him, so the best she could do was embarrass him when guests were at the crib, even if the guest was a twelve-year-old Filipino kid who was about to watch a bomb named Jessica obliterate everything he knew about moms, women, or any organism carrying eggs, for that matter.

I had to get away.

Joey loved basketball, playing Twisted Metal, surfing, and alternative rock. I would tell him, "Damn, son, you Filipino, you should be the b-boy, rockin' snap-backs, listening to Pac, not me!" but that was Orlando. There weren't many Filipinos in Orlando so they didn't have an underground smell-road, no places to gather and just be Filipino. Every year, what Filipinos there were would go to Lake Cane Park and roast a pig, eat some adobo and garlic rice, but they weren't militant about maintaining their identity like the Chinese were. Joey was free to just do him, which meant being an easygoing dude with shoulder-length hair and grunge steez. Also, his brother, Carl, had this dope Italian girlfriend, Joanne, so he didn't make fun of white people as much as me. I was rocking Starter jackets and Levi's, but Joey was the opposite; he rocked Airwalks, flannel, and things I'd never seen. I remember this fool listening to Alanis Morissette and I'd ask, "Man, you can just go outside and hear white women whine in the cul-de-sac, why you paying money to hear that shit?" But that was Joey, Filipino in Orlando with a California state of mind.

Joey was happier than me. That might've been because he had dope parents. They gave him everything he needed and most of what he wanted, but also made sure he got his work done and was a good kid. I thought to myself, Well, that's easy. Why is it so hard at my crib? Why can't we just wake up, eat some SPAM, watch the Lakers, and be like Filipinos. Then I realized, I'd rather stand in a horse stance holding a twenty-pound bucket of rice over my head than rep the Lakers.

I loved going to Joey's house. When I met white kids' parents, they always asked me bullshit questions about race, where our family was "from," and used words like *Oriental*. I was like a toy in their house, but

Joey's parents were Asian so it felt like family. I never felt like I had to carry the burden of the whole Chinese diaspora, or that everything I did was a statement about my people and where we're from. Whenever I got to stay at Joey's, I'd talk to his dad about basketball, food, the news, what I wanted to be when I grew up. Joey's mom liked me, too, but she could tell I was a troublemaker. Joey's dad covered for me and said things like "dee boys are boys," but she was still suspicious. Dr. Vano was hilarious and had the ill accent. I remember one morning he told me about getting circumcised in the Philippines.

"Eddie, you don't believe how painful this is."

"I got circumcised and I don't remember it being so bad."

"Oh, that's because they do it to you when you leetle boy. I got circumcised when I was fifteen!"

"Dad, why do you always have to tell this story!"

"Joey, why you embarrassed, this is natural, everyone is circumcised these days."

"Yo, it's cool, man, let him tell the story."

"So, in the Philippines, you go to the doctor when you're fifteen and they cut your foreskin."

"Does it hurt?"

"Of course it hurts! It hurts so bad, we would all run to the beach and jump in the salt water to clean it!"

"Wait, you just jump in the water with bloody dicks?"

"Yes! And you come out, your penis looks like a tomato!"

"Dad, I'm eating, man!"

"Yeah, just like Joey's Vienna sausage there, ha, ha, but beeger, much beeger!"

Joey would get embarrassed and take his food in his room so I went along, too.

Joey's pops was a Laker fan like most FOBs who grew up in the Magic era, but Joey was a die-hard Orlando Magic fan. I loved Shaq in fourth grade, but Orlando was full of idiots who didn't know the game. When Shaq became a free agent they ran an article in the *Orlando Sentinel* asking if he was worth $100 million. No doubt he's worth $100 million! God-damn, Juwan Howard got $100 that summer and he was a six-nine power forward that got his buckets with line-drive fifteen-footers. Your boy Shaq was rippin' backboards just eatin' everybody's food, there was no question he was worth $100. In the stands, you'd always hear people complaining about how much athletes made, wearing their Washington Mutual polo shirts. One time, I even turned around and said to a guy, "Every one of my friends could do your job, but not one motherfucker between Orlando and Houston can do what Shaq does, so fall the fuck back and watch the show." Surprisingly, no one said a word after; motherfuckers started leaving the crazy Chinaman alone.

When draft time came around, Joey would get excited and I'd tell him every single year that they were just gonna draft the best available white guy and I was right. Go back and look: Geert Hammink, Brooks Thompson, Brian Evans, Michael Doleac, Matt Harpring, Mike Miller, Curtis Borchardt, Zaza Pachulia, Travis Diener, and the whitest NBA player of all time, J. J. Redick. I was surprised these fools didn't draft Frederic Weis twice.

I couldn't fuck with the Magic. I went for the Suns, Hornets, and Knicks: Barkley, 'Zo, and Patrick. I had a problem watching ball at Joey's, though. No matter how hard I tried, I'd be yelling at the TV, cursing, making fun of the Magic, and Mrs. Vano always overheard. In front of his parents, I spoke good English, kept it clean, but around Joey I was just wildin'. There was nothing two-faced about it, but Mrs. Vano didn't really like it.

She started to see a change in Joey once he started hanging out with me. He left 2Pac *All Eyez on Me* in his mom's car one day and she got real upset when she heard it so, of course, I got blamed. We'd always fuck around in class and end up in detention, but it was just hijinks. I never felt like I was transforming Joey into a "bad" person; I was just helping him live a little more. One week got especially funky, though. There was this science teacher we hated, Mr. Mazza, a passive-aggressive dick that always assumed we were fucking around when we weren't. So, in the great self-destructive tradition of minority adolescents everywhere,* we figured, "Why not cause trouble, he gonna assume it anyway." This was when Biggie's "Big Poppa" was a hit, so when he walked into class I'd always yell, "I love it when you call me Fat Mazza!" and we all laughed at the fool.

That Friday, Fat Mazza gave us an assignment. It was the dumbest thing I've ever seen a teacher do: "All right, class, this week, I want you all to design a weapon using the things we've learned in class about force." We couldn't believe it, this fool really gave us free rein to make weapons, test them at school, and present them in class. Mazza made it clear we weren't allowed to make explosives or use materials like knives, BB guns, paintball guns, and so on. It had to be something that would represent the principles of physics, but not actually hurt people. For the rest of the day, all anyone could talk about was the weapons they were going to build. Some people wanted to make potato shooters, others catapults. Joey and I were trying to figure out what we could do that would really wreck shop, but we were blank.

After school, his mom took us to the mall so we could get ideas. We went straight for the comics shop. *Punisher* always had the best weapons but they were all guns. The X-Men had wild mutant abilities that they clearly weren't selling at K-B Toys. Comics weren't very helpful, it turned out. We went to K-B, though, and found a Nerf slingshot. It was meant for shooting small toys or tennis balls but we wanted to move more heavy-duty objects. I'm pretty sure we went to Sports Authority, where we found a metal slingshot with a heavy, rugged sling. The joint could launch anything easily a hundred yards. But we decided that slingshots are boring. We still needed to figure out what we were going to shoot. All night at Joey's we played Twisted Metal 2. The next morning we woke up for breakfast and of course it was eggs, toast, OJ, and Vienna sausage at Joey's. But then it hit us, the answer was right in front of our noses, fucking up our sense of smell.

SPAM.

"Son, a SPAM launcher!"

* Chris Jackson, my editor, got my back with this one!

"Oh, no way, dude, that's crazy."

"Naw, for real, a SPAM launcher. We would *wet* people."

FOR LUNCH, PEOPLE usually sat around in the grass, went to the cafeteria, or took lunch in class, but a few of us played basketball every day. In the winter, when it got a little cold, we all wore North Faces and played football in the grass by the parking lot. But that day, for once, there was no basketball.

We had a motherfucking SPAM launcher.

Everyone was mad excited. We set it up at the free-throw line, loaded a brick of SPAM in the tray we made, and shot the shit right at the backboard. SPLASH!

"Damn! That shit is nasty!"

"It's stuck to the backboard, man."

"Again!"

We shot free throws, three-pointers, and half-court shots with this funky-ass SPAM launcher. It was late May in Orlando so the weather was already ninety-plus degrees. As the SPAM fell to the blacktop, it started to sizzle. Everyone walking by started to cover their faces. It smelled like we were cooking dog food. At this point, I wasn't on the football team anymore and a bunch of the guys were wearing their white home jerseys around school since it was a Friday. We saw this one kid we didn't kick it with anymore walking with his girl like a punk-ass Friday night lights jock.

"Yo, hit that motherfucker, man."

"Naw, naw, you gonna fuck up his jersey, son. That shit is crispy."

"Fuck that jersey, we don't play on the team no more."

"All right, do you."

Blap! We meant to shoot the kid, but missed and it went down shawty's shirt. The girl totally bugged out and ran to the office all crazy with high butt kicks like O-Dog in *Menace*. We couldn't stop laughing 'cause this girl's running around campus and a brick of SPAM just pops out the bottom of her dress like a newborn shitburger. We knew we were fucked, but it was definitely worth it. We were living our suburban version of

Mobb Deep's "G.O.D. pt. III" skit:* "Yea, yea, hit him out the window, son!"

Before we knew it, Miss Lacey, the music teacher, came by in high heels. If there was ever one teacher that I felt bad for picking on it was her. She wasn't mean; she just had no idea how to communicate with kids. She'd enforce rules to a T and didn't understand when to just let kids be kids and look the other way. To her credit, the school never should have made people like Joey or me take music class and have us sing. They used to give us sheet music on stands. She was one of those people that thought kids didn't know what sex was yet, so we would remix the songs, talk dirty to sheet music while girls would be singing, and hump the music stands. Everyone loved it, but Miss Lacey would go crazy screaming to stop. One day she got so upset, she just ran out of class in her high heels screaming, "I quit! I quit! I don't know what to do with you anymore!" Poor woman slipped on the stairs and we all felt bad. We were like, "Yo, come back, Miss Lacey! We just playin' with you!" Of course, on SPAM launcher day she was the first on the scene.

"What is that smell?"

"It's nothing, Miss Lacey."

"Eddie! Joey! I know it's you!"

"Hi, Miss Lacey!"

"What are you boys doing? What is that?"

And of course, we just ripped a can of SPAM over her head.

"Naw, it ain't me, Miss Lacey!"

There she went, running to the office to tell on us with a brick of SPAM just lying next to her. It was hilarious. Joey was usually pretty worried about getting in trouble, but that was the first time I remember seeing him really, really enjoy one of our dumb-ass stunts. He didn't even care he was getting in trouble and I loved it. I was always telling Joey to just wild. Life fucking sucked anyway.

I took my own advice in every phase of my life except girls. Annabelle Masterson looked like money. She had good hair, an ass, stellar middle

* What up, P!

school titties, and green eyes. Annabelle came correct with all that expensive Ralph Lauren. I mean, we had Polo or Sport, but this girl wore RALPH. Purple label. We had the joints with bright-ass colors and big logos on it. Annabelle had the leather boots, the jackets with embroidery, plaid, not the hood Polo we were coppin'. I swore she rode horses and shit.

We had never even talked to this girl. We never even talked to any of her friends for that matter. The only person I knew that talked to her was my homie Chris Sullivan, because he ate lunch with her friends sometimes. I knew Chris from football and he was a knucklehead, so that was my mans. Chris and Joey decided to take my crush on Annabelle into their own hands. All I ever did was talk about what I'd do to her, but I was too scared to actually approach her.

Three weeks before our last year of middle school, Joey and Chris wrote a letter to Annabelle with my name on it saying all the things that I had been saying plus some other killer bars. I believe my favorite was "I just want to get inside and eat your dingleberries." After two years, the student had become the teacher. Joey went over the top, all-in. At first I was embarrassed that Annabelle knew I was fiendin', but I couldn't stop laughing. Not surprisingly, Annabelle didn't like the letter at all and took it to the office. It was signed with my name, so at first people thought it was me—but eventually the truth came out and Joey and Chris ended up in the principal's office. They were suspended for a few days.

Joey's mom lost her mind. She got so mad at Joey that she forced him to go to confession. Even though it was his idea, I was implicated. I understand. Joey was a good kid, never causing trouble, never talking back, and along came this wild-ass Chinaman with mental SARS that totally fucks his world up. If you're Joey's mom, you're not going to like that kid very much. I guess she felt about me the way I felt about Robin Givens: the bird ruined Mike! My mom got a phone call about the situation, too, and I was under review by the school just because I kept getting involved in so many situations.

They couldn't expel me for the Annabelle letter because I didn't write it, but I was near the stove enough that they wanted to speak with my parents about whether or not I'd be able to attend in ninth grade. They never had the talk because our report cards came the same week. For the first time in my life, I got a D. My mom didn't even think twice and pulled me out of the school. She'd called 'nuff:

"I'm not spending my money so you can go fuck around with these rich kids. You're going to public school."

I didn't want to leave. Joey was my first really good Asian friend, my A-alike. I loved that motherfucker.

THAT SUMMER I went to the Dennis Scott Basketball Camp and got kicked out after the third day. Everyone at the camp had Chinese jokes. I remember after one game, this blond-haired boy, Sean, came up to me with his brother and yelled at me, "Ching Chong Eddie Huang sitting on a jumbo gong!" During a game, another kid came down the floor and laid one up on me real nice. After he scored, he had something to say, too. I can't remember what he said, but it was in the "ching chong" category of low-IQ slurs. It got me heated. So, the next time he was on a fast break, I ran his ass down and chucked him into the wall when he went for the layup. The kid started squirming and I knew I was done. I changed my clothes and just waited outside for my parents.

People had jokes, but at this point I was meaner, so I didn't even think twice. You said some shit, I threw you into a wall. Teachers, counselors, psychiatrists, family, and friends couldn't understand. I was a nice kid, smiled a lot, had a genuine interest in books, culture, and anything that I could get my hands on to read. But there was this switch that would go off. Between getting hit at home and all the things people said about me, I just couldn't take it. I couldn't walk away. I was determined to get even. I wanted to hurt people like they hurt me.

That summer, we moved to Bay Hill. In Orlando, there were two famous subdivisions. Arnold Palmer's Bay Hill had the best golf course in central Florida and hosted the Nestlé Invitational. On adjacent land, there was another subdivision called Isleworth, which had a shittier golf course, but almost all the houses were on the lake. Isleworth is the joint Tiger Woods lived in when his ho game got put on blast. We didn't just move into Bay Hill. Pops built a house, on a peninsula, accessible only if you drove through a gate at the end of Bay Hill and then over a bridge. #Money Team. Emery and I were shocked. There were no warning signs. For our entire lives, my dad was a hardworking small business owner and my mom was clipping coupons. Neither of them spent much money on us. Realizing that they had money was like finding out I was adopted. Who were these people? By that time, Pops had two restaurants: Atlantic Bay Seafood and Cattleman's Steakhouse on I-92. Both were doing well, but we had no idea they were balling for real.

Southwest Orlando was full of athletes, Palestinian landlords, people like the Magnusons who blew up overnight for inventing PVC patio furniture. Pops fit the bill. For the most part, it was white people, but there was one token minority in each subdivision. The Lebanese Khatibs lived one division over, the Maalis were down the street, Barry Larkin lived in the cul-de-sac, and the Neilsons from New Orleans were across the street. Sixty percent of the families were *Real Housewives of Southwest Orlando* types with platinum blond hair, BCBG shoes, and Botox. MILFs ran down the street with those rhinestone Bebe shirts, the uniform for every over-the-hill gold digger desperate to make their shit shine.

These families were twenty-first-century forty-niners digging for gold in the Orlandos, Phoenixes, and Dallases of the world. Carpetbaggers with no culture or moral compass, enabled and empowered with new money. The rush was real in those cities, all vying to be the next L.A. or Vegas. Disney, Exxon, and America West put cities on their backs. I didn't understand why my pops went down to Orlando until he blew up. That summer, it was in plain view for us all to see. His plan worked: that chink fucking made it. I'd say I was proud of my dad, but the first night in the house he made it clear we had nothing to celebrate. My dad was watching Emery and me as we ran around from room to room in the new house, hooked up our PlayStation to the new TV, and toasted our new life with Capri Sun. We were hyped. He wasn't smiling. With no advance warning he grabbed us both and kicked our asses. The money was his, not ours, and he made it clear.

My dad built a room where he put punching bags, speed bags, a bench press, and sparring equipment, just so Emery, Evan, and I could work out and spar with each other. He never wanted us to stop fighting, even if it meant fighting each other. We were never going to get soft, never going to give in to the cupcake life. My dad was still a G at heart, but unlike the American gangsters whose dream is for their kids to never look in the rearview, Dad did everything he could to make sure the money didn't change us. I'll give him that.

That fall I started my fifth school in seven years, Dr. Phillips. When I walked on to the school bus, I saw a bunch of preppy rich white kids, but there was also a Cuban girl; Neal, the big Jordanian; the Palestinians Maali and Muhrad; the Dominican Easy Eric; and me, "Chino." From jump, I knew the diversity at Dr. Phillips would be good for me even if it came in the Sizzler Buffet one-of-each format. The other thing that came clear was that I wouldn't be throwing kids into the ground like it was Dennis Scott summer camp; these motherfuckers were big. After my first day of school, I sat at the back of the bus. A few minutes after I sat down, this tall Palestinian dude, Maali Maali, came up to me and said, "That's my seat." I was literally a foot shorter than Maali and he had a full-on beard. I still hadn't shaved in my life and I had a photo of Bugs Bunny and Michael Jordan on my T-shirt. The Chinaman those days was in no position to fight grown-ass men. But of course, I couldn't back down.

"It's my seat now."

"Oh shit, son! Little man steppin' to you, kid!" screamed Neal. He was even bigger than Maali, but at least he smiled. Within seconds, there was a huge crowd at the back of the bus, ten deep with kids from my new neighborhood. "This n!gg@ got a Bugs Bunny shirt on, son. You gonna fuck him up?"

FYI, Palestinians and Latinos in Orlando all called each other "n!gg@" and black people called us "n!gg@," too. Palestinians ran shit so they could call you, your mom, your brother, your sister, and themselves whatever the fuck they wanted to. And apparently, everyone wanted to be "n!gg@s."

Then another Palestinian came on the bus with a tape deck in his backpack bumping Nas's "If I Ruled the World." We all used to buy tape decks, throw in a tape of music we recorded from 102 Jamz, and put them in our backpacks, which we'd wear on our chests to broadcast to whoever was unlucky enough to be in the vicinity. Most of us didn't bother with Walkmans 'cause we wanted to play our shit loud. Muhrad was doing the worst Lauryn Hill I've ever heard in my life. Dude was singing at the top of his lungs with his Palestinian Ebonic accent "If ahhh Roooo-led the Wooorrld!!!!" Then he saw me.

"The fuck is the deal, n!gg@, this kid is in your seat, Maali!"

"N!gg@, I know, he fuckin' deaf, b, I told him to get the fuck up but he ain't movin'. I can't fuckin' fight kids."

There was one white girl that got to sit in the back, Emily Huyzak. Maali and Neal always kicked it to Emily, a tall blond girl, cute, always dressed well. For real, I got most of my game just listening to Neal rap to her. Dude would come across the aisle, try to touch her legs, throwin' all kinds of wild-ass game at 6 A.M. Shit was better than the morning show on 102. On that first day, I recognized her. There were photos of her at my orthodontist's office so I figured it was my orthodontist's daughter. When she came on the bus, she screamed to Maali, "Oh my God, are you guys picking on kids? Ha, ha, what's his name?"

"I don't know, the n!gg@ ain't talkin', he just stays in my seat!"

Before anyone else could say anything, I shouted toward Emily, "Your dad is my orthodontist! Dr. Huyzak!" They all started laughing.

Maali wasn't a bad dude. He just ran the bus and the route. No one fucked with him and no one sat in his seat. My only out was if this white chick held me down.

"A'ight, a'ight, little man. You can have the seat, but when the bus driver comes, you gotta throw this shit at her." Maali pulled out a blue pen and broke it so that it leaked ink. The bus driver came, I hit her in the head, I got suspended from the bus for a week, and everything was cool. From that point on, those guys always looked out for me. When this fool Joe said he was gonna roll up to my crib with a burner, they cornered him at school, beat his ass with a giant umbrella, and took care of it. No one believed the kid even had a ratchet, but Muhrad made sure if he did, it wasn't comin' out.

———

LATER THAT WEEK, I was walking around the neighborhood to see if there were other kids out. No one was really around, but there was this big white house that looked like Colonel Sanders lived in the joint. For real, shit was country. It was all white with a rocking chair, benches that hung from the roof, a brick driveway, and them Southern window shutters. I saw this kid cleaning the pool so I walked toward the back. I just wanted to see if homie wanted to play basketball, but I was unsure if we'd even get along. I mean, his house looked like a fucking plantation. He saw me wandering around his backyard.

"Hey!"

"Wassup?"

"You live here?"

"Yeah, I just moved in."

"What's your name?"

"I'm Eddie, you?"

"Warren . . ."

There was a bit of silence. Neither of us knew what else to say. I looked at this kid and he looked like Tom Sawyer cleaning a pool in Orlando. He looked at me, sized me up, and then dropped a heat rock.

"Eh, yo, this is weird . . . but do you listen to Wu-Tang?"

It was one of those moments I'll never forget. Motherfucker saw right through me and I loved it. We couldn't have scripted that shit any better. I was all about the Wu, but at private school I had to beg people to listen to *36 Chambers*. There was only this one Indian kid that would rock the black shirt with the yellow *W*. All of a sudden, I go to this new school, new neighborhood, and people are trying to tell *me* about it. I was excited; this kid Warren was real. He was supposed to clean the pool so I helped him out and as soon as we finished, he called his boy Romaen, this Persian kid that lived over the wall. He was in my PE class, too, so I knew who he was.

"Romaen, what you doing, man?"

"Yo, son, I got this recording from the Playboy Channel Hooman ordered. You gotta peep this shit. Pac got hos butt-ass naked with Jodeci in a limo drinking champagne and shit."

"Ha, ha, I'm with this new kid, Eddie. He said he has PE with you."

"Oh, the Chinaman? Yeah, that kid let me hold *The Sporting News,* that's my dog."

That day, Warren showed me how to hop the wall to Romaen's. We lived in this neighborhood called Isle of Osprey, but if you walked to the back, there was a wall that divided us from Isleworth. Sometimes you could see Shaq on the lake jet-skiing. He'd have a kid drive a motorboat and he'd follow in his Jet-Ski to ride the waves. Life was funny in those years; we saw a lot of new money just stuntin' in the neighborhood.

As soon as we hopped the wall to Isleworth, we saw security cameras and those sensors that shoot lasers everywhere we looked. Warren taught me to slide down the wall so we wouldn't set anything off. The first back-yard we were in had dogs and sensors so we just crawled under the sensors to get away from the dogs. They were supposed to be guard dogs, but they were some lazy-ass Rottweilers that just sat there. Then we were in someone else's yard, but there were people chillin' in the pool so we ducked behind bushes and crawled around again until we could see the road. Once we got around the bushes, we just bucked it toward the road and luckily no one saw us. Everyone had alarms, but they were sleeping. Money had them under a spell. Once they spent the money on a problem, they never thought about it again. It was hilarious. Two kids randomly crawl and buck through your yard, but you don't even flinch. Three months later on TV, we saw that house with the Rottweilers on *Lifestyles of the Rich and Famous.* They were talking about how ill the security and dogs were. We just laughed.

Once we got to the road, I turned around to look and couldn't believe what I was seeing. Every single one of those houses could have been on *Cribs.* Benzes were the Chevys of that neighborhood. Most people were pushing crazy vehicles: military-issue Hummers, Rollses, Bentleys, I saw a Lamborghini, Range Rovers on twenty-twos. Kids were rollin' around in golf carts, women were getting mail in Manolo Blahnik stilettos, it was like

Monaco in Orlando. We walked up to Romaen's crib and his mom had just made him salmon and jasmine rice. It was delicious. After watching uncensored 2Pac videos from the Playboy Channel, we went outside to play ball and Romaen just kept "Hit Em Up" on loop the whole afternoon. Between games, I sat on Romaen's driveway, drank my Gatorade, looked around the neighborhood, and thought to myself. Damn . . . Pops, you came up.

7.

THE CHAIN REACTION

A couple of months into the school year, Romaen, our friend Ben, and I tried to join the debate club at school just to battle the smart kids. By default, I played the role of Will Hunting, which made Ben the half-Mexican Affleck and Romaen his Persian brother, Casey. At that point, I'd say we were like a lot of fourteen-year-olds. We all had Anarchy A's on our backpacks and crew names written across the straps, like P.T.C.* There was a childlike playfulness to our rebellion. We were just kids having fun. Everything seemed OK, but looking back, I'd say that day with the Debate Club was our last dance, a final, fleeting attempt to do things through the ivory tower.

We went in like a bunch of assholes as usual, but it was a big thing for us. No one invited us to go, we didn't know what it was about, and none of us had done anything like Debate Club before. It reminded me of my

---

* Romaen, Warren, Ben, and Josh came up with the name P.T.C., which stood for "Poon Tang Clan." Everyone thought it was really original, but I saw a VICE documentary called *Epicly Later'd: Menace Crew* that was about the infamous Menace Skate Crew in Cali. They had a skate deck called Poon Tang Clan and it was cool to see that on an entirely different coast, there were dudes in khakis and chucks doing the same juvenile shit. U-n-i-t-y!

boy Deshawn looking at the YMCA pool: the only thing worse than admitting you want to swim is admitting you don't know how. These days I wish there had been an adult in the room who understood where we were coming from. That stepping our feet in the door itself was an olive branch. No one grows up wanting to be a degenerate. We wanted to be like the other kids. We wanted to go to college. We didn't want to be hooligans, but we also wanted to debate in our own distinct voices. We didn't talk like the other kids, but we still had things to say.

Everyone sat in chairs as the president of the club gave this dry, convoluted orientation about how serious debate was and that the goal was to compete in Lincoln-Douglas–style debate or some shit. We didn't want all the posturing; we just wanted to play ball.

"Yo, we just want to debate about legalizing marijuana, g! Fuck this other shit," screamed Romaen.

Ben and I couldn't stop laughing, but the president in his blue blazer and oxford shirt decided to make an example out of us.

"OK, you want to debate legalizing marijuana?"

"Yeah. That's why we're here."

"Well, that's certainly a novel topic that no one has ever tried to approach."

His debate cronies all chuckled. I knew what he was doing so I jumped in.

"We know it's not original, but we want the exercise of the discussion. Our way."

"Your way? Well, that's admirable and we welcome your participation in Debate Club, but that topic is probably better served in the columns of *Hustler* or *Playboy*, not a Debate Club like ours."

"Man, fuck this shit. Let's get out of here."

That was it. We left embarrassed that we even tried to join something corny like Debate Club, yet also relieved that we wouldn't be trying to fit into something the rest of the semester. That's how it went for us. We'd all been through enough cultural cleansing situations that we knew something like Debate Club was going to try to remodel us, but I'll never forget what happened when we left.

These were the days before cellphones, so I called my mom on a pay phone to tell her that we finished early, and she came to pick us up. We had waited about fifteen minutes on the curb when she finally pulled up. As soon as I got in the front seat, I turned the radio to 102 Jamz. I had enough blue-blood Debate Club talk for the day and wanted to hear the countdown. But there was no countdown that day.

"For those of you just tuning in, we are sad to announce that Tupac Shakur has died."

"What the fuck?"

"Pac died?!?!"

We all knew he got shot, but Pac was invincible. He'd been shot before and survived, so none of us actually thought he'd die. The motherfucker was supposed to regenerate like Wolverine. It was almost a week since he got shot and we figured he was already up walking around. I remember the moment. None of us cried, we weren't really sad, we were mad. Mad that Pac was dead. Mad at the world. Mad that the one thing that really spoke to us was taken away before we even had a chance to really know him.

Pac was unlike any other rapper. In the era of hip-hop where the art form was under siege for its lyrical content and motifs, Pac was the one guy we all pointed to and said, "Tell me this isn't someone we should respect. Tell me this isn't positive. Tell me he's not an artist." He was a bona fide role model regardless of his contradictions. If there was one rapper that you could see joining a debate club it was Pac. There was always pressure to wild out, but Pac was that dude we looked at and for a few seconds we could see ourselves with three-piece suits and glasses writing "The Rose That Grew from Concrete" and shit. He was a reminder to all of us that "it's bigger than hip-hop."*

A FEW YEARS ago, I saw a photo of all our homies taken in Ben's backyard. We were just a bunch of cornballs at a fourteenth-birthday pool party but sixteen years later, Joey's dead, so-and-so smokes crack, and most of us

---

* Shouts to Dead Prez, *Let's Get Free*, y'all.

got two strikes. Suburban or not, something most definitely went wrong and we're still trying to figure it out. But if you ask me, Pac and that dickhead at Debate Club had a lot to do with it. We never tried to join a club, after-school activity, or anything productive, for that matter, ever again. The Honor Roll wasn't something we wanted to be part of. We gave up on doing it their way, we wanted to get free.

"YO, SON, YOU know dat dat kast comes back out today, right?"

"What's dat kast?"

"N!gg@, you don't know 'bout dat kast?"

"Whatever, man, you didn't know what Hurricane Starang was."

"Oh, hell naw, dog, this is the dirty dirty, you can't be tellin' people you don't know 'bout dat kast . . ."

Outkast was another one of those groups that you didn't hear on the radio, but people were certified crazy for *Southernplayalisticcadillacfunkymusik*. I got clowned all day because I didn't know " 'bout dat kast," but I didn't care, I just wanted the album. Romaen had an older brother, Hooman, who could get it for him, but Warren and I needed to find another way.

"Warren, you know *ATLiens* comes out today?"

"Yeah, man, we gotta go to Best Buy before it sells out."

"My mom won't take me, though. What about yours, dude?"

"Hell, no, my mom ain't gonna take us to go buy dat kast."

"I got an idea."

Back then, there was a subscription service from Columbia and BMG records where if you agreed to buy their album of the month, they'd give you nine free CDs of your choice. We pulled a bunch of subscriptions out of music magazines, then signed up using fake names and credit card numbers. Somehow, some way, they never checked if the credit cards went through but we always got the CDs in the mail. Between the two of us we got thirty CDs apiece and then recorded and swapped to double our collection. That's how we got *ATLiens*.

"Eh, yo, what are *Atliens*?"

"Yo, stop playin', man, you for real?"

"Man, how the fuck am I supposed to know, I'm Chinese."

"Son, it's A-T-L. ATLANTA, motherfucker, and they aliens. It's not that hard."

"Man, fuck you."

"You a funny ass, Chinaman, you know that?"

I was always a hip-hop head, but back then Romaen could school me on shit. Not only did he have Hooman, but he'd been around kids who listened to the same shit all his life. On the other hand, I'd been a loner caught up in the culture all by myself for fourteen years. Like the one kid in the hood who watches anime, I was the Chinese kid in Bay Hill doing the Bankhead. But if I didn't know something, my homies would hold me down. Romaen, Easy Eric, Warren, Baber, Samer—I never had friends like that besides my brothers.

Private schools are funny. Everywhere you go, people are socially competitive, but different circles value different things. Rich kids care who your parents are, what they do, where your clothes are from. In public school we cared what we wore, but every one of us had homies in the crew dressed like straight assholes. Your boy with the giant North Pole pullover in Florida or the fool rockin' RZA goggles. We would all crack on those dudes, but they could still roll. At private school, their passive-aggressive techniques were advanced. They had shit like the silent treatment. With public school, if I didn't like the way you dressed, I told you, and if you had something to say, we'd just battle. You could look like Bushwick Bill, but if you were witty, had jokes, or a way to get money, pussy, or beer, we fux'd with you.

Warren and I were trading places. He used to go to Southwest Middle School with everyone, but in seventh grade his parents pulled him out and he had to go to First Academy, where I went in third grade. What were the odds? He went to TFA and of course, who's his best friend? My boy Chris Nostro, who I used to chill with. I remember Warren called Nostro on the phone one day.

"Yo, Nostro, you remember this Chinese kid, Eddie Huang?"

"Wait, the Chinese kid that went to TFA in third grade?"

"Yeah, that's my boy! He lives across the street from me now."

"Oh hell, no! I remember when he put Edgar in the microwave, dude, ha, ha. That shit was wild. What's he doing in your neighborhood? He got money now, too?"

Neither Warren nor I wanted to accept the fact that overnight, we'd become the "rich" kids at school. Warren was somewhat apologetic about it and I was, too. If someone needed money for lunch, I'd just hold them down because I remember being that kid even though my parents weren't actually giving me money. I was just as "broke" as them but perception was a bitch and even at that age I didn't want people catching the vapors. At Trinity, I used to eat this kid's matzo and peanut butter because my mom didn't give me enough money for lunch but I didn't say anything. It bothered me a lot because people at public school thought I was spoiled, but I'd spent my life being the dirty kid at school wearing his dad's old clothes.

Romaen and Easy Eric took my swag into their own hands. I always liked shopping for sneakers, Starter jackets, and Polo, but I would lace my shoes up high, not match, or just rock my shit goofy. I remember one day for lunch Baber clowned me, too.

"Eh, boy, your parents work at Champs Sports or something?"

"Oh hell, naw, Baber, this motherfucker paid! Stop clowning him, dude."

"I'm not clowning him, Romaen, he wearing a Champs Sports Polo, son! They wear that shit at the register!"

"Man, it's a Nike polo I got for ten dollars!"

"Aw, damn, man, we gotta go to the West Oaks Mall. Son, you can't be steppin' out like that."

"Like what? It's Nike for ten dollars."

"Baber just told you, son, it's ten dollars because it's the motherfucking uniform, b! What made you think that shit was fresh? It's navy!"

Easy Eric had paper because his father died in the Air Force and he got a six-hundred-dollar check every week. He spent it all on kicks and clothes but he'd sell us his shit after he wore it. Dude had mad style; I got a lot of my steez from Easy. He had all the Tommy, Polo, Nautica, Wu-Wear,

Mecca; that was our shit. We were all little fourteen-year-old kids rockin'
tall tees, baggy jeans, and Timbos. I mean, it was Florida, we didn't need
six-inch Timbs, but we all read *The Source* and wanted to look like Ca-
pone 'n' Noreaga posing in front of Queensbridge. I switched it up when
the six-inches got played out and rocked the Beef and Brocs.*

There were only two places to cop Mecca, Wu-Wear, Pelle Pelle, or
Karl Kani. We had to go to the Magic Mall, owned by this rapper White
Dawg, or to the Jamaican store, Nappy Gear, in the West Oaks Mall. The
difficulty was an advantage; they only had a few sizes of each design, which
made it harder for people to jack your style.

The must-have item of the late nineties in Orlando was the Air Penny
II. After we'd been brainwashed by a million Lil' Penny commercials, we
were literally fighting at Foot Locker the day they were released to cop a
pair. I'd never seen anyone fight over shoes without the Jumpman, but for
three years, the Penny 1, 2, and Foamposite changed the game. Everyone
wanted a pair of those shits with the wave on the side, ice-cold soles, and
the one-cent on the back. That shoe was the one. I didn't have the money
to cop a pair, but Easy had two pair of each color so I just waited till the
second week, when he scuffed the first pair, and bought them for half
price. That Dominican had some stank-ass feet, but I didn't care. I rocked
those Pennies till they were talkin'.

Warren loved Mecca, but besides a few Mecca tees and silver-tab jeans,
he wasn't as materialistic as Romaen and I. He was a different cat. I'd come
home from school and see Warren walking around the street with no
shoes, sitting in the grass, or fixing his boat. There was this Sunfish sailboat he had in the backyard that he loved. One day, he let Chris Nostro
and me take it out. Before we left, we all got high hitting this bong we made
out of a plastic Mountain Dew bottle. Warren wanted to steer the sailboat.

"Yo, you guys are way too high to steer this shit."

"Naw, man, you worried we gonna break your little Sunfish?"

"Ha, ha, ha, yeah, Warren, this shit is cheap, man. We ain't gonna
wreck this, anyway. I been to sailing camp!"

---

* Green and brown Timbs.

"My aunt gave me this sailboat. Just let me steer it."

Nostro started laughing so hard he fell off the side of the boat into the water and then got stuck under the boat.

"Dude, what if he dies! He can't get up under the boat!"

"Why doesn't he just swim around?"

" 'Cause he's high as shit, man, and doesn't have his life vest on."

We started bugging out. Nostro was under the boat for a good forty-five seconds and then we heard him bumping underneath it.

"I'ma flip the boat!"

So Warren and I flipped this sailboat over, which is usually OK, but then it slid out, hit a dock, and a few pieces broke.

"I'm alive! I'm alive!"

"You fucking bitch, you couldn't even swim under the boat?"

"Yo, I think I inhaled plastic! I've never been this high. I thought I was gonna die!"

We ruined Warren's boat, just like we'd mess up Warren's house, or leave beer and weed that his mom would find later, yet he never got mad. Warren was the best friend I ever had. He was a wild-ass kid who would jump off his roof into the pool or off the bridge into five feet of lake water, wrestle a wild alligator in the dark, and break his collarbone snowboarding. He was never good with words, but he had this smile that'd do the talking for him. I never understood why he would put his life in danger, stand in the back of Jared's pickup truck going forty-five down Apopka Vineland, or just go sit in the woods by himself. But I realized, Warren was looking for something.

Warren and I both came from families that worked really hard to get where they were. He was unlike any white people I'd ever met.* In a lot of ways, he was just like me. He respected his dad for how far he'd come, but didn't want to eat off his pops. Mr. Neilson was a lawyer and Warren would work in his office, but it's not the life he wanted. Just like my dad had me work in the restaurant as a busboy, but neither of us wanted to be our dads.

---

* I'm sure there are others like him, but at that age I hadn't met them.

Two or three days a week like clockwork, one of us got disciplined at home. We knew something had gone down when the other didn't pick up the phone after dinner. A lot of times, Warren would come by the house and I was sleeping because I just didn't want to deal with shit anymore, but he'd wake me up to go run around the neighborhood.

I came into ninth grade an upset, stepped-on, defensive Chinese kid who felt white people were out to get me, but Warren showed me a new perspective even if we didn't always agree. At the time, I was libertarian because I was reading Ayn Rand; I know, it's horrible, but I simply didn't trust the government, I hated people like C. Delores Tucker, and felt that money was the third party that won every time. In my mind, if money was winning, what chance did government have against it? We just needed to stack paper ourselves.

Warren, on the other hand, was a Republican because of his dad. My parents were the same way; they'd always tell me to vote for whoever wanted lower taxes. I'd argue with Warren, but it's a funny thing with people. Even if you argue, when that person isn't around to say their piece, you say it for them. You may not even link with their point, but out of loyalty you make that man's point for him 'cause he ain't there. Years later, in college, surrounded by cynical liberals like myself, I'd say things that I swear came out of Warren's mouth and it helped me understand that old saying that no man is an island. People ask me what my greatest strengths are and I say perspective. The best way to get that is to meet people that are polar opposites; you learn the most from them. There are pieces of you that are inherently yours, but everything else is a collection of the things you've seen and the people you've met. In the end, we're like the Triumph beat: who's next on this RZA track? Step up and drop a verse on my story. That's the illest.

One day in tenth grade, this girl Emily Connors came over to my crib after school to kick it. She used to see my boy Ben, who lived down the street from us. It was pretty unanimous in ninth and tenth grade that if you liked shawties with curves, Emily, half Cuban, half white, was the one. She was also the only other person in our crew in the gifted program with me, not that it mattered. We were all family.

I was walking Emily out of the crib that day when we noticed these Indian kids cruising up my block. I remembered them from Lake Highland in sixth grade. The kid driving's initials were A.K. and so his vanity plates read AK-47. We ignored them and said our goodbyes but when Emily got in her car and tried to pull out of the driveway, these Indian fools pulled their ride up to block her. They didn't just casually block the driveway. They drove up onto the grass, cut the turn tight, and sat one side of wheels on the dip on the front of my driveway and the other on the grass. Alim thought he was slick, cheesing, and refused to move. I called Romaen, Warren, Austin, and Ben. While we were waiting for them, eight-year-old Evan saw this dude parked in our grass and got pissed. He came out with a paintball gun and just started blasting this fool's Jeep to fuck up his paint job. Of course, the Indian kids called their people, too. In the end there were twenty-plus fourteen- and fifteen-year-old kids in my driveway. It looked like a Ruff Ryder Proactiv commercial with a bunch of skinny punks in white tees staring each other down.

"Yo, it's one-on-one, man, Eddie versus one of y'all."

"What, you pussies don't want a piece?"

"I'm saying, we doing you a favor, we got you by at least five people. You gettin' off easy one-on-one. Keep it clean."

I didn't give a fuck so I pushed AK's boy first. I wanted to smack both of them so I figured just go for one and the other will fall back, but these Indian motherfuckers had heart. As soon as I pushed his boy, AK punched me in the face, a closed fist studded with rings, and I went down. I couldn't believe the shit. I looked at my friends, but all of them just stood there while it went down. The only one out of our crew that did anything was my brother Emery, who went running at AK with a pitchfork, but Ben held him back.

When my dad got home that night he was so mad I almost got a second ass-kicking. Warren, Ben, and Emery were all still at the crib and my dad just kept talking about how fighting isn't about fair. It's about winning. Warren kept shaking his head, but Ben and I were all ears. He talked about how in Taiwan they never fought one-on-one or if they did, it was a trap just to jump people. Warren didn't agree, but he wasn't sitting there with a broken nose. I never wanted to get hit again and from that point on, I got busy.

The next Monday at school, I showed up with a broken nose and black eye. That fool AK got me good. We couldn't go to Lake Highland to even things up with AK because private schools were so small; we'd never get in and get away without getting caught. But AK's friend M-Ron—the one I pushed first—went to Dr. Phillips and Ben found out his schedule.

English class was my first class after lunch and when I sat down I noticed everyone acting really weird. Kids who usually spoke to me or said wassup just moved to the side. I figured it was 'cause I had a black eye so I said to this one kid, John, "Damn, man, is my face that bad?"

"Naw, you didn't hear?"

"Hear what?"

"Your boys got that dude that lumped you up."

"For real?"

"Laid him the fuck out in the middle of the lockers, then changed clothes and left school. Kid is all fucked up in the office."

I couldn't believe it. Ben and our boy Jared took what my pops said to heart. What kind of parent teaches kids things like this? My motherfucking dad, that's who. If we were gonna run around causing trouble, talking shit, and starting fights, we had to be ready to finish them. From then on, if one of us was in a fight, we all were.

Pops didn't just let me run buc wild, though. He understood why I had to defend myself, but there was no excuse for stealing. One day Warren wanted to get his friend Kurt a birthday present and decided he'd like this giant tiki pole he saw in someone's yard. I thought it was kind of fugazi, but whatever, I was down to steal some shit. We pulled your average midday smash-'n'-grab, throwing the tiki pole into a car and then driving it home, figuring no one saw it. A few hours went by and nothing happened, but then there was a knock on my door. It was Officer Randolph.

I never liked cops, but this dude wasn't so bad. He was always patrolling the neighborhood, stayed out of our way for the most part, but when something happened, he'd come to our cribs first.

"Hi! How are you, Officer?"

"Good, how are you, Mrs. Huang?"

"Good, good! Can I help you with something?"

"Is Eddie home?"

"What he do now?"

"One of the neighbors is missing a tiki pole that was on their lawn, just wanted to see if Eddie knew anything about it."

"Ahhh, I see. Give me one second."

"Sure."

Mom closed the door politely, but as soon as I heard it click in my room, I covered my ears.

"HUANG XIAO MING NI GWO LAI NI TSE GU WAN BA DAN!"

"OK, OK, hold on, I'm sleeping."

"SOOSIN! NI GWO LAI!"

I paced around my room thinking if he'd let me go playing stupid or if he'd come search my room. Meanwhile, downstairs, Pops had to stop karaoke-ing to come talk to the police so he was pissed, too. He put his leather slippers on and walked toward the door.

"Hi, how are you today, Officer?"

"Good, just waiting to speak with Eddie."

"Yeah, he's on the way down right now."

Dad was a lot more savvy and knew that yelling in Chinese bugged everyone out. That was the difference between my parents. If my mom was mad, you'd hear wild and crazy Chinese. If it was my dad, he got his white man voice on.

"Eddie, would you please come down and speak with this officer? Thank you."

I ran down the stairs.

"Hey, how's it going?"

"Good. There was a tiki pole taken out of Mrs. Hogan's yard this afternoon. Did you happen to see anything?"

"Oh yeah, we thought it was trash in the front of her yard! I got it upstairs."

"Really? You thought it was trash? Because it was standing upright in the middle of her lawn."

"I mean, yeah, I'll give it back. It's not a big deal."

"She said she saw Warren from her window helping you grab this tiki pole. Where's he?"

"I don't know."

"Did Warren help you take the tiki pole?"

"Why don't I just get you the tiki pole?"

"Eddie, was Warren there with you?"

"He's across the street, you can ask him while I go get the tiki pole."

Fifteen minutes later, we managed to drag the tiki pole down the stairs. I went outside and Warren was standing there with Mrs. Neilson and my parents.

"Look, you boys know that wasn't trash, and you stole your neighbor's property. Luckily she doesn't want to press charges, but this is burglary any way you slice it. Do you understand?"

"Yes, Officer Randolph."

"Huang Xiao Ming Gui Xia!"

I'd never heard my dad scream Chinese in front of white people. He thought it was rude.

"No, Dad . . ."

"GUI XIA!"

Everyone's faces turned. My dad was a respected person in the neighborhood and always maintained his cool with people outside the family. Warren was nervous, Mrs. Neilson was dumbfounded, and Officer Randolph tried to intervene.

"Mr. Huang, is everything . . ."

Before he could finish, I did what my dad asked and kneeled on the concrete driveway. I kneeled right down in front of the officer and bowed three times.

"I'm sorry, Officer Randolph.

"I'm sorry, Officer Randolph.

"I'm sorry, Officer Randolph."

"It's quite all right, Mr. Huang, I see you have this under control. I'm sure the boys won't do it again."

"No, they won't. I'm very sorry they did this. It's not right."

"No, it's not, sir. We will see you around the neighborhood. Have a good evening."

I had never seen an officer so shook in his life. Warren's eyes got huge, looked at his mom, looked at my dad, and everyone took off still fearful for my life. I mean, in the middle of a gated Orlando subdivision, there was a Chinaman kneeling in the driveway for all passersby to see in all his shame. For hours, my dad left me out there as punishment. People had no idea what to make of it. Were we a cult? Was it religious? Was the rapture coming? I saw the faces in cars as they passed, laughing and pointing in pure shock at this ancient Chinese ritual that had somehow landed off Apopka Vineland Road. I wasn't mad at my dad. I deserved it. For our people, this is how we paid the price and I accepted it. I'm just glad there wasn't Instagram back then.

AROUND THIS TIME, Warren started dating this girl down the street, Julie. She had this red Toyota and would drive us to school, but she totally fucked up Warren's taste in music. Dude went from Wu-Tang and the *Menace II Society* soundtrack to Modest Mouse and Incubus. I wanted to puke in my mouth every morning listening to that shit. I started bringing my Discman in the whip just so I could avoid listening to songs about water and wine or whatever it was Incubus kept going on about. In the end, some people can only keep up the "hip-hop thing" so long.

I think hip-hop is real for a lot of white and Asian kids, but there's a point of diminishing returns. That's when they make an upward assimilation. I didn't listen to hip-hop for strategic reasons. I loved it, I needed it. Watching my white and Asian friends move away from hip-hop opened my eyes to this rite of passage that I was never going to join—the ascendance into whiteness. It's a funny position being an Asian in America. You're the dude who can cross the union line. Your community actually wants you to sell the fuck out and work in law, accounting, or banking. But I realized then that I wasn't going to cross the picket line just to get a nut. I was down with the rotten bananas who want nothing to do with that. We live to fight the good fight.

I started kickin' it with dudes who skipped school and skated. I couldn't skate, but I could smoke the shit out of some weed and we liked the same music. Mike Muschewske was the ringleader and a fucking animal. This kid looked like he was eleven for most of high school, but he barely went to school, had all the video games, girls at his crib around the clock, and we all got to kick it. His mom was cool with it and kept mad food in the kitchen and he had this ill cocker spaniel that bit Austin's nose off one night when he dropped acid and kept teasing the dog. Every day, it was me, Muschewske, Lil' Cra, Justin, Austin, and Chaz hanging out at Chew's.

Justin called me "Gourmet," 'cause every time we got high, I couldn't just eat the chips or cookies. I made ill stoner food, like Doritos sandwiches, where I took ham, turkey, and cheese and rolled it up on plates, then sandwiched them between Doritos. I'd microwave cookies and eat them with ice cream, bake macaroni and cheese with crushed Cheetos on top, real disgusting Scooby snacks. A few years later at a bachelor party in Miami, after hitting Miami Gold, pissing off the VIP balcony onto the dance floor at Voodoo, and copping frozen chimichangas at 7-Eleven, we went back to our hotel. Total fail, because we didn't have a microwave in the room, but I didn't give up. I told my homies, "Ay yo, let me get the ironing board and iron!"

I put the frozen chimichangas on plates and started ironing the shits. Fifteen minutes later, we were eating chimichangas with crispy exteriors and I was officially the Iron Chef.

THIS WAS MY downward assimilating crew and my parents definitely weren't feelin' it. I first spotted Justin at school, walking across the campus wearing those ugly-ass Pippens with the word "AIR" plastered all across the entire shoe, and recognized him from Sea World Summer Camp when we were in third grade. We were supposed to train mice to walk through a maze but Justin and I didn't have the patience. There was a giant python tank at Sea World so we would take the mice from class and feed them to the snake. We got caught, but even then, Justin was using the line he'd be using seven years later: "It's cool, man, nothing's gonna happen. My dad is captain of the SWAT team." Anytime we got busted for shit, if we were with Justin, we walked. He was our get-out-of-jail-free pass. So we went buck wild.

Orlando's first Best Buy opened on Sand Lake Road around that time. It was a big deal. Our city had made it. So every Tuesday, a bunch of us would go in the spot with double-sided tape around our waists. All the mom-and-pop record stores and Sam Goody's had big-ass alarms on rap CDs. They knew the deal, but Best Buy was slow. Every CD just had a security sticker that you could peel off. We'd just peel off the stickers and stick the joints to our waist under our clothes. Every week we brought home five or six new albums. Eventually, they caught on. Instead of putting stickers on the hip-hop joints, they put rent-a-cops at the ends of the aisle. We tried to outsmart the system: We'd take the CDs from the music section and leave them in different parts of the store. Then we'd circle the store like we were looking for something—a washer-dryer, a new coffeemaker—and pick them up on our way back out. This time, I could see a rent-a-cop following me.

He thought he was slick, but I saw that fool. I led him into the appliances aisle and ditched the CDs into a dryer. With nothing on me, I just went toward the exit, but they arrested me anyway.

"Yo, the fuck you touching me for, son? I didn't do shit."

"Then who put these CDs in the dryer?"

"Since when is it illegal to put CDs in dryers?"

"We have you on camera transporting these CDs into the dryer. That's attempted robbery!"

"It's not like I transported hookers over state lines; it's CDs in the appliance aisle, son. You're wildin'."

"Don't get fresh with me! You tried to steal a Sporty Thievz 'No Pigeons' single!"

Game recognize game, that rent-a-cop kinda shot me in the heart with that one. Talk about spot blown, getting called out for trying to steal the "No Pigeons" single is pretty much the Urban Dictionary definition. That was like the time Muschewske bought the Lord Tariq and Peter Gunz album, quite possibly the worst, most anticipated album of all time, the pariah of the Bronx. #Dejavu. The rent-a-cop let me go and five years later in college, someone stole my two-hundred-CD collection out of my whip. I had never even loaded the music onto my computer. My life's work lost, but it was fair. Karma is a bitch and I never paid for those joints.

Every weekend, Justin, Mike, and I would go to parties and wild out so much that people called us Fouls. Someone's parents would be out of town and they'd invite the whole crew to come party 'cause we were the only ones that really threw down. These people that opened up their houses basically rented us like hookers selling "cool" but they had no idea what they were in for.

One weekend, this girl Melanie threw a party. It was kind of a dope house, there were a lot of drinks, and at least eighty people were packed in. We were having fun, but I was toe up. I'd been drinking this jungle juice Mike made and saw all these herbs with board shorts and frosted tips. Most of the people that hosted house parties were first-timers. It was the cool thing to do, but they weren't down so we'd toss the whole crib. Why? 'Cause they never talked to us, said sideways shit when we weren't around, and stigmatized us as black sheep. Any chance they'd get in class to tell on us for being late or being high, they would, but as soon as the parents left town, they wanted to be us for a weekend. They assumed we'd steal their shit and piss in their milk, but they STILL let us come party 'cause they needed us. For one night they wanted a "pass" to wild out with the derels. I wasn't about to be nobody's Bojangles 3000 so I set it off.

I went to the bathroom, where there was a long-ass line so I just whipped my dick out and pissed in the kitty litter. I never peed in a litter box before so I had no idea it would get so full, so quickly. The shit sloshed over the sides. I thought it was mad funny so I showed it to Mike and that's what started the chain reaction. Mike and Justin would always one-up me so Muschewske took two boxes of cereal, poured them on the kitchen floor, then followed it up with a gallon of milk. Melanie's man bugged out. "Dude, what the fuck are you doing?" Deadpan, Muschewske, with a blunt in his hand, doesn't even trip: "I'm makin' breakfast, bitch."

Meanwhile, I was out back where Melanie had a bunch of rabbits in a cage. I cut them loose. Get free. To Zion! Justin poured out a big bag of chips in the yard and the bunnies went apeshit for the Doritos. When the rabbits, roaming the yard, looked up from their Doritos buffet, their faces were dusted orange from the cheese powder. Once the party blew up, we left leaving the tourists to clean up. Welcome to Jamrock!

Warren was disappointed in me. He was friends with everyone and didn't understand why I'd tear people's cribs up with Mike and Justin. Part of it was just being crunk, but I hated these people. They'd judge me in class, call me a burnout behind my back, but that one weekend their parents were gone, they'd call me and my friends to party because they were fucking tourists. Warren was torn because no matter how close we'd become, his reference group was still white. He didn't understand that I didn't hate white people. I hated *whiteness*.

"Dude, you're just as racist!"

"Man, I'm just getting even."

"No, you aren't. These people haven't done anything to you. They invited you to their party and you fucked their house up and cut their rabbit cage open! What the fuck, man?!?!?"

"Stop being a bitch, son. They're not like us. You're white, but you spend time with them, you'll see, once they know how you think they'll toss you out with the water, too. We're different."

"How do you know that? You don't even talk to these kids."

"Man, your boy Cory told me last week he still wishes there were plantations and gentlemen! He thinks it'd be more 'civilized,' g. What the fuck is that?"

In my mind, Warren was too forgiving. We should have punched Cory in the face for saying that shit. The way I saw it, everyone liked Warren 'cause he was everyone's favorite white boy and I was his wild-ass gremlin sidekick. I don't fault Warren; we were just dealt different hands. He wanted me to play my 3, 4, off-suit like his double-cowboys* but Mama didn't raise no fool. I could never win playing a white man's game. Warren

* Kowboys . . . get it? Two Kings.

never would've let me get away with fighting his boy Cory, so I'd organize *Fight Club* in the sparring room. That way, in the context of *Fight Club,* I got to punch a gentleman in the face.

THE PREPPY WHITE kids would never see Warren as the "other" and they'd never see me as one of "them." If they did try to see me as one of "them" it wasn't in my true form; it was as a reformed, assimilated, apologetic version of myself that accepted the premise that my people were barbarians with FOB scars* and they were the people on the hill. At one point, I tried to detox myself of whiteness. I hung out with Baber, Samer, Abbyshek, Neal, and my boy Kalpesh. They were the first friends I made in high school anyway. Baber was Muslim and so was this other kid in my gifted class, so I started reading the Koran just to see how others viewed religion and society. I could never be Christian, but I found some level of solidarity with Muhammad. It's the age-old problem for Asian Americans. You dig and reach and beg for anything that was made for you, but it's just not around.

After a few months reading the Koran and not partying, I knew it wasn't for me, either. I had a lot more in common with Baber, Samer, and Abbyshek (who was Hindu, not Muslim) concerning family and values than Mike or Justin, but it wasn't enough. A lot of the things that bugged me about Christianity were present in Islam, too. I realized that organized religion wasn't going to solve my problems.

My search wasn't over, though. My parents were bad Buddhists, but I wanted to really do it right so I read about Siddhartha, too. I got into it and fasted on just water for seven days, writing things in a diary just to see if it affected my thinking, but the notes were basically "Day 1: Mo-fuckers is hungry . . . Day 2: MOFUCKERS IS REAL EXTRA LIFE OR DEATH HANGRY." I wasn't about to go out eating vegetables, telling myself that life is suffering. To me, life wasn't suffering, it was a game where you tried

* FOB shots—get familiar. When you get a tetanus shot abroad and it leaves the ill scar.

to eliminate all the shitty days and live for the good ones. Buddhists seemed like a bunch of kale-eating losers accepting defeat to me. They were the soccer moms and dads with kids on the team that never won a game, yet wore Birkenstocks and hemp clothing to every game telling their uncoordinated kids that they were still winners.

That's when I found Taoism and it made a lot of sense, 'cause it made no sense at all. This dude Lao Tzu was the original RZA writing cryptic shit you brought your own meaning to with mad double entendres and metaphysical language. For the same reasons I liked hip-hop, I liked the Tao Te Ching. You didn't pray to anyone, you didn't submit to anyone, and it was what you needed it to be. It wasn't a religion, it was a philosophy. As basic as it seems now, that's when I flipped the script and stopped reading anything religious. There isn't a God in the sky that pulls the string. I told myself that there is something bigger than us but that it was egotistical and presumptuous to personify what that was. No one knows what's on the other side, but I read anything and everything if it was founded on things we actually knew. I wanted to trade in reality and save up for the unknown. Maybe we die and we don't take anything with us, but if there is a human spirit, wouldn't the intangible things be the ones we get to keep? My memories, my knowledge, my know-how, my soul. All that shit, I didn't know where it'd go, but whether it came with me or not, I listened to Nas and "stayed chiseled."

Around this time, I turned sixteen. I was excited because I wanted to get a whip. Every weekend, I worked at Cattleman's with Warren and Ben and was trying to get my dad to help me with a down payment on this used BMW Hatchback from 1990. It was only $20K and I could make the payments if he held me down on the down payment. I wasn't totally confident it would happen; in fact, for two years I hadn't gotten shit for my birthday, not even a cake, because my mom said I was a "bad kid." That I understood, but I hoped they'd help with the car because I needed to get around.

The day of my birthday, my dad pulls up at home with a brand-new Benz SLK, the hard-roof drop-top roadster Benzo, the first year it came out. My heart sank. I knew that shit wasn't for me.

"You like my new car?"

"Yeah, it's cool . . . Does this mean you're not helping me with the down payment?"

"No money, I just bought this car."

What a dick. I understood him not helping me with the down payment, but he didn't have to pull up on my birthday with a new Benz for himself. I didn't understand. Even my mom and Emery thought it was kind of fucked-up. I mean, there's stuntin' and then there's that. Looking back, I wish I never made a fuss because what happened after was worse. I should have just accepted that most kids don't get cars. It's one of those suburban privilege moments that I'll be embarrassed about forever: feeling entitled to a car.

I made a stink about it so that weekend, he agreed to go to the used car lot and at least go look at the Bimmer hatchback with me. That's when he went over the top.

"Fine, you can have the Benz."

"But I don't want the Benz."

"You don't even have your license yet and can't drive for another six months anyway! We'll just call it your car."

I knew my dad was a Jedi, but this was the ill, Homer Simpson makes Bart smoke all the cigarettes at one time switcheroo. Like, "Oh, you want a car? Here's a CAR!" See how much you like it now.

"Dad, I appreciate it, but that's too much. I can't drive that car. It's O.D."

"Look, I drive it for six months, then you drive it for a year and a half, and I'll sell it when you go to college. No big deal."

I like to think my pops meant well, but the car bugged me out.

Everywhere we went, he'd tell people about how he spoiled me and gave me the car like he was the World's Best Dad, and it pissed me off. All those years getting whipped by five-pound Busch Gardens rubber alligators was wiped out and made right with one really fucking over-the-top car that I never should have got in. Kids from school all sweated that car when I pulled into the parking lot during summer school. I remember John Whitehead said something that really woke me up.

"Damn, son, you shinin' so hard right now."

"For real?"

"Kid, you just pulled into the parking lot, top down, bumpin' 'Picture Me Rollin', you win!"

"That's not winning, man. My dad bought this car. I didn't do shit for it."

"But own it! That's you."

"Naw, man, it's not."

People didn't understand . . . or maybe they did and I didn't. They were right. I could have owned the car, stayed in Orlando, worked for my dad, run his restaurants, and never had to worry about money ever again, but that wasn't me. That's not what life was about to me. I didn't read the Koran, starve myself for two weeks, read the Tao Te Ching, and struggle for answers every day just to give up for a car. I remember not having money, I remember having money, and neither had a bearing on who I was as a person. It affected how others saw me, but not how I saw myself. Everyone talks about how they'd love to be ballin' or how only rich people complain about having things; they're right. You can't possibly know until you have it, but trust me, it only means something if you earned it. If it's truly yours. Otherwise, you're just a punk-ass kid bumpin' "Picture Me Rollin'." I couldn't even listen to that song for years.

8

PINK NIPPLES

I hated the gifted program. The kids were cool and being treated like we were X-Men was really dope, but the teacher was horrible. Junior year, we had to take courses from this conservative Christian woman from FSU. Our curriculum was nontraditional, since we were "gifted," so she broke the year into two semesters. The first semester she would choose one topic that we studied and explored for eighteen weeks. The second semester we would pick our own topic, study it, and give a fifteen-minute presentation at the end of the semester. The topic she picked was the Holocaust and everything seemed fine.

But the first day we started, I knew something was wrong. The first couple weeks, the lessons were taught based on photos from a summer vacation she spent going to Holocaust sites and museums. This was hipster irony before hipster irony. Every photo we saw was of her in some horrible Seminoles T-shirt and visor, white short Americana smiling, juxtaposed against the background of Holocaust sites. The tone of the photos was totally fucked and it became comedy, which no one wanted to admit because we knew it was wrong.

She'd tell us stories about what tour guides told her and for weeks, there was no through line or message, just her own Christian guilt on display for thirty gifted English students. We had Jewish kids, white kids, black kids, and an Asian kid in class; to a man and woman, none of us thought the subject was being treated with the proper respect. The first project she gave us was to draw our feelings about the Holocaust on tiles. She wanted to mimic the AIDS quilt, but as a Holocaust tile mosaic to decorate the room with. I had no idea how to approach this shit, was worried if I'd offend someone, and we were also being graded on our "feelings." It was totally fucked. I ended up drawing a picture of Hitler standing on a big pile of poop.

"Eddie! What is this?"

"Hitler on top of shit."

"What does this mean? What are the feelings you are trying to convey?!?!"

"That Hitler and his ideas are a giant pile of shit."

"This is not a feeling. You did not follow the assignment."

"It is a feeling. I feel he's a piece of shit. Don't you?"

"Go to the office! I'm not putting this tile up."

Literally, twice a week, she sent me to the office because I'd point out how ridiculous her photos and lesson plan were, but she really lost it this time. She was screaming, shouting, and pushed me out of the class like I had SARS. Usually she at least let me grab my bag, but I didn't even get that courtesy this time. People in other classes heard the screaming, saw me standing outside, and knew something happened.

"Ha, ha, yo, E, what'd you do this time?"

"I drew Hitler standing on a pile of shit."

"What?!?"

"Yeah, I gotta go to the office. See you later, man."

While I was in the office, people from class started telling everyone about the tile I made. Other people drew Stars of David, people holding hands, doves and olive branches, but the one everyone wanted to see was Hitler on a Pile of Shit.

The last month of the semester, our project was to enter a national essay contest about crimes against humanity. She forced us to write about how the Holocaust was the greatest crime against humanity ever committed. I didn't disagree, but I felt it was an infringement on free speech and undue coercion. You can't force someone to agree with your conclusion and then grade them on it! Especially not in a classroom full of Holocaust tiles juxtaposed with Seminoles paraphernalia.

"I agree with you. There isn't another crime against humanity that I can objectively and definitively say is a 'greater' crime against humanity, but that's not my point. We should come to decisions ourselves. You can't MAKE us say it!"

"I'm not making you say anything, it's true."

"No, you can't objectively say that. It's unfair to Native Americans, victims from the Rape of Nanking, and pretty much any black person brought to America against their own free will! This is bullshit."

"That's it! Go to the office."

"That's all you have, the goddamn office and your Christian guilt!"

"Eddie! Go to the OFFICE NOW!"

I was right, the administrators couldn't force me to agree with her, and I got to write an essay that did not conclude the Holocaust was the greatest crime against humanity. My essay ended up being about how it is unproductive for anyone to argue that there is one single greatest crime against humanity. There's nothing "great" about any of them. The one productive thing that came of that semester, though, was an introduction to Jewish history. When it came to choosing law schools five years later, I chose Yeshiva without any hesitation.

GIFTED ENGLISH SUCKED, but during the summers, I took college courses at Davidson or Duke University in North Cack-a-lack. I'd fly into the Charlotte airport and see white rocking chairs with old white people kicking back in V-neck sweaters, flip-flops, digging into some vinegar pulled pork. I felt like I accidentally walked into a photo shoot for *Southern Living*. When I got out of the bus and onto the Davidson campus, I was hit by this ill wave of whiteness: green, dense, manicured grass, all khaki everything, shawties with headbands. I could smell the fucking mustard wafting from the cafeteria. There was no way in hell they had Jamaican beef patties for lunch in that joint. I told myself the first thing I'd do was call Emery to ship me a case of Tower Isle Patties to hold me down.

Landing at Davidson was like hitting the reset button. The kids were all right. Even the nerdy prodigy-like ones were down-to-earth and just there to have a good time. I got into TIP (Talent Identification Program) because I scored in the top .25 percent of the nation on my PSATs in eighth grade. Of course, my math scores were ill but my verbal scores weren't, so I enrolled in this class, Writing with Aristotle, taught by a professor from the University of Georgia. He was a dick, but he had good taste in books. Our first few lessons were on propaganda. He showed us the contrast between Martin Luther King Jr.'s "I Have a Dream" and his "Letter from Birmingham Jail"—one an appeal to emotion, the other to logic. It was eye-opening. My whole life, I felt lied to by parents, society, the news, etc., but I could never explain why. All along, from the time I was a kid, people tried to satiate my inquisitiveness with propaganda, appealing to emotion or tradition or threats, instead of reason. I was just their pawn.

ONE DAY ABOUT two weeks into the summer, the professor came in with packets of five pages stapled together and dropped them in front of us. I looked at the title: "A Modest Proposal" by Jonathan Swift. I remember the first time I heard Michael Jackson's *Bad,* I remember the first time my cousin played "Fuck wit Dre Day," and I remember the first time I read "A Modest Proposal." It was like going to the gym early in the morning and hearing the first basketball hit the floor, *dumph.* From that first drop, you can feel that the game is on.

When I read Swift it was like I could hear this dead motherfucker. It wasn't writing anymore, it was live. I could feel how he felt with someone standing over him his whole life. He was sick of it. There was some real hate behind his words. Swift was beyond "Letter from Birmingham Jail."

At a certain point, people don't deserve "Letter from Birmingham

Jail." All they get is hard dick and bubble gum. Swift reminded me of Ghostface on the intro to "Biscuits."

Who the fuck brought me this chocolate shit, man. I said a banana nutriment, man.

He reminded me of Ghost because it was frenetic, funny, desperate, and reasonable all at the same time. People look at Ghost and think he's nonsensical, but he's not. He makes more sense than anyone else in the game, but at a certain point, being straightforward sounds nonsensical because the rest of the world can't shoot straight. When you feel like you're the only one in the world going crazy, it's probably not you, it's them. What else can you do when everyone else becomes paralyzed by social ketamine? You kufi-smack them in the face! That's what I learned from Swift. Everyone knew what England was doing to Ireland wasn't right, but Ireland didn't have a chance. I respected that Swift knew he couldn't win, knew England wouldn't care, but told his story in the most raw, real, and personal way possible. Eat our children, eat them, that's exactly what you're doing anyway! You want them? Eat them. He made sure that if England was going to keep doing what it was doing, that their government and their people did it consciously. There would be no mistake about what exactly was going on.

When we talked about "A Modest Proposal" I felt like I was running circles around everybody. I understood that shit better than the professor 'cause he was just a fan. I wasn't an Irishman, but I knew how it felt to have someone standing over you, controlling your life and wanting to call it something else. From the people at Christian Fellowship to First Academy to my parents to Confucius to thousands of years of ass-backwards Chinese thinking, I knew how it felt. Everything my parents did to me and their parents did to them was justified under the banner of Tradition, Family, and Culture. And when it wasn't them it was someone impressing Christianity on me and when it wasn't Christianity it was whiteness.

Those other kids had more vocabs than me and more knowledge of the

American canon. At that age, I didn't know what *Citizen Kane, Gone with the Wind*, or even *A Christmas Story* was. There were so many gaps in my American cultural understanding because we just didn't get it at home. It always hurt me writing or debating because I didn't share their references, but that summer I was determined that it wouldn't stop me. I wouldn't try to talk about things they knew anymore. I would use the references that made sense to me and make them catch up. Before I ever read a marketing book in college, I understood what "pull marketing" was. Unlike the other kids, I wasn't memorizing words or events. I was speaking from experience. For the first time, I wasn't arguing just to argue. I wasn't wildin' out 'cause I was bored. I finally found another mind I fucked with and it was just my luck he was a dead-ass Irishman.

I was never the same after that night, though. Swift gave me confidence. He didn't use flowery language, ill vocabs, or references to obscure historical events. He had wit and that was it. Like Mark Jackson had a teardrop and AI had a crossover, Swift had satire. Seeing me that day must have been like watching a twelfth seed in March Madness. Reading "A Modest Proposal" was the moment I realized, "Dogs, you can win this game. You got these motherfuckers, b!" You look up at the clock with six minutes left and you're only down two. Never did you ever think you'd be in that spot, but you look around and everyone else is complacent. They're confused how they're in that boat with you, but while they're shook, you come with the full-court press and see a way out. Everything comes clear and you see exactly how you're gonna win the game: by doing you.

I found my voice and no one was going to take it from me. It wasn't Swift's voice, it was mine, but he gave me the confidence to let it go. My dad urged me to fight, but Swift taught me how. It wasn't just sparring in the kung fu room or wearing a belt. I started to study the mechanics that writers and orators used: complex sentences, allusions, metaphors, framing, satire, parody, alliteration, syntax, logos, pathos, and ethos. It wasn't enough to be right; you had to know how to argue. I started reading classic essays like "American Scholar" or Tolstoy's "What Is Art?" There was a formula to being persuasive and I wanted to figure it out.

There was a girl that summer, too, Brandy Jenkins, a bad Southern thing with dirty-blond hair, and I wanted to see if she had pink nipples. Allen had hooked up with this white girl and he always told me about pink nipples so I wanted to see them for myself, too, but the curiosity was deeper. I remember accidentally walking in on my mom once changing and she had brown nipples, so I obviously didn't want anything to do with something that reminded me of my moms. If I was gonna see nipples, I kinda wanted pink so that they wouldn't be screaming "MOM" and make me puke in my mouth.

I remember the first day of summer session, everyone was up on her. We had the same class together and I kicked it to her, but she liked this white dude who played soccer. I was a little salty for a minute, but once I read "A Modest Proposal," I stopped thinking about her. Every day, I worked hard in class participating in discussions, taking notes, and then doing the reading at night. After class, I would ball with my boys Jerel and Zack. All the floors would play each other in basketball. In Orlando, I never got on the court at school 'cause we had people going to the NBA. But in North Carolina, I was on one. Back then, Jerel and Zack would say I played like Penny. Anyone from Orlando would have laughed, but—can I live?—I could handle in the half-court, had a ratchet and a postgame. We could pick-and-roll but I really liked to dish out of the post or play high-low with Jerel, who was already six two at the time. I remember I got everyone with my spin move. I'd drive hard to the right, spin, and hit a floater; no one stopped it that summer. Once I gained weight, I started playing more like Mark Jackson, but that's depressing so we'll save it for another chapter.

After a week or so, Brandy stopped fuckin' with that boring-ass white boy. We started eating lunch together. There was no history between us, no commonality, no expectations, just two strangers in North Carolina tryin' to kick it. I really liked her a lot. She was smart, funny, and didn't just go along with things I'd say. She pointed out inconsistencies, disagreed, and had this ill Southern drawl. I'd never met a girl that was as confident as her, either. She knew everyone liked her and never tripped. She was on all the time. We got to know each other, but nothing really moved it past friends until the Counselors versus Campers basketball game.

Our floor had all the best players except one dude that played small forward on another floor. I forget his name, but he was one of those long, thin, jump-shooting small forwards. He did a good job on the glass, ran the baseline, and hit mad fifteen-footers. The counselors were six to seven years older than us, but Jerel and I were convinced we could get 'em, even though the campers never beat the counselors. Jerel, Zack, and I practiced every day after class. When the game came around, we all had goofy-ass T-shirts that had our names tagged with Sharpies.

The first play of the game, the counselors brick and Zack rebounds but I bring the ball up. Jerel's already down the court in the post so I give him the ball and he draws double. Homie was easily our best player so all the counselors collapse and I fill on the left baseline. Jerel hits me with the pass and I nail a twelve-footer to go up.

We lead the whole game by two or three points when their point guard comes down the court. I meet him a foot outside the three-point line. He drives right then tries to cross over, but I see it so I eat this motherfucker's lunch. Ball goes through his legs, I scoop it, and head down the floor on the fast break. I have a clear path and the counselor's on the floor, but he lifts his leg up and trips me—I jump up onto the counselor but then we all get separated.

They canceled the rest of the game but we didn't care. Everyone knew we won and all the campers were upset on some *Bush v. Gore* steez. Brandy and her friend Gwen even started barking at the counselors and I remember thinking, This bitch is pretty thorough! The girl definitely caught feelings.

My knee was kind of fucked-up so I was sitting on my bed in the room when Brandy came through with Gwen, Jerel, and this chick Sheila. I didn't want to move around 'cause I cut it up pretty bad. Being in high school, the girls were extra-dramatic about some small shit, but I wasn't trying to stop it! That was the first time Brandy asked me about back home. They all knew I was from Orlando and Jerel was from Deerfield Beach, but we never really talked about what our families did. I actually had some photos of my friends and me so I showed Brandy. There was this photo of Emily and me on a Jet-Ski that she saw.

"Who's that?"

"Oh, that's my man Ben's girl that he used to see."

"Why is she with you, then?"

"We're just friends; it's not that serious!"

Brandy was wide-ass open and it was pretty funny. She went upstairs after a few minutes with Gwen, but before the end of the night Gwen came back down.

"Eddie . . ."

"Wassup?"

"Do you like Brandy?"

"Yeah, she's cool."

"No, like, do you 'like' Brandy?"

It always cracked me up how people used *like* in high school. But I couldn't front. I was all about her that summer.

"I told you weeks ago I was into her! She is always acting like we're just friends, though, so I don't try."

"Well, she really likes you."

"For real? Why didn't she say something."

"Because you're supposed to, you idiot."

I had to admit, I was a straight goon with girls. I never curbed my personality for anyone and everyone always talked about just being yourself around girls so I did. Problem was, just being myself was probably a little too raw. Most of my game came from shit Warren, Romaen, and I heard from skits on *Doggystyle*. Romaen was always tellin' that "Deez Nuts" joke whenever he could. Emery loved that skit from DMX before "How's It Going Down." Luckily for Warren, girls just jumped him; kid didn't even need game. I was funny so that was my game, but I sucked at closing. The next day, Brandy stepped up.

"I like you and I'm taking your keys."

"Oh, really?"

"Yeah, come get them later."

And she put them down her shirt. Even a goonie goo-goo like me knew how it was gonna go down. I have to say, I was pretty fucking excited and happy that the first time I'd see titties live and in person would be so premeditated. I had hours to think about it, prepare for it, visualize all the fantastic things I'd do to those titties . . .

After dinner, we snuck off and went to her room. She had on a white top, sun coming in from the window in her dorm room, and cutoff jean shorts that her butt poked out of. Brandy was no pro herself, but I remember looking into her light blue eyes and feeling comfortable. I kissed her and she put her tongue in my mouth first. Everything we did, she initiated because I had this irrational fear every time I was alone with white women that some parent or cop would bust in and arrest me for infecting them with yellow fever. Honestly, all the way until my freshman year of college, every white girl I made out with, I let make the first move because I thought I'd get arrested.

But that evening, white people really weren't so bad after all.

We made out for a few minutes and then she took her shirt off. I went for her bra and surprisingly, it only took a couple of seconds of fumbling and off that went, too. And there they were . . . pink as motherfucking Laffy Taffy and soft as Swiss Miss pudding. My dick felt like a bound foot in my jeans trying to get out, but I figured that wasn't happening so I did what anyone in that situation should do. I dove headfirst into her boobs and put as much of them in my mouth as I possibly could. It was like being at Golden Corral. I wanted it all, plates and plates and plates of titty, PLEASE. I didn't want it to end, but I heard someone in the hallway.

"Oh, shit!"

"It's OK, Eddie, the door is closed."

"Naw, I don't want to get arrested."

"Arrested?"

"Never mind . . ."

She kissed me again, but I figured my time was up and kissed her back hesitantly before leading her to her clothes. It was kind of hilarious, but my first time hooking up with a girl, it was me that said "no more." This guy, Eddie Huang, what a bitch.

The last week of the summer, we got reviews. Everyone else's parents came to pick them up, but my parents never did. I liked that. Once you're past fourteen, you should be able to take a plane, not get your shit stole, and set up a dorm room. If you can't do that, you're going to be a biscuit anyway and your parents should save their time and money 'cause you are definitely not winning *Survivor*. The one advantage of coming, though, was that the professors would have conferences with parents. Brandy's dad came, but she kept him on the side and didn't introduce me. But at the dance during the last week, one of the counselors saw me and Brandy with her legs open so they bugged out and told the other counselors and our professor. Without getting detailed, the professor told her pops that we were messin' around, so this dude writes me a letter. I remember one classic line: "I have a shotgun and I will use it."

I really liked Brandy, but more than that, I liked what I could be with her. I needed to get away from my family and Orlando. There was an individual inside me that wasn't Chinese, that wasn't American, that wasn't Orlando. Just a kid trying to get the fuck out, tell his story, and arrange the world how it made sense to him. I started to think about whether I was who I was or I was just a reaction to something arresting me. I wanted to get free.

As soon as I got home, I picked classes for my next year of school. Instead of taking Spanish like everyone else, I took Latin because I wanted to learn the history of language. I took creative writing, humanities, and since I always got in arguments with the gifted teachers, I dropped out of the program and took regular English and Integrated Math. They were basically English and math classes for kids that were going to get vocational degrees and GEDs. I made a conscious choice to surround myself with like minds instead of always feeling insufficient for someone else's reference groups and masters. I started avoiding Warren's friends. Life was too short.

I read books, cut down on the smoking/drinking, and had my mind right. But, on the weekends, I'd still wild out, hang with my homies, and be a retard. I was never going to be a monk, but my consciousness was slowly rising. I remember one thing that I really regretted was hog-'n'-jogging from Steak 'n Shake one night. We ate, I was gonna pay, but Warren and Mike wanted to hog-'n'-jog so I went along with it. Nothing serious, we did it a few times before, too, but this girl Sheila Jimenez said something to me at school the next day.

"You're a real punk, you know that?"

"What?"

"I work at that fucking Steak 'n Shake you ran from! My coworker had to pay for you guys' food."

"I don't give a fuck."

"Well, you should. Not everyone is rich like your parents, you fucking asshole."

I'd been called a lot of things, but that really cut through all the bullshit. She was 100 with me and didn't even want my money when I tried to pay later. That was the turning point for me. I realized I couldn't have it both ways. I was either a good person or a shitty one. There wasn't one logical explanation for why it was OK to hog-'n'-jog. We used to say it was OK to steal from Blockbuster or Best Buy because they were big corporations, but this time we got it really fucking wrong. I never wanted to be that wrong again.

The two teachers who really made an impact on me that year were Mr. Barrows and Mr. Feddell. Barrows was the humanities teacher. A lot of the same kids that were in gifted and honors classes would take his class because you got college credit, but I just wanted to read the books he assigned. We got to read *Siddhartha,* the Tao Te Ching, and Socrates. It was like a hybrid humanities-philosophy class. I hadn't been in class with those gifted/honors kids for a year so it sucked being around them again. They weren't actually smarter than the kids in my regular English class, either. It doesn't take much to get good grades. You memorize what the teacher says, write it down, and spit it back out. In regular English, it was like watching a movie in a theater in Brooklyn. Everyone had something to say and they were loud about it. People were from different parts of Orlando, different ethnicities, and no one agreed on anything. In Mr. Feddell's English class, we had so many hip-hop heads we'd all talk about how lyrical Shakespeare was, compare him to Pac and Nas. For the first time, I became the teacher's pet. Without a bunch of gifted/honors kids fighting to kiss the teacher's ass, I got to actually have a real discussion with Mr. Feddell. Instead of playing the contrarian, I just spoke my mind about *Hamlet, Macbeth,* and my favorite, *Julius Caesar.*

English was mad fun. Half the class worked at McDonald's or Chick-fil-A after school and would most likely get GEDs, but for one hour every day, we really got into Shakespeare. Most of them weren't reading between the lines, but they definitely understood it. Especially when we talked about Brutus, honor, and loyalty. *Julius Caesar* is the epic street tale. It's all about betrayal, loyalty, honor, and going out like a G. Feddell couldn't see it, but we did. We loved *Julius Caesar.*

I started to realize that books weren't meant to be understood one way or the other. We took *Julius Caesar* and made it mean something entirely different than Feddell, Harold Bloom, or maybe Shakespeare ever expected. I remember Feddell was such a purist he'd cross-check all his thoughts with Harold Bloom but that was his weakness. You don't need validation from anyone, not even the author. Just like we did with Nikes, breakin' 'em out, wearin' 'em with no laces, tying the Air Force 1 straps backward, etc. Like the Fab Five coming through with black socks, baggy shorts, and intimidation, we didn't have to do it the Man's way. That's how we resisted assimilation. Every time people tried to feed us soma, we freaked it out. It was around this time that I stopped feeling helpless, became less nihilistic, and realized that if I didn't want it their way it didn't have to be, but that I'd really have to work. It's harder to resist, but there's honor in it.

THEN IT HAPPENED. Emery was at the mall with his homies one weekend. Nader, Emery, Yuel, and Raul, they called themselves Windmill because of the break-dancing move. Yuel was Hawaiian-Japanese dred, Raul was Latino, and Nader was Lebanese. Emery's United Nations crew was chillin' at Hooters with some girls when these two white boys kept eyeing them, talking shit. Once they left Hooters, the guys followed them. They didn't want to ditch the girls so they kept walking, but these dudes wouldn't give up. Finally, they told the girls to go home and Emery led everyone into FAO Schwarz, where the kids followed. They went to the sports section, got junior baseball bats, and beat the shit out of the two trailing them. The next week at school, Emery was just eating lunch in the cafeteria when some kid ran up from behind, punched him in the face, and took off. I got home that Friday and Emery had a broken nose so my dad was like, "You already know."

I had no problem getting the kid, but that weekend was rough. Sunday morning, we woke up to a car crashed right through a wall on Apopka Vineland Road, a mile from my house. The bricks were all scattered, the wall was shattered, and there was a champagne sedan stuck halfway through the wall with the other half hanging out. As soon as I saw it, I knew it was my man Ricky Santo's car. Ricky was a year younger than me, but one of my good friends. I'd always watch sports with Ricky and he was also the first to put me on to Mos Def: *Black on Both Sides*. He was a two-sport star at Dr. Phillips, playing baseball and football, which was a big deal since a lot of our players ended up at D-1 programs. But more than that, Ricky was one of the most likable dudes. He never beefed with anyone, always smiling, and when news broke that he was in critical condition with head and neck injuries we all bugged out.

We went to school the next day and before first period, the principal was on the intercom telling us to have a moment of silence for Ricky. I was just walking into school so I stopped right inside the entrance as thousands of us stood frozen for Ricky. I lifted up my head, opened my eyes, and to the right I saw Emery coming out of the bathroom and that motherfucker that punched him was waiting. I was shook from the moment of silence, but I knew what I had to do and dropped my backpack. Warren was right behind me so I knew he'd scoop it. Those were the days right after Columbine so we all had to wear student IDs around our necks. I took my ID off, wrapped it around my hands, crept behind this kid, and yoked him right in front of Emery.

All the Tangelo Park cats hung by the bathroom so as soon as they saw it, you heard the motherfuckin' bird call. Kids surrounded us and formed a wall so the cops couldn't break it up. Emery froze for a second, but then reared back and mashed him right in the face. After letting him get the first shot, I put the kid in a headlock and started punching him right in his left eye over and over. Emery kicked him from behind, then we threw him headfirst into a wall.

The kid fell in a pile, but the cops still couldn't get through. I lost all self-control. When I got into fights, my hands would always shake and feel light. I could never feel the punches until after when my knuckles were cut and swollen, but every time I hit this kid it was heavy. I beat that kid like he was Ms. Truex, Edgar, Reaganomics, the Counting Crows, and *Moby-Dick* all rolled into one. I heard the kids surrounding us start to talk.

"Cot damn, y'all."

"Oooofff. This some *Rocky IV* shit, boy."

It really was like the Russian versus Apollo Creed. The Red Chinaman pummeling Mr. America. I stood over him, looked at the cops finally breaking through the crowd, and stepped right on this kid's balls.

"Ohhh, hell naw. Huang done gas-pedaled this n!gg@?!?!"

"That's too much. You already know that's too much."

"Ha, ha, yaaaooo, don't fuck with these Chinamen y'all! Do not fuck with these Chinamen!"*

Usually I was quick to run when cops came, but I just stood over this kid. I don't know what got into me, but I just never wanted anyone to fuck with me or my family again. I was sick of it.

The cops grabbed me and I spit my gum in one cop's face and that's when I'd gone too far. They arrested me, walked me out of school, and sent me to booking. Things done changed.

---

* I remember going to Chik-fil-A two days after the fight and the entire staff giving me pounds 'cause they had watched the fight. No one ever fucked with any of the Huangs after that.

9

LEN BIAS BROKE
MY HEART

I still remember the shoes I had on that day at booking: Carolina Blue Jordan XIVs. They made me take the laces out because they had metal tips, but it was cool, the XIVs looked good broken out anyway. Plus, a lot of kids in booking were walking around with tongues floppin'. I got lucky: since I was still seventeen they sent me to juvie. It wasn't bad at all, looked like a doctor's office with linoleum floors and holding cells with skinny dudes in long white tees. I wasn't worried; I didn't do anything wrong. Someone punched my brother in the face so I stomped him out.

It definitely didn't faze my dad. I've never seen a parent so proud to pick his kid up from holding. "You dumb-ass . . . You're not supposed to get caught!" he said with a smile. Around this time, I had become closer with my dad. He had stopped hitting me at home, we talked on the regular, watched Magic games together, and I was working at the restaurant a lot more. Once his restaurants were successful and that was off his mind, he could handle my mom. She didn't get to him as much and the house was a lot more calm. Every day, she would still wild, but my dad learned to walk away. He just rolled around in a bathrobe and boxers all day eating fruit and watching NBA games he recorded.

Just to keep me out of trouble, he'd been scheduling me for work every Friday and Saturday night, but it didn't really help. If anything, it made things worse hanging with servers, bartenders, and cooks. Now I could get beer, weed, Xanax, acid, whatever, any time I wanted it. Once I got arrested, though, I knew I'd have to chill; I didn't have that many chances left. The kid I knocked out never came back to school. Romaen saw him one time and found out his face was broken. I felt bad about that, but figured he should have thought it through before hitting Emery. We all chose to fight that day, just happens he took the L.

Emery was different, though. When the cops came that day, he took the kid who was knocked out and flipped his unconscious body on top of his own, which made it look like he was the one getting attacked. He never got arrested.

Emery saw what happened to that kid and basically quit fuckin' around cold turkey. His friends were still wildin' but he just stayed his ass at home, stopped listening to hip-hop, and got a little shook. He wasn't scared of fighting, but became more wary of the consequences. I remember him saying to me, "That could have been one of us, man."

He was right, people could catch you at any time. Emery was now getting turned off by my style, my music, my friends, and the drugs. I was doing a lot of ecstasy at the time and Emery got scared enough to tell my dad. The day he found out, he didn't hit me, he didn't yell, he took me out on the lake in our canoe, and we just kicked it. I thought he was gonna "Fredo" me, but he kept it real. It was one of the first times I really opened up to my dad.

He didn't judge, he just listened. I explained that it wasn't like I had a drug "problem." I was just partying. I did it for fun. Kids love glo-sticks! But my dad knew this was one of those moments he had to be a dad even if it contradicted his own wild times as a kid.

"You remember I always talk about Len Bias, right?"

"Yeah, you hate Len Bias and Lefty Driesell."

"No! I LOVE Len Bias and Lefty Driesell but they broke my heart. That goddamn Len Bias throws everything away. He could have been Michael Jordan, but that dumb-ass kill himself right after the NBA draft. I never been that sad in my life!"

I couldn't say anything.

My dad was always an independent man. His family was poor, he ran the streets, and his mom spent most of her time playing mah-jongg. Like me, alone in the American wilderness, he just had his homies and the street in Taiwan. His father didn't work and spent most of his time translating the Bible after seeing horrific acts during Chiang Kai-shek's reign. Dad took care of himself and didn't want to depend on people and he didn't want them to depend on him, either. I didn't notice until we both started working at Cattleman's but we're one and the same: horrible trainers. You'd always hear the same three words come out of our mouths when people asked for help.

"Figure it out!"

We always had to figure it out, so you can, too! We didn't have the luxury of people explaining why I couldn't use my left hand or why his family had no money. We just figured it out. But love is a funny thing.

Growing up, he loved the Bee Gees and basketball. That was it. When he came to America, went to university, and got to be part of a community—Terrapin basketball—he turned obsessed. Len Bias was the only person that gave Jordan a run for his money and when YouTube came around, the first thing I did was pull up old Len Bias videos, but my dad couldn't even watch. Bias broke his heart and he hated being vulnerable to others. Len Bias was dead to him and he never wanted to think about it again. In a lot of ways, Len Bias mirrored his approach as a father. He was scared of heartbreak and tried not to show how much he cared about us. It was no problem for him to show love to acquaintances and business associates that came to the house. The show is easy when there aren't real feelings behind it. My mom would always complain that he was cold and didn't express himself well to his family, but was a maestro with strangers. None of us understood, but I finally got it that day. He was scared.

Pops hated not being more in control of my life, hated how I made mistakes, hated how in many ways he couldn't just live my life for me. It took a lot of self-control for him to not be like my mom. He knew he got a lot of his character from independence, struggle, and failure. That was the plan for me. Run out into the wild and hopefully return in one piece. It all worked in his head, but when the plan looked like it was falling apart and I came home with bad grades, bad manners, or a bad attitude, he kicked the shit out of me. As much as my friends thought I was Will Hunting, I wasn't. I had a dad and he loved me. He just hated that I made him vulnerable. And when Emery told him about the ecstasy, he broke. Not in a weak way. Pops broke open.

The dam burst and he unleashed an avalanche of fear, talking about all the worries he had. How he would play Len Bias's story over and over in his head as a father scared that one of his kids would go out like that. He really believed that it could happen and even though he let me go out and do my thing, he just prayed I was strong enough not to lose total control. He made me promise that I'd stop doing ecstasy and never do coke. The weed, the beer, the Xanax, fine, but stay away from the sugar. I thought it was funny, but I figured, what the hell . . . Your dad asks you for one thing in life, anything, and it's not to do coke? We're gonna grant that wish. I got off easy. Thanks, Len Bias.

We rowed the canoe back home that day after our talk and I felt good. I had a reason to stop doing things that I knew were self-destructive and sometimes that's all kids need. A reason to live. Some people have the birds and the bees, others have the cat's cradle, my epic talk with my Chinese dad was Len Bias. I look back and it's funny. You think it's gonna be Confucius, Lao Tzu, or maybe even something Grandpa passed on since he was such a great man, but no. Even as an immigrant who came over in his twenties, when it came time for the talk, my dad found the inspiration in an African-American basketball player. Like father, like son.

I REALLY GOT into working at the restaurant after that talk. I wasn't so focused on defying my dad. I just wanted to make him proud 'cause I knew he cared about me. His chef was this cool Jamaican dude, Chef Andy. He had the ill machine-gun stutter and accent so it was always entertaining when he spazzed on people. He'd say shit like, "Ttttakkke tttthhhhaaattt, bbbbbboi." Warren and I also worked at my dad's other restaurant, Co-Co's, which served fusion Floridian and Caribbean food that this guy Chef Henry concocted.

I wasn't a big fan of Chef Henry. He was dirty to me. He had gnarly hair flying around on his head, nasty shit under his nails, and he'd still insist on tasting things with his fingers. It was American kitchen culture. Shit, it was American food culture. People would take pride in having hands covered by buffalo wing sauce or BBQ stains on their face. I remember watching meat heads in the dining room eat thirty-two-ounce porterhouses, challenging each other to see how much they could eat. The way those people experienced food didn't make sense; it was gross to me. I always loved food, but it didn't bring me any extra enjoyment to eat it or cook it like a frat boy.

I DIDN'T RESPECT Chef Henry and he didn't like me. Mainly because I was the owner's son, but also because I didn't respect his food. There were a lot of goofy fusion things that he made and all his recipes were overcooked.* Warren worked with me and Chef loved him. I would always choose the tasks on the prep list requiring more skill and Warren would gladly take on the dirty ones. He took pride in doing the more physically demanding tasks, but I'd rather butterfly shrimp or clean the New York strip because I wanted to learn. Additionally, I liked working on the proteins so that I could make sure we weren't wasting my dad's money. Dad would cut the New York strip himself a lot of the time, but when he wasn't there I'd watch it for him. Since that day eating soup dumplings on my sixth birthday, everyone knew I understood flavors and if someone showed me something once, I wouldn't forget it. Chef could see it, but he resented

---

* Overcooked doesn't mean it's actually overcooked in terms of temperature. It's overcooked in the concept. Like things Dwight Howard wears with epaulettes and zippers all over the place. That's overcooked.

me. He'd rather have someone like Warren who worked hard and followed instructions.

I learned a lot from him, though. That guy taught me how to make sauces on the sauté station, bread proteins, clean meats. All my technique prior to working there came from my mom and it was straight Chinese. We'd use a lot of bone stocks, cornstarch, scallions, ginger, dried chilis, and aged Chinese rice wine. The biggest surprise to me in an American kitchen was the use of butter. It was everywhere! Regular butter, infused butter, heavy cream, all things that you'd never see in an Asian kitchen unless you cooked Southeast Asian, but even then it was coconut milk.

I also kept my shifts at Cattleman's, where I worked as the expediter. I loved expediting because you could control the whole operation and identify weaknesses. I expedited almost every Friday and Saturday night at Cattleman's where we did $10K on average nights and up to $15K on big ones. The expediter stands on the side of the pass opposite the line, which is where the food is cooked using a grill, sauté, fryer, or whatever. The tickets come in, you put them on the speed rail, and as the food comes out, the expediter finishes the dishes with garnish, wipes the plates clean, and organizes the tickets. In a lot of ways, the expediter is the catcher calling the game. You tell the kitchen what to fire, what to hold, what to refire. The waiters and managers need to tell you what's going on in the dining room, who's in the weeds, which tables are causing problems. If you have a table that doesn't have patience, you bump their ticket up in line, turn and burn 'em. If there's a table that's cool, drinking wine, having appetizers, you slow their meal, give a little extra, send a dessert. You want them to come back. My dad put me there to keep an eye on quality as well. If something came out that was inconsistent, I'd send it back.

When I started, I was a slow expediter because I kept burning myself. Most expediters were in their mid to late twenties and had been working in restaurants their whole lives. They had reptilian skin. Nothing could burn them. I sucked until I started wearing two gloves at a time. Such an easy fix and it made all the difference. There were people who were faster than me, but they made mistakes and didn't pay as much attention to food cost or customer service. They just wanted to do their job, get the food out, and finish the tickets. Since my dad owned the place, I tried to stay aware of all the other factors and started to see how difficult it was to be the owner. Every single person in the restaurant needs to do things exactly how you teach them or you lose money. Additionally, they need to think like you and more than that, they need to care like you. It was an important lesson. I saw how managers would give people manuals, train them, and write them up, but it was empty. If you really wanted good employees that would have your interests at heart, they needed to buy in. You needed people who wanted to grow with your business and see themselves as valuable members on the team. My dad was the master at that.

He knew where everyone was from, their background, their struggles, their boyfriend or girlfriend, their hobbies. He took a real interest in people's lives at the restaurant and even made the down payment for one of his manager's homes.* No one called him boss or Mr. Huang. He wanted them to call him Louis, but they respected him so much they insisted on Mr. Louis. There were numerous people at the restaurant that had been at Cattleman's over ten years and two employees literally worked there until they died. I still go home now and see the same bartenders and servers I grew up with. If they don't work there, they still drink there.

On the other hand, my mom was the guard dog. Every day my mom would hunt down the parts of the operation where people were losing money or did their jobs wrong. These people were stealing right from under us and if they weren't stealing, their laziness was costing us money. Fines from the health department, giving the wrong portions, ordering the incorrect amount of meat or produce—things fall apart every day at a restaurant, but as a manager, the key is to understand and accept the human element. No one is perfect and if they were, they wouldn't be working for you.

---

* R.I.P. Bill. His manager, Bill, was a great guy who really helped my dad in the early years. Pops paid the down payment on his house and Bill was doing great, but he had a nasty coke habit. He would come work for us three years clean, go off the rails, then come back two years later, etc. My dad always welcomed him back, but it ended badly when Bill OD'd. These are the things you see growing up in a restaurant.

People don't make much working at restaurants so you need another way to motivate them. Servers have motivation because they make the most, but your kitchen, your busboys, your dishwashers, these guys don't see shit and they work ten times harder than the servers. My mom wanted to fire everyone, but my dad understood that you have to have the proper expectations at restaurants. You understand people's strengths and weaknesses, and put them in a position to succeed. There are numerous positions in a restaurant; it's your job as the owner to find the right fit.

My favorite thing to do was watch the Haitian guys make ribs. I loved barbecue my whole life but had no idea how to do it. Southern food was one of those things that always eluded me. It drew me in because of the play between savory, sweet, and aromatic. Compared to other regional American food I ate, there wasn't any comparison. You could see from the motley of dishes in the Southern American canon that it was created out of necessity and there was genius in how they made do with scraps. There was an honesty to the cuisine that I gravitated toward and I'd skip school in the mornings with my friends just to eat biscuits 'n' gravy. It wasn't until I became a chef that cooks would say to me, "You got nice moves."

"What are nice moves?"

"You know, like that thing you do with the dried shiitakes. How you wash them, soak them, then use the infused water to give vegetarian dishes umami."

"That's just cooking, g!"

"No, Chef, that's a nice move."

In cooks' terms, Southern food simply had a lot of nice moves. From the pickling to the smoking to the frying, Southern food really spoke to me.

Just like Charles Barkley, Jonathan Swift, hip-hop, and *Married with Children,* I saw parallels with Southern food and my home. Mom loved pickling things and one of the first recipes I learned from her was this quick garlic pickle we'd always have in the fridge. Those were the only pickles I knew until I started seeing things like chow chow, pickled okra, old pickles, young pickles, and everything in between. The first time I saw boiled peanuts on the side of the road in Georgia, I said, "Grandpa used to eat these!" I thought some Taiwanese people were gonna jump out from behind the barrel, but instead it was some dude with no shoes and a pair of overalls. Apparently, Southerners liked boiled peanuts, too. But the most familiar thing was to take little bits of smoked meat to flavor vegetables, starches, and soups. In the old days, meat wasn't plentiful so Hunanese people got really good at smoking meat, especially duck or ham hock. One of my dad's favorite dishes was a plate of leeks stir-fried with bits of La Roh or smoked ham hock. I remember watching collard greens come at me across a counter in a pair of dark brown hands. It was unfamiliar until I took a bite and recognized that the flavors easily could have come from my father's hands, carried in a melamine bowl with plastic chopsticks.

The Haitians at Cattleman's taught me how to make ribs, but it wasn't until years later that I realized how un-Southern their technique was. Yet, seeing it done the wrong way, knowing there was something off, and then learning to do it the right way taught me a lot about food. With food, there's a right way to do things, but it's probably only right for you. You may like *char-siu* pork roasted in an oven hanging from hooks like the old Chinatown joints. Or, you may like to sous-vide and finish it on a high-heat grill like me so you get the caramelization of sugar with a bit of char. They're both acceptable ways to make *char-siu* pork, but whatever method you take, there's a right way to roast it in the oven and a right way to sous-vide. Style isn't an excuse to cook without a standard. Style just determines the set of rules you choose.

I have to say, the Haitian guys chose a really shitty style, but my mom and dad loved it because the technique was familiar. They would boil off the first,* but the liquid was infused. It would have bay leaves, oranges, onions, garlic, carrots, liquid smoke, scotch bonnet peppers, sugar, etc. We would throw all the ribs into this boiling stock and cook off the first. A lot of the technique revolves around cooking the "stink" off of pork and then

---

* When people from Asia or the Caribbean cook, there is usually a "cooking of the first." Jamaicans, when making oxtail, will soak them in a solution of water and vinegar to let the blood out, then also flash-boil them to "cook off the first." At our home, we'd flash-boil everything before braising or stewing because it was bad form if the meat had a "stink." Andy Ricker tells me that in Thailand they won't even eat lamb because of the smell.

slow-cooking the meat so the juices you want come out later. After boiling the ribs, we'd finish them in the oven with BBQ sauce. It was definitely not barbecue in the traditional sense, nor was it delicious. I'd say to myself, Why do they insist on calling this barbecue? Why don't we give up on BBQ and just do a red cooking braise with the ribs? Or even my mom's winter melon and sparerib soup! No one listened and I became the "crazy" one that didn't like "barbecue." I had a lot of fun cooking with those guys, but I still needed someone to teach me real Southern American techniques.

Warren and I reconnected through the restaurant, too. Once he started working at Cattleman's in the kitchen, we got to hang out like we used to. We'd become so close by that time that we didn't even ring each other's doorbells. Warren had the code to my garage door and vice versa. Warren would still surprise my mom all the time, but my dad loved it. Whenever Warren came in, we'd set him up a plate, a chair, and some chopsticks, which he got really good at because he followed instructions. My mom used chopsticks the wrong way, holding them with her knuckles instead of fingers, so we all picked it up, too. Warren learned from my dad and those red chopstick paper instructions so he was pretty nice with them. I remember my brothers or Mom mumbling in Chinese when Warren would go to the bathroom, "This guy is taking the food so fast!"

"Bu yao fan!" (Don't be annoying!)

"I'm not annoying, he's eating everything!"

"He is our guest! Let him eat."

"He's here every day! When is he gonna stop being a guest?"

"Eh! You guys always complain white people make fun of our food, then we find one that likes our food and you complain he eats too much! White people can never win with you guys!"

"What are you talking about?! White people win at everything! If they didn't lose with us, they never would!"

"Ha, ha, ha, bunch of assholes, man! Bunch of assholes . . ."

I remember for Thanksgiving at our house we would just eat hot pot or some strange spread of sautéed Chinese items, cranberry sauce, sweet potato casserole from Boston Market, and sushi from Publix 'cause I guess it really made the table pop. These days my Jamaican friends have turkey but it's flanked by oxtail, beef patties, rice and peas, cabbage, etc. My Cantonese friends have turkey with lobster steamed over *e-fu* noodles, salt fish fried rice, and stir-fried squid with yellow chives. I fux with Diasporic Thanksgiving and consider it more American than duck sauce, but at the time, I felt left out of the American experience. Our family really didn't like Thanksgiving until I went to Warren's and finally understood what it was about.

Every Thanksgiving, I'd walk in through Warren's garage door and get hammered by the smell of roast turkey, chicken cacciatore, biscuits, boudin balls, and of course Mrs. Neilson's green bean casserole with fried onions on top. That was her dish. I remember seeing it come out of the oven with golden fried bits of onions on top, covering a stack of fresh green beans mixed in with cream of mushroom. It was a simple dish. Mrs. Neilson even used canned cream of mushroom, but I'd never had green bean casserole so it was a revelation. I took a plate home to my mom that had a little sample of everything on it.

"Mom, look, it's Thanksgiving!"

"Oh, I don't want American food."

"Try it! It's really good! I promise."

"No, no, no, American food makes me feel funny. Too much salt and cream."

"Mom, come on, you are missing out! I ate it and it's awesome."

Whenever I brought home American artifacts to share with my mom, she'd shut me down. My parents were not the type to humor their kids; they always kept it too real. It literally took three Thanksgivings as Warren's neighbor for my mom to finally try the green bean casserole I brought home every year.

She was sitting at the kitchen table just drinking tea so I put the plate down and she picked around the green beans with her chopsticks. With a few swift moves, she transferred the green beans to her bowl and lifted them to her mouth, then stopped. She turned them around in her chopsticks, took a whiff, glanced one more time as if to find flaws, and then bit carefully. I saw her eyes widen like Scratchy getting shocked by Itchy. It was a cartoon within a cartoon, Thanksgiving within Thanksgiving moment as my mom experienced New Orleans in a ceramic bowl with edges adorned by Chinese key.

"Oh! Oh! Oh my God! What is this?"

"I told you! Green bean casserole."

"Casser-who?"

"Casserole, Mom. Like when Cantonese people put stuff in clay pots. That's a casserole."

"What's it mean, though?"

"I dunno, it's just casserole."

"We need more! How do we make this casserole?"

"I don't know, I'll call Warren."

Later that day, Warren came over with a huge dish of green bean casserole for my mom. He was so happy she liked it since she was so picky most of the time. For the first time, my mom was eating food from a non-Chinese home and she loved it. Who would have known it would be Mrs. Neilson's green bean casserole?

From that first Thanksgiving in 1998, I started cooking at our house every Christmas and Thanksgiving. I read cookbooks, talked to Warren's mom, and watched a lot of Food Network. It's embarrassing, but I would watch every single Food Network show leading up to Thanksgiving. Most of the year, I never watched the station, but I was determined to put together an all-American Thanksgiving.

I watched Emeril one year make an infused butter, let it cool, then he'd get under the turkey skin and spread the butter between the meat and skin. With a little seasoning salt on top, he'd wrap it in foil and send it to the oven. The turkey was flavorful, the skin was insane, but the white meat was still a bit dry. Plus, the flavor wasn't in the meat. It was on top of it. I liked how braised meat took on the flavors throughout every piece inside out. Somehow, some way, I needed to get up in the guts.

I started thinking. What about that Haitian thing where they boiled the turkey in infused water? No, it wouldn't penetrate something as big and dense as a fifteen-pound turkey. But I thought about marinating it so I went online and searched for "marinating" and "turkey." What came up was this thing called "brining." I had never heard about it before. We'd marinate proteins by letting them sit in spices, soy, rice wine, aromatics, and so on, but not usually overnight or beyond three to five hours. Brining is different because of the time spent and the higher levels of salt. The goal isn't just to get the flavors into the meat, but also to add enough salt, retain water, and in turn keep the protein moist. I tried it.

Moms helped me out. We dumped a bunch of salt water into a bucket and brined the turkey that year, then rubbed the infused butter under the skin just like the year before. That year the turkey came out with crisp skin as usual, but salt carried the flavors throughout the meat and maintained its moisture. Very important lesson every good cook learns early on: master salt. It doesn't matter how great your aromatics or spice mixes are: if you don't have the proper salt levels, the flavors won't travel. I also made a stuffing from scratch that year instead of buying Stove Top. It was easy, I bought Popeye's biscuits, let them dry out for a day, then sautéed some loose country sausage with butter, sage, rosemary, thyme, salt, cracked black pepper, tossed in dried biscuit crumbs and finished with a little cream, sugar, and a pinch of chili powder. Once again, dinner proved to be more than the sum of its parts. Thanksgiving is my favorite American holiday because it was the first one I felt like a full participant in. I earned my way in.

Legally, I've always been a citizen. I was born here. But, even now, you'll never see me hold an American flag, own a USA bumper sticker, or rock a Dream Team jersey that doesn't say Barkley on the back. I been here eight years and I rep New York; that's it. I get down with New York because it's international. As for the rest of this thing we call America, I get down once a year. Thanksgiving. That's my day as an American and it's enough. Fuck countries and boundaries; you can call me international.*

Unfortunately, my parents weren't feeling the whole "international" thing. Shit, they didn't even want me to go above the Mason-Dixon line for school. If it was an Ivy League, sure, but you know the kid wasn't getting in. I didn't want to, either. My first choice was Georgetown just be-

* What up, Theo! #LVRS

cause of the basketball squad, but if it was academics, I wanted to go to Syracuse. Being a sportscaster was as close as I would get to the game so I applied to the Newhouse School of Communications that Marv Albert and all those other fools went to. I wrote my application about Charles Barkley and how his voice had a bigger impact on me than his game. There was a narrative in sports and I wanted to join that story even if it was off the court with a headset on.

The only problem was that I had to report my charge. Initially, the police were going to charge me with assault, but I was granted pretrial and pled down to a disorderly conduct that would be expunged after I did community service at Teen Court. When I applied to Syracuse, it was still on my record, so all my teachers helped out and wrote recommendations. They knew I was turning my life around and supported the kid. I was accepted around Christmas of my senior year and I couldn't have been happier. For once, there was something society approved of that I also wanted to get down with. There was no shame in being a sportscaster. It wasn't a "white" job, something that would change who I was. I'd get to be around the game I loved *and* get paid. I remember running to find my dad in the living room when the big white envelope came in the mail.

"Dad! I got in . . ."

"Where? Georgetown?"

"Naw, man, stop playin'. Syracuse!"

"Syracuse? Syracuse is far! You in New York is trouble!"

"I learned my lesson, I've been good."

"YOU WERE IN JAIL five months ago and still have community service! What you talking about?"

"If this was Georgetown, you'd let me go. They have the best communications school in the nation. All the ESPN dudes went there."

"Why you going there then? You not going to be on E-S-P-NNNNNNN." As he accentuated his N's, I clenched my teeth. By this time, I knew what was coming.

"Well, they gave me a scholarship so I'm going!"

"Yeah, right! You think you're going to be a sportscaster?"

"It's better than selling steak!"

"Yeah, you talk trash about my steak! Go ahead. I pay the bills around here, don't forget that! What have they done for you? You worship these ESPN, these basketball players, gimme a break. They'll never let you on ESPN with that face! Hilarious! Sportscaster, my ass."

My dad was full of shit. Right in front of him on *ESPN News* every day was Michael Kim, a Korean American. I pointed to him as evidence, but he laughed at me.

"You are nothing like that Korean."

"What are you talking about? He's evidence!"

"Evidence of what? That ESPN likes Asians? There's one of him already; they don't need another."

"Dad! He's not on ESPN just 'cause he's Asian. There's room for more."

"You look at him. You both Asian, but you tell me you're similar? You have shaved head, tattoo, crazy sneakers, you think ESPN putting you on TV? Fucking kidding me, man!"

Once again, my dad knew something I didn't. Looking back, I realize it wasn't just that I was Asian. I was a loud-mouthed, brash, broken Asian who had no respect for authority in any form, whether it was a parent, teacher, or country. Not only was I not white, to many people I wasn't Asian either.

10

SPECIAL HERBS

Pittsburgh was my first time in a walkable city and I finally didn't need that goddamn Benz. We sold the car and off I went. My Da A-Yi, First Aunt, lived in Monroeville, just outside of the city, and owned Quality Furniture out there. My cousins Allen and Phillip also went to Pittsburgh, and we were all excited to be reunited. It would be the first time in nine years we'd be living in the same place—I was suddenly back like cooked crack and that's how they treated me.

As a kid, Allen was the leader. He was the oldest, he was wild, he had made jokes, and I looked up to him. But by the time I got to Pittsburgh, his reprogramming was complete. He was a nihilist in the sense that nothing was worth his effort anymore, but the worst kind because he was alive just enough to be jealous if you found something to be passionate about. Besides getting a job, paying his bills, and watching DVD porn, he really didn't care about anything. He was a coupon-clipping, self-haircut-inflicting, George Costanza-esque Chinaman. Things would piss him off, but he wouldn't say shit until he got in Jerry's apartment, where only a few chosen Elaines and Kramers got to watch the meltdown.

"Yo, cuz!"

"Yeah, yeah, wassup, man?"

"Since when you start wearing New Balances son?"

"Word, you like them? I got them for seventy dollars!"

"You stay chasing deals, man, you need to get your Bo Jackson game back on."

"Oh, my bad, am I not cool enough now? What are all your 'homies' wearing these days? Show me how to be down, Eddie!"

"Stop playin', man, you're the one that put me onto Bo Jacksons, now you steppin' out like an English teacher with cats and shit, b!"

"I don't know, man, I just can't keep up with you 'brothers' these days. I'm just not black like you."

"Whatever, dude, let's go eat."

My first night in the 'burgh Allen and I went to this joint Fuel & Fuddle, an independent T.G.I. Friday's–type place with an "international" menu that made me want to take a shit right on the table. These fools were serving hot trash like pulled pork egg rolls or seared tuna wasabi nachos. You know the joint. Every neighborhood with a mini-mall has one of these things run by the kid from CIA who couldn't cut it in New York but still wants to stunt in their hometown. Allen was cheap like my dad: he loved it 'cause everything was half off after 11 P.M., but I couldn't subject myself to the shit. I don't do coupons or Reeboks. Life is too short to half-step.

After dinner we walked outside and I noticed a huge line snaking its way toward the doors of Primanti's, an unassuming restaurant across the street. I was still hungry because I hadn't eaten much at Fuel & Fuddle, so I got in line.

Every kid was walking out holding a giant triple-decker sandwich wrapped in white wax paper. Every sandwich stacked like a g-pack except it had vinegar coleslaw, fries, meat, cheese, and three big pieces of white Italian bread. I literally got a boner in line I was so excited. Their slaw was slick, snappy, vinegary, and just peppery enough. The fries were fresh, creamy on the inside, crispy on the outside, and the bread was thick, buttery, and soft. They'd toast it on the griddle just a little if you wanted for a light crisp. I would take a bite and gas-face everyone around me it was so fucking good. People in Pittsburgh thought I was a gremlin that fell in water or some shit, 'cause I was running around all crazy over this sand-wich. With that three-pound sandwich in your hand, you feel like the man: "Fuck you and whatever you got poppin', I'm killin' life with this sandwich right now, b!" Later that night, I would tell anyone I ran into how good the sandwich was and they were like, "Dude, I grew up here, I've had the sandwich, calm down."

Without even meaning to, I now lived in a food city. I didn't know they existed in America; my only fully immersed food experience prior was Taipei. Pittsburgh wasn't Paris, Tokyo, or Taipei exactly, but, Fuel & Fuddle aside, it was a long way from Holando's Denny's and Perkins cir-cuit. From that first Primanti sandwich, I was open; I spent the rest of my year rolling around Pittsburgh looking for new food experiences. I could smell them making fresh waffle cones at Dave & Andy's from two blocks away. The ice cream was so banging, I'd eat it with no gloves on in ten-degree weather. They had the ill pistachio and cookies-and-cream, every-thing with creamy, rich, fresh natural flavors, it was like eating Mariah Carey's ass with a spoon circa the "Honey" remix.

Then there was Mad Mex. Hands down, the best wings I've ever had. I like buffalo wings, but I prefer my hot wings with flavors like spicy gar-lic, or Japanese Izakaya wings at Kasadela, or BonChon Korean fried chicken, but the first time I had anything of that ilk was at Mad Mex. For breakfast, we had Pamela's, with pancakes crispy on the outside like dollar bills but fluffy on the inside. They were so light you felt like you could throw 'em like Frisbees, but they also had a crazy buttery, rich flavor, which contrasted with the light texture and thin crisp. I'd get the banana walnut pancakes with a side of corned beef hash.

In October I took a trip to South Street in Philly to cop new kicks be-cause there weren't any good stores in Pittsburgh. It was the first time I'd ever seen sneaker stores that carried all the OG and retro kicks, every sneaker Saran-wrapped on the wall. I'd seen Japanese sneaker stores like this in magazines, but to bump into one accidentally on South Street was life-changing. The first pair I bought were white and silver Jordan V ret-ros. Down South, we bought white Air Force 1s or white Jordans, but I realized with the quickness you can't be rockin' white up north. Once the weather hits, your shoes are done. I started wearing shoes with a lot more colors and blacked-out panels. My Timberland game switched, too. I got off the Beef and Brocs, back to the six-inch nubuck joints. For the first time, there was actually a purpose to rockin' Timbs.

The first kid I met at Pittsburgh was a dude named Mark Mariz, who introduced himself to me as "Goombah." He was pretty much what he said he was, a fucking goombah. Goombah was from Buffalo, and had a ton of Rogaine 'cause that Italian hair loss thing was killin' his game. Goombah knew as much if not more about hip-hop than me, but he consumed it in a different way. Most of my homies back home that listened to hip-hop found real solidarity with the stories in the songs. Austin was in rehab and I actually saw his pops punch him in the face at the crib. Ben was adopted and never fit in with his fam. Jared got beat at the crib and his parents were getting divorced, too. With Warren and me, you already know. I'm not saying hip-hop is the HRS Anthem, but there's pain and for kids like us, we related to it. You don't go to school and talk about what happens at home, you just try to be normal 'cause that's all you see then one day someone passes you *The Chronic,* you take a hit, and like Professor X with Cerebro on, you realize there are others out there like you. That's it.

Goombah made me realize that we all connected with hip-hop for different reasons. Goombah was one of the first kids I met who listened to everything, could recite lyrics from the most obscure backpack tracks, but was just a nice white kid from Buffalo who was down with the culture, if not the lifestyle. He hadn't seen the shit we'd seen, but I hadn't seen the shit B.I.G. did, either, so who was I to judge? I just liked that Goombah tried to appreciate the music in an earnest way even if it didn't come naturally. Goombah taught me that culture could be just as powerful if you absorbed it as a metaphor, not a list of commandments. You could live through it, learn from it, find yourself in it, and let it change you—a poem not a script. Hip-hop was my escape, but I realized that at times I was guilty of reading another MC's route as my own way out.* Like they say, you learn more from Goombahs than wise men.

* NOT A DIDDY ALBUM REFERENCE. Thank you.

My best friend at Pitt was my boy Graham. A Philly cat with a con-man father, two turntables, and a microphone. Before I met Graham, I didn't even know what backpack rap was, but Graham introduced me to the Outsidaz, *Soundbombing* I and II, Jurassic 5, and Blackalicious. We had another friend on the floor, James, a Cali guy who was the older cat so he could get us beer, weed, whatever. Then there was Cliff: he was a local dude from Pittsburgh and word got out that he had a gun, so people didn't mess with him. There was this buffalo wing joint that Cliff delivered pizza and wings for so he was able to get a concealed weapons license. If you deliver pizza and carry cash, you can hold one.

I met Cliff outside of a house party run by frat boys. Some girls had invited us—James, Graham, and me—to the party but we got there late. I didn't know Cliff at the time but he arrived at the same time we did. The frat boys were cranky at our late, uninvited asses and maybe they could smell our contempt for their little Greek clubhouse. They were crunchy and it looked like they were going to turn us away but Cliff wasn't having it.

"Man, fuck this shit!"

Cliff goes in the back, pulls out the ratchet, and just licks off three through the roof.

"Oh shit! Run! Run!"

"AHHHHHH!!!"

Girls were running, everyone was shook. And, of course, the shit was hilarious to me. We all bounced but I saw Cliff later, in the lobby of my dorm tower.

"What up, son, that's you with the ratchet?"

"Ha, ha, yeah, man, fuck those frat boys."

"Yeah, bull, that's what I'm sayin'. You had them runnin' like roaches!"

"You think anyone saw me?"

"Hell, yeah! I saw you! Ditch that piece for a week."

Cliff lay low and, understandably, didn't hit up many frat parties after that. He didn't care, though. He was like me: We didn't understand frats. You went your whole life meeting friends, hanging out, having fun without needing to pay some motherfuckers, go through Hell Week, and wear shirts with Greek shit on 'em. If it was that ill, we would have been wearing Greek shit in high school, but it wasn't. I'm convinced that frats are the beginning of the end for most of the people who end up running the world. It teaches them to give up individuality, independence, and even their paper for acceptance.

Just like in Orlando, the derels found each other and opposed the cornballs with curved brims,* but that's the way I wanted it: the flavor was in the margins. I really didn't get along with kids at college; most were pretty sheltered, bubble boys and girls, who didn't know what I was talking about half the time. Even though I had Graham, I started to realize I might not have been ready to leave home. I liked that there were people in Orlando that knew everything and understood me. I didn't have to explain why I was weird, I just was. I had become so close with Ben by the summer of 2000 that I tried to commit perjury so he would be acquitted of an assault charge, until his lawyer stopped me. I look back on it now, not having spoken to Ben in eleven years, and laugh that I almost threw my life away for him, but he would have done it for me, too.

Things only got worse. Prior to bid day on campus, people may have been herbs, but they knew it and owned it. Goombah knew he was a goober, but once he joined a frat, overnight he started flexing like he bought some big-dick-willy game on eBay. For a guy who arrived on campus with Rogaine six weeks ago, he was pretty fucking brave. Watching bid week unfold, with all its talk about tradition and brotherhood, felt like watching a White History Month special with a bunch of meatheads handing out hood passes. No one was safe and we started to lose people, like it was the Rapture. Goombah disappeared, girls we hung out with got caught up with sororities, and everyone wanted to be at frat houses Friday night.

I got bids for two frats 'cause I was wild and played football with some of the "brothers." Outside of their frat identity, they weren't so bad, but once some asshole came around calling Jackson "Action," or Steven "Scuba," they'd have to play the part. The worst was when my cousin Phil joined a frat. Something about watching my older cousin walk around

---

* The biggest giveaway I'll never have anything in common with someone is a hat with a curved brim. Flat brim, 59/50, leave the stickers, kid!

with a PKA hat on his fat head being hazed by white "brothers" pissed me off. It must have been how our grandparents felt watching the British or Japanese herd their people around in water lines. OK, maybe I was imposing my own meaning on the image, but there was something wrong with it either way. White people making my cousin carry their shit, wear their colors, and walk with his head down. It took every ounce of self-control not to go apeshit on his brothers and, when I was done, beat the shit out of Phil, too! It made Allen and me so mad that it finally brought us back together. Like watching William Hung sink your entire race with each word of "She Bangs," we died every time Phil walked through the towers surrounded by frat brothers.

I couldn't stand the Greek system, but Graham, James, and I were still curious to know exactly how it all worked—I went to a bid meeting at one of the frats so I could report back to Graham and James about what kind of embarrassing shit actually went down. It became a theme in my life. I always had friends on the periphery but the people we hated would always pick me to cross the line. I'd fake the part for a second to infiltrate, gather intelligence, and then ditch it, laughing on my way back to the outside. That's the perk to being Chinese, you can walk through walls and no one really notices. The older cats that gave me the bid told me that I wouldn't have to go through Hell Week like the other kids because I was already friends with them from football. But, once we got to the pledge meeting, they switched up their story.

"OK, all the people who just received bids, stand against the wall."

"Stand against the wall?"

"Yeah, Huang, stand against the wall like everyone else. You're a pledge!"

"Wait, I'm supposed to pay y'all to be my friends and I gotta stand against this wall while you sit?"

"Eddie, just do it, dude. It's tradition!"

"Yo, you told me I wouldn't have to do this shit like the other herbs. You already know me!"

"Everyone stands against the wall! We all had to do it."

My argument with them went on for a good five to ten minutes before

I left. It was funny, to me, how they shit their pants like Justice Scalia trying to maintain tradition—the tradition of crushing individuality through pointless humiliation even though they themselves didn't believe in it. There was vindication in going, lifting the curtain, and confirming every bitch-made notion I had about them. In the end, you get a bunch of conformists all united in a cartel that asks them to sacrifice one year of their lives to feed someone's ego, in exchange for the ability to do it the next three years to others.

Without any good parties, I got a taste of student activism in spring semester. I didn't intend to get involved; something just set me off so I spoke out. I saw other groups get holidays off or school benefits for their organizations like Hillel or the Black Students Union, but the Asian Students Association didn't even call for Chinese New Year exceptions for attendance. Growing up, my parents would let us stay home on Chinese New Year because there were things we had to do. Sweep out last year's luck, pay respects to our ancestors, reflect on last year, and look forward to the new one. It wasn't just a national holiday, it was a spiritual one. I figured being at a public university with exceptions for Yom Kippur and Good Friday that Chinese New Year would make the cut, but it didn't. Every club had things they negotiated for, but the Asian clubs were always just happy to be vocational organizations. Everyone went and joined the club for resume filler, but when there was actually something to speak out about, no one wanted to be the punk that jumped up to get beat down.

Lucky for them, I gladly played the punk. As a freshman, I sent a letter into the school paper and they ran it. My letter wasn't about how the school should give us Chinese New Year off. It was all about Uncle Chans and how they fucked the game up for Asian people. For too long, I wrote, we've been lapdogs. The people who don't want to offend anyone. We hide out in Laundromats, delis, and takeout joints and hope that our doctor/lawyer sons and daughters will save us. We play into the definitions and stereotypes others impose on us and accept the model-minority myth, thinking it's positive, but it's a trap just like any stereotype. They put a piece of model-minority cheese between the metal jaws of their mousetrap, but we're lactose intolerant anyway! We can't even eat the cheese. I called out the Asian Students Association for not saying anything to the school, for not fighting for their identities, and for spending the budget on bullshit mixers and networking events without any substantive cultural programming.

When people don't give you the time off work or school to celebrate the most important day of the year for your people, you lose yourself. How are you supposed to maintain your identity in America without your holidays? If not all of them, then how about one? It wasn't just about Chinese New Year, though. I was sick and tired of half-assed potlucks thrown by ABCs (American Born Chinese) who didn't even know how to cook Chinese food. These same ABCs couldn't speak Chinese and didn't care— but you don't have shit without your native tongue. African slaves were forced by threat of physical punishment to abandon their native languages, but a lot of us just gave ours up with a shrug—these Uncle Chans convinced us to assimilate, shut the fuck up, and play the part. What they didn't understand is that after you have the money and degrees, you can't buy your identity back. I wasn't worried about degrees, but I cared about my roots. Even if I hated what it meant to be an Asian in the American wilderness, I respected the Chinese home I was raised in. Usually I wasn't so vocal about Asian identity, but without my parents around, I felt a sudden duty to say something myself. It's funny how annoying I thought my mom was, but as soon as she wasn't around, I carried the torch for her.

At school, there were Chinese New Year events, but they involved shitty lion dances, takeout Chinese food set over Sternos, and a bunch of conservatively styled Asians with a few flavorful Filipinos mixed in. I actually got along with the Filipino cats because they were frequently left out when the model-minority net got dropped in the water. People weren't fishing for Pinoys and they got to build a lot of their own identity in America. Just like Joey's parents and the other Filipinos in Lake Cane Park setting up shop, a lot of Filipinos were free to do their own thing because there wasn't so much institutional or communal pressure to be one type of Pinoy. One of the board members was an older Filipino guy named Brandon who DJ'd a lot of the parties in Pittsburgh and he tried to get me to join the board, but I declined.

"Yo, that article was powerful, man! We need that voice on the board."

"Respect! I'm glad you fuck with it, but I'm not an institutional cat. I'll complain about it, but I'll never be part of it."

"I don't get it, dude, we'd be giving you a platform?!"

"Look, man, I'll never be 'Asian' enough for the people in this club."

"Son, you playin' yourself, you mad Asian! You know everything about the food, you speak fluently, you been back to Taiwan, you more Chinese than all these cats."

"Yeah, but it's different than what these ABCs expect. My pops isn't an engineer or doctor; he got an automatic he used to put on my head while I watched cartoons."

"What's that have to do with anything?"

"Everything! Dude, do you listen to the people in these meetings? They're all dying to live under the bamboo ceiling and subscribe to the model-minority myth; I'm not OK with that shit. They don't understand that in China, Taiwan, or the Philippines, we can be whoever we want. In America, we're allowed to play ONE role, the eunuch who can count. You seen *Romeo Must Die*! Jet Li gets NO PUSSY!"

Whenever I tried to articulate what I really felt about being Chinese in America, my dad said I sounded like a slant-eyed Malcolm X. He'd always tell me not to talk like that in public because Americans would try to silence me. In Florida that made sense, so I played dumb, but college was supposed to be the place where you could have liberal ideas so I figured I'd drop the "dumb" act and speak my mind.

After a year, I decided to transfer home to any college in Orlando that would have me, but before I left Pittsburgh I got a lesson on Italian food that changed my life. It was .45-cal Cliff who taught me. The university was in the Oakland section of Pittsburgh, but Cliff was from the other side. One day after playing ball at Trees, he took me to the Italian diner that he grew up eating at. I scanned the menu looking for my standbys—chicken parm or sausage and peppers—but before I could figure out what I wanted, Cliff summoned the waiter over and ordered for both of us.

"Two orders cavatelli and red sauce."

"Can I get some sausage in mine?"

"Fine, we'll allow him the sausage in the cavatelli, but let's also get two slices of cake."

The cavatelli came out different than I'd ever seen before. It was chewy, with good texture, and lopsided. You could tell they were handmade, which was a rare treat. But the sauce seemed boring, just stewed tomatoes with a little basil and salt. No oregano, no rosemary, no ground meat, just a few pieces of Italian sausage sprinkled in. I didn't get it.

"Yo, Cliff, why is the tomato sauce so bland? It's just salt and tomatoes, kid."

"Just eat it."

I didn't want to diss his food so I just kept eating it . . . and eating it . . . and eating it. It was endless. I'd never had to chew that much eating pasta, but it had its charm. Every bite gave perfect bouncy, textural mouthfeel that remained amazingly consistent from piece to piece. Just chewy enough without being dense or heavy. The sauce was inoffensive, it was there, but unobtrusive. By the time I finished the bowl, I wanted another. Cliff nodded. His bowl was empty, too.

"Another two bowls, same thing, please."

In that little Italian diner tucked onto an anonymous street in western Pennsylvania, I learned that there were universal food truths. Every culture had dishes that prized the simple and traditional over showy flavors and elaborate presentations. The things that may not seem worthy on first look, but over time become an indispensable part of your life. If you grow up in an immigrant culture, there are going to be foods you eat that other people just don't get. Not the universal crowd-pleasers—the fried chickens and soup dumplings—but the everyday stuff. We Southerners, for instance, love grits, boiled peanuts, and fried okra but nobody else understands. For Chinese people, it's things like rice porridge, thousand-year-old eggs, or tomato and eggs. Simple things that don't impress at first look, but instead offer nuance: strange textures and sublime flavors that reveal their charm over the years. The things people left off menus, only to find an audience during family meal.

Whether it's food or women, the ones on front street are supermodels. Big hair, big tits, big trouble, but the one you come home to is probably something like cavatelli and red sauce. She's not screaming for attention because she knows she's good enough even if your dumb ass hasn't figured it out yet.

The best dishes have depth without doing too much. It's not about rounding up all the seasonal ingredients you can find, it's about paying close attention to the ones you already have. You don't need anything more than a few tomatoes, onions, and maybe a country rib, but simple tomato sauce requires patience: you sear the country rib, wait the twenty-five minutes it takes to caramelize onions, boil the tomatoes, peel the tomatoes, and then watch them stew the requisite hour and finish with just the lightest touch of fresh basil, salt, and olive oil. What more do you need? Patience, attention, and restraint are the keys to good cooking. That night, I learned everything I needed to know about food eating a bowl of cavatelli and red sauce with some Yinz pizza delivery boy rockin' a do-rag. America, I fux with you.

My food education continued that summer, when I went to my friend TJ's crib in Lewiston, New York, right outside of Buffalo. TJ's mom made the best sausage and peppers I'd ever had from an oven. I had never seen sausage and peppers roasted before because usually people did them on griddles or sauté pans. Her food was the other end of the spectrum, but every bit as delicious. I watched how she roasted garlic to the perfect consistency. It's harder than you'd think: not enough time and the garlic is too sharp; if you over-roast, the garlic is mushy and too sweet, but done right it's rich, meaty, and laced with a sweet caramel tone that lingers. Fold that into your sauce, hit it with some dry white wine, fresh herbs, peppers roasted until tender but not soft, and you have the perfect sauce. Her food jumped off the plate. The flavors were big, deep, kid-dynamite-Mike-Tyson-knock-you-out-the-box shit. But, again, she didn't add any crazy herbs or vegetables. It was classic sausage, peppers, onions, and unassuming fresh herbs done right. Every single aspect was considered. I loved seeing food at that level in someone's home. You pick through the dish to see how the flavors were created and you realize at every layer of the dish, it was all about patience and awareness. If any element was ignored or dismissed, it wouldn't be the same. Those sausage and peppers were like Wu-Tang, nine crazy motherfuckers all on the same page firing at the same time. Perfection.

TJ's people later took me to their favorite spot for pasta and I revisited the revelation I had with Cliff: boring red sauce, lumpy handmade gnocchi, and flake salt on the table. No server coming around with cracked pepper or parmesan, just eat the shit as is. It reminded me of my mother's minced pork on rice, the de facto national dish of Taiwan when you inexplicably don't want to eat tofu cured with rotten cabbage (stinky tofu). The gnocchi was "q q"* just like a well-made bowl of short-grain and sweet rice that provided the perfect canvas for minced pork. I remember how Moms mixed the pork belly with ground shoulder as if she were Voletta Wallace on that Jamaican rum and whiskey. Minced pork stew employed things like five-spice, fried shallots, rice wine, and rock candy, but at the finish line, it all came together as one simple, unassuming gravy that revealed its character bowl after bowl just like red sauce. Cliff and TJ taught me a lot about Italian food and it became one of my favorites.

I remember riding out of Pittsburgh in Allen's Civic the last day of school. I said peace to Graham and Cliff thinking I'd see them again, but it wasn't so. When Allen and I crossed the bridge over Three Rivers I looked down and saw all of Pittsburgh. I always loved coming into Pittsburgh, coming down the bridge, and around the bend descending into Oakland, but it was a relief to get out that day. College just wasn't live enough for me. It felt like some fantasy world incubating the future gentrifiers of America while the rest of the world did its thing. The whole idea of a campus felt unnatural to me. A lot of kids liked being insulated, but I hated living in a reverse retirement home with a bunch of kids who constantly asked me how to fade hair and cop ecstasy. I wanted to go home. I

* Taiwanese people are fond of describing dumplings, rice, or any flour-related items as "q q" when they have a bouncy al-dente-like quality to them. Rice in Taiwan, unlike America, doesn't always come out soggy and limp.

missed my family, I missed the Gunshine State, and I missed my homies. I couldn't wait to get home and hotbox Mike's Toyota Celica with a fat philly blunt, eating Triscuit sandwiches and frozen bagel pizzas and playing NBA 2K with Pastor Troy screamin' "We ready!" through the speakers. What I didn't realize was that there was nothing left for me in Orlando.

11

THE END OF
THE BEGINNING

When I got back to Orlando, it was like nothing had changed. Warren was gone, but Justin, Romaen, Austin, Lil' Cra, Muschewske, Ben, and Jared were all still around, just chillin'. I burned all evidence of Aeropostale* and got back on that flip-flops and socks with shants game. When I told them I was going to Rollins College, they all started laughing. We never went down near Winter Park 'cause Rollins was the "country club," a pipeline school for kids from New England boarding schools who couldn't get into the Ivy Leagues. If you had paper and bad grades, you could go to Rollins. It was mentioned in *American Psycho* and the most apt quote I ever heard was "Rollins is where you send your daughter so nothing happens to her and if something does happen to her, it's from the right guy." I didn't care. I figured I'd just take class, mind my own business, and hang with my old friends. College wasn't for me.

Sadly, the same shit I tried to escape was alive and well even at a small liberal arts school. Every single party was thrown by frats. It didn't bother

---

* Pittsburgh reps Aeropostale *hard*. It was like Gap for EBT Yinz who ain't had jobs since the seventies. We got a lot of it cheap, though, 'cause they'd unload the surplus in the student union.

me though 'cause I'd just roll with my homies and crash the parties. That first night at Rollins we realized something; we could get money here.

"Yo, Denny, these kids are marks."

"You tellin' me? I came with the footballs,* they eatin' 'em up."

"I'm sayin', let's get this paper."

Denny was my boy since eighth grade; we played on the same YMCA basketball team but in high school he dropped out and just hustled with all the Lake Cane kids. Denny introduced me to Danny Diaz and this Chino named Allen who didn't even go to school. That cat was a futuristic China-man with gold fronts and a pit bull named Jade. It was one of the first times I saw an Asian kid that was rotten-banana'd out like me and we recognized each other from jump.

Allen had a crib out in the woods off Sand Lake Road that you couldn't see from the street. It was just him, his girl, and Jade. Allen wore that deep yellow Asian 24k gold that everyone wanted. Twenty-four-k is pure gold, it's easy to break 'cause it's soft, but if you ball that's what you need. Every-one knew you had to go to Chinatown if you wanted that cheez-whiz Cuban link. Russians stay on that 18 to 20k, broke mofuckers cop 14, but Asians wanted that 24k pure soft yellow. I remember when Ghostface came to UCF and the first thing his manager, Vel, said to my brother Evan was, "Where you get that gold g? Shit is deep!" Allen and his 24k were always on point and consistent so I never needed another connect.

I didn't have a car when I came home so I got a dorm room at Rollins and used it as home base for my hustle. Most kids at that school weren't local and got their work from this Indian kid Samir, who lived off-campus. He was pitchin' borax to the entire campus, but wasn't really serious, a Winter Park kid selling turkey bag† bullshit and stepped-on yack. Through Allen and Denny, I set up like Duane Reade on campus: I had Xanax, Vics, e, and sour diesel. Cokeheads were extra and I wasn't trying to come up that hard so I stayed out of the coke game. If they wanted the white girl, I sent 'em to my boy PC, who posted up at the gas station.

A month in, I found this kid Troy Perkins. He was on full athletic

---

* Large-dose Xanax.
† Outdoor weed shows up in turkey bags. You want that indoor super chron.

scholarship to Rollins but for some reason he rolled with this Tibetan kid, Yani, who was loud and reckless. I remember the first time Yani ran up on me at a party talkin' about wanting work and having customers ready to go. I told him he needed to calm down, look, and listen. After a few weeks of getting to know them, I started keeping the work at Troy's house off-campus. No one knew where he lived, the school never messed with him, and his complex was quiet. For about fifteen months, I kept the work at Troy's and we never had problems. All he wanted was a cut.

Yani, Troy, and this kid Joe Randall all wanted to hustle but they were new in town and had no contacts so I was the only source they knew. If I was really going to make bread, I needed a crew. That's where this Irish kid Krazy Kris came in. Kris was wild. He was a lot like Graham: he was from Philly, DJ'd, had turntables and stacks of records, and made his own tapes. On top of that, he was in a frat, which gave us a direct line to the biggest marks.

The first few weeks were the hardest. I ended up giving dimes away like Bourbon Chicken at the mall so people could get a taste. Most people are already copping from someone else. The only reason they'd check me out was to try something new—and if I didn't have that, they already had someone else to call. I'd smoke whatever went dry. Everything I served was sticky, fluffy, no sticks, no stems, no seeds. When business was slow, my trick was to throw a piece of lettuce in every ounce. Never failed, it'd add weight, keep the weed fluffy, and no one could tell the water came from lettuce.

Every game is the same. Baos, birds, or bud, you do everything you can up front to get them in a habit, then just don't do anything to disturb it. Set a pattern, get them into an expectation about how you gonna move, and everybody settles in. The key is not to run with people who can't be consistent. Joe Randall was the weak link and I had to keep him focused because he didn't actually need the money. When it comes to those dudes, you gotta keep an eye on 'em, don't give them more than they can handle, and try to contain it. If he sold short bags, was late, or just didn't show for some people, I'd send them to Krazy Kris the next time. Once Randall saw he lost people, he got his shit together. Same strategy in restaurants: if you fuck around and don't close down or work the line properly, you lose shifts. Never fails, the dude's next shift is always perfect. I pay people the respect of talking to them the first time, but if they don't get it, I stunt their money. Who knew selling weed to frat boy marks was this serious? My crew was on some Little Giants shit. If you think it's hard to find good delivery boys at Chinese restaurants, try teaching New England boarding school toy dogs to move like pit bulls. Worst in show.

The two things I hated dealing with were snitches and bum ninjas who couldn't pay. We had a situation once where Krazy called me saying someone wanted an ounce and a half out of the blue. It was a lot more than recreational, but still not any serious weight so it didn't make sense. Sometimes if people wanted to make brownies they'd cop a half, but 1.5 just smelled funny.

"Yo, dawg, he's cool, man. He's on the swim team."

"Swim team?"

"Yeah, that kid Andrew."

"I got English with him. The fuck is he doing with one-point-five?"

"I don't know, he throwing a party or something."

"Isn't he in that house with the collar-poppin' motherfuckers? If he wanted work, he could get it from Kaywan. Turn it down, man, don't smell right."

"For real?"

"Yeah, trust me."

Two weeks later, Kaywan, a Cape Cod aspirational peon who hung with the J. Crew–lookin' frat motherfuckers, got busted serving the swim kid. Those kids were the worst. Bunch of cokeheads with ribbon sandals, rollin' around with croakies, popped collars, and sweaters around their necks. They styled themselves like the ruling class, but they were weak— halfway addicts who'd turn to rats in a second to save their skin. Kaywan was an Arab from Louisville who acted his way through Rollins, where anyone with swarthy skin could pass himself off as Freeway Ricky Ross. The truth was that none of his tree was good—and he was a glorified errand boy for another dealer. Didn't stop him from getting popped when swim fan snitched on him.

———

A FEW WEEKS after Kaywan got busted, some of his customers needed tree so they came to me. One dude liked to cop eightballs and quarters. He'd get up then blaze when he came down. Fool was a mark, coppin' every three days real consistent, but people get funny around Thanksgiving break.

"Hey, man, I want a quarter but only have fifty. Can I give you the other fifty after break?"

I didn't have a layaway program, but I didn't want to get stuck with a quarter over break, either, because I was going home for the weekend. So for fifty dollars, I broke my own rule and let him get it on credit.

The first day after break I called this fool and he didn't pick up, but I knew I'd see him. Around 6 P.M., I ran into him in the computer lab.

"Your phone broke, motherfucker?"

"Hey, Eddie, wassup, man! How was break?"

"Son, it's fifty dollars, just pay it."

"All right, cool cool, I'm just gonna go get it from my car."

It was stupid, fifty bucks was bullshit, but the point was if we let this motherfucker get off on us, other people would, too. To be honest, people should have been smarter. I'd get in fights over random tomfoolery, but I already knew I wasn't going to really hurt anyone. It wasn't worth it. I'm surprised more people hadn't already tested me. I wasn't like other hustlers. I treated it like a job and kept it friendly 'cause I had the best product. I didn't need to goon out, but this fool was testing us so we had to do something. I thought to myself . . . How can I make this dude fear us and tell other people without actually doing something *too* illegal?

I told Randall to be outside the back of the library 'cause I knew this dude was full of shit. By the time I got around the back, Randall had him gripped up.

"You trying to run, son?"

"No, man, I was going to my car."

"Naw, this dude was trying to run to his crib."

"Get the fuck in the car."

Just to fuck with this dude, I had my six-foot-three homie Farama, from Sierra Leone, with us. Funniest thing about the situation was that Farama was Kevin Garnett dark so these Rollins kids assumed he was the muscle, but he was the only one of my friends who was actually a good kid. His family was aristocracy in Sierra Leone, he went to a New England boarding school, and just started running with us because we played ball together. Poor kid ended up masked up with a stunt Glock in the back of Randall's car because we knew the Cape Codder would be shook just from seeing a black person. Even when we were planning it we could barely stop laughing, but we had to get our faces straight to make it work.

The stunt Glock belonged to Justin's dad—it was a training gun for the SWAT team that shot blanks, but until someone pulled the trigger, you'd swear it was real. No one was ever shooting anyone at Rollins—the truth is I was the Kanye of hustlers, knew I knew more about Polo than Gaston Glock. But I kept the stunt piece because it solved problems. I always figured it didn't matter if the gun's fake if the piss in this motherfucker's pants is real.

"Oh shit, man! Is that a gun?"

"It doesn't have to be if you pay me my fifty dollars, bitch."

"Dude, it's not that serious, we don't have to do this."

"We ain't doing anything. We're just talking, why you shook? If you got my money, there's no problem."

"I don't have it, though!"

"How the fuck do you not have it, you rich motherfucker!"

"My parents didn't give me my allowance this week yet!"

"Allowance? You twenty-one, how the fuck can you say 'allowance' with a straight face, b? Get a fuckin' job. Gimme your phone, man."

"But if I give you my phone, I can't call you."

"Then gimme that watch."

This fool didn't have fifty dollars, but he was running around with a gold and silver link Tag Heuer—it was worth more than three thousand.

"Man, my grandma gave me this watch!"

"Ha, ha, you hear this kid? You watched too much *Friday* talkin' 'bout your grandma-ma, bitch. Gimme that watch."

If you've seen *Friday,* you remember Chris Tucker's line 'bout his grandma-ma giving him his chain. We were dying in the car, if he didn't give up the watch quick, we wouldn't have been able to keep the act up, it was so funny. I might as well have been Ben Affleck with socks showing at a law firm screaming "Reee-tain-eeeerrrr."

"Fine, here's the watch, but can you drop me off at home?"

"Yeah."

We dropped him off and then everyone wanted to wear the watch. None of us had ever had anything that nice. Everyone wanted to take photos with it but I knew that was the kind of silly self-incrimination that got people locked up. Still, I rocked the shit out of that watch. Two weeks later, the kid got his fifty dollars together and called me.

"Hey, I have your money, meet me with the watch."

"Naw, it's cool. Keep your money, I like this watch."

I made this kid chase me for three weeks trying to get his watch back just so he knew how it felt. In the end, I sold it back to him for three hundred. Pay your bills!

Rollins was a resort. We did whatever we wanted and ran the place as freshmen (technically, I was a sophomore in age, but it was my first year there, you know the deal). One day, I got caught up and didn't make it to Troy's crib after I picked up the work so I went to my coming-of-age novel class with two ounces. This girl Connie that sat next to me got my attention.

"Eddie!"

"Wassup?"

"Wassup??? You have a giant bag of weed on the table!"

"Shit!"

I didn't even notice, but I had left my bag open when I got my notepad out and the weed was just sitting on the table when Dr. Jones came in. Luckily she didn't see it.

That class opened my eyes. It was one of my first classes in the English major and looking around the table, I saw what it was really like to be wealthy. In Orlando, we had new money, but like Chris Rock said, we were rich, but we weren't *wealthy*.

There were kids in class with their own yachts, sailboats, and European chalets. These people moved different. They had mastered the art of saying nothing. You could ask them a straight question like "Don't you think we should have welfare?" And they could go on for five minutes, waxing poetic, and say absolutely nothing. They were masters of leading you in the wrong direction, taking you on a ride, and dropping you right back where you were when you asked the question. These were the real hustlers.

"The welfare of the poor is of course a serious problem that affects the condition of the nation, but it's debatable how to solve the problem while properly incentivizing people to participate in a capitalist society. You don't want a situation where your tax dollars are incentivizing stagnant behavior."

READ: I don't care about poor people and I'm assuming that everyone on welfare is some single mom with five kids who keeps having them to get more money on her EBT card.

But there were also people there who came to the school because it had a good reputation for liberal arts. There was a rich history at Rollins—it gave rise to the Black Mountain College movement and was an innovator in interdisciplinary study and breaking down a lot of the traditional education structures. I didn't know anything about the history of the school until I got there and hung out with professors. Here I was running around with a bunch of knuckleheads serving the whole school, yet, when I was in class, I saw a whole other life for myself.

Dr. Jones's class struck a nerve. Reading coming-of-age stories like *The Perks of Being a Wallflower*, *Catcher in the Rye*, *Huckleberry Finn*, and *The Liars' Club* helped me answer a question I'd had for a minute. For years, I wanted to know if there was one person, one voice, one individual inside me. All my life people would call me a chink or a chigger. I couldn't listen to hip-hop and be myself without people questioning my authenticity. Chinese people questioned my yellowness because I was born in America. Then white people questioned my identity as an American because I was yellow.

No black or Spanish person ever called me chigger, but hustling all of a sudden got white people off my back. I was the same dude with a different job, but now I was finally "authentic"* to white people, and it made me realize it's all a trap. We can't fucking win. If I follow the rules and play the model minority, I'm a lapdog under a bamboo ceiling. If I like hip-hop because I see solidarity, I'm aping. But, if I throw it all away, shit on my parents, sell weed, pills, and strike fear into unsuspecting white boys with stunt Glocks, now I'm authentic? Fuck you, America.

After class, I was still spending my weekends back home on the Southwest Orlando side with my old homies. I went out with Lil' Cra and Muschewske to Point Orlando one night. We were up in the club, chillin', drinkin.' I dropped a Xanax bar so I was nice. Not super twisted, just zonin'. Everything was kosher, but as we left, I saw that kid M-Ron that fought me in my driveway.

"Ay yo, Cra, that's that dude."

"Which one?"

"That kid from my driveway in ninth grade. Remember?"

"Oh shit, for real?"

"Yeah, I'ma get him, son. Hold me down."

"A'ight, I got you, man, no doubt."

I always had a padlock on me in case we got in a fight, 'cause you wanted to throw a heavy punch. You put your finger through the middle of the lock and make a fist around the joint. That way, you won't break your hand and it's like having a brass knuckle. I saw this motherfucker in his wack ass Kenneth Cole shoes and a Ben-Sherman-looking shirt. Kid grew up to be just like all the other sellouts in the neighborhood chillin' with some spiked hair, 9 to 5 bros. He was walking with two other dudes when I walked up to him. One of the Rollins kids I was with was this kid named Mike Harris. He was supposedly from Boston and talked a lot

* Best skit on authenticity, The Clipse's *Hot Damn*: "One thing about me, I'm an authentic bitch."

about how he put in work back home, knew Israeli street fighting, could speak with his hands, etc. Blah, blah, blah, you know how it goes: college boy thespians.

"Harris, I'ma run up on this kid. Cra got my back, but hold me down if the other dude tries to creep."

"What do you mean?"

"What do you mean what do I mean? I'm sayin', hit the big motherfucker if he moves!"

"Uhhh, OK."

I walked up to the dude right in the middle of the parking lot.

"Hey! Hey, man!"

"Huh?"

"Yo, wassup, man? Long time no see!"

"Do I know you?"

"You don't remember me, dogs? It's Eddie, man!"

CRACK!

I whacked this motherfucker right in the teeth with my right and he crumbled to the fucking concrete like a sack of soybeans. One of the best punches I ever threw. He didn't just fall, he stumbled twice, tripped over the other leg, and then yard saled.

"Ohhh, look at you now, son. Remember the name, motherfucker: Eddie Huang."

BAM!

I pulled the classic bad guy shit that always fails. Remember, kids, if you knock someone the fuck out, don't stand over them, don't take your mask off, don't tell 'em your name, and DEFINITELY don't let their giant A-Rab friend kick you in the back of the head.

"Oh shit! Eddie, get up, man, the cops are coming!"

Lil' Cra had one, but Mike Harris sat in the fucking car while we threw down. All that talk about Israeli street fighting and how he could kill a man with his bare hands was just sales puffery. That's why real motherfuckers hate college kids, man. Hormones got you actin' wild in the club in front of girls, but push comes to shove and you're sitting in a Toyota Celica smoking Parliament lights like a fuckin' female. I got up and everything was spinning. The kick wasn't that bad, but I didn't expect it, so I hit the concrete parking lot facefirst and started bleeding everywhere.

"Stop that kid! Stop that kid!"

I saw pork so we bucked and jumped in the whip. Muschewske got us the fuck out of there before we could get arrested. Me, Cra, Muschewske, Harris, and this chick Jerry all got away.

"Damn, son, why you didn't get Eddie's back!"

"Yo, I might have killed one of them, man. I can't get involved like that."

"Dead ass, you really gonna stick with that bullshit Israeli street fighting story? No one fucking believes you, dude. If you gonna bitch out, at least lay the fuck all the way down and stop frontin' like you've ever done the damn thing."

"Eddie, you're bleeding everywhere!"

"For real, Jerry?"

"Take your shirt off, I'll stop the bleeding."

I took my shirt off so that she could press it against my face. The shit was dripping blood everywhere, but I really didn't feel shit 'cause I was on bars.

"A'ight, so, I need to know, y'all saw me knock that motherfucker out the box, right?"

"Ahhh, you definitely got him, b! Most definitely got him."

"Yeaaah, I been waitin' years to hit that motherfucker, man."

"Are you idiots serious? You're missing half your face right now!"

"Yo, it's worth it, though. That's the only L I ever took."

"Uhhh, I don't know what kind of crazy math you guys are running, but this whole situation on your face is definitely an L."

"Ha, ha, Jerry, you wildin'!!! This is nothin'. Plus, I got hit from behind, this isn't on my scorecard."

"Yeah, all I see is W's today!"

"Let's go to the 7 and get some more beer."

"Dude, you are GIVING blood right now, we're going to the hospital."

"Naw, naw, naw, I can't go to the hospital. I got pills in my system. We can just put neosporin on this."

"Hell no!"

"Jerry, for real, we can't go to the hospital."

"Um, no, we're going to the hospital."

Eventually, Jerry won out and we went to the hospital. But, first, I chilled out in the Chick-fil-A parking lot down the street, had some food, drank some water, and brushed my teeth at a gas station so I didn't have alcohol on my breath. Jerry and Muschewske checked me into the hospital and told them I hurt myself skateboarding. We both had Etnies on and shit so it made sense. They bought the story, didn't bother with blood tests, didn't notice my breath, and took care of my injuries.

I wasn't mad at all. Whether I was missing half my face or not, it always bothered me I never swung on those kids in ninth grade, and now I did it. Revenge is always expensive, but you get what you pay for. Everything was roses sitting there on the hospital cot when I realized I forgot about my coming-of-age novel class.

"Fuck!"

"What? We're good."

"Naw, my *Huckleberry Finn* paper is due tomorrow!"

"Yo, fuck school, man, you can turn it in later."

That night, I made a decision.

I made Mike take me back to school and drop me off in my dorm room, and I wrote my paper on *Huckleberry Finn* for Dr. Jones's class. It finally became clear. There was no ending! Twain copped out. He didn't finish! As much as I loved the book, I couldn't let him get away. Where was my ending? More important, I looked myself in the bloody-ass face and said to myself: "What's your ending, asshole?"

The next day, I rolled into Dr. Jones's class about fifteen minutes late. Considering everything that had happened, I figured she would cut me some slack. I opened the door, walked in, and kids literally puked in their mouths. I stunk like weed, I had bandages all over my face, and my elbow was still bleeding. I tried not to make a commotion, but Dr. Jones stopped and just stared at me walking in.

"Eddie, are you OK?"

"Yeah, yeah, I'm totally fine. Sorry I'm late."

She didn't want to get too personal in front of the whole class, but she gave me the concerned screw face. I sat in my seat next to Connie and pulled out my paper. After a few minutes, I was comfortable enough to look around the room and realized something.

"Yo, Connie, is this family day or some shit?"

"Uhhh, yeah, Dr. Jones has been talking about it for weeks, remember? She brought her kids to class today . . ."

"Fuck, are you serious?"

"Look in the back, dude."

"I'm cool, though, right? I fell off a skateboard."

"Eddie . . . I don't know how to tell you this but you are really really not cool right now."

And she smiled. I loved Connie. She was judgmental, but never acted on her judgments. She'd tell you you were an asshole. She'd tell you what she thought, but she'd still kick it with you. Connie wasn't one of those people that operated on stigmas and stereotypes; if she saw something that seemed off, she'd dig deeper where others would run. She was mad understanding and whether she'll admit it or not, probably also just liked being around random ignant shit like me.

"Connie, I don't think I'm gonna make it. I gotta fuckin' puke. Can you give my paper to Dr. Jones?"

"Yeah, but I'm calling you after class."

"Gimme a few hours. I gotta take a nap."

"Whatever."

I got back in my room and passed the fuck out. I woke up five hours later to a full voicemail box:

"Eddie, it's Dr. Jones. I need to talk to you."

"Umm, dude, are you really going to leave your paper with me and then not pick up when I call to see if you're OK? Call me . . ."

"Ay yo, it's Chew. You got that motherfucker last night, son. Let's get it innn tonight!"

I called Dr. Jones.

"Hello?"

"Hey, Dr. Jones, it's Eddie."

"Eddie . . . Nice to hear from you. I have a bone to pick."

"What happened?"

"It's about your paper."

"You don't like it?"

"No, I haven't been able to read it."

"Why? It's all there."

"Well, I'm looking at your paper and there's freaking blood all over it!"

"For real? Oh, should I bring you another copy?"

"Yes, yes, Eddie, you should bring me another copy. But I don't want it right now, bring it to the next class, and by the way, what the heck happened to you?"

"Uhhh, you really want to know?"

"You can tell me."

"I saw this kid that I got in a fight with in ninth grade so I hit him, but his friend kicked me in the back of the head so I hit the parking lot with my face."

"Are you serious?"

"Yeah."

"Eddie . . . I don't know if you think this is funny or OK, but it's not. You can't keep doing this. You know I love you, you're a smart kid, but it's one or the other. You can't have it both ways."

"I know. I mean, yo, you won't believe me, but I left the hospital just so I could write that paper and turn it in this morning."

"Of course I believe you! I can't believe you came to class! It's insane. You have this dedication, but then you do these crazy things. You make money writing papers for other kids,* you hit someone in a parking lot, then you hit the parking lot with your face. What are you thinking?"

"I don't know, Dr. Jones."

---

* I had admitted to Dr. Jones that I was making money writing papers for other students. Never told her who, though.

––––––

BEFORE IT GOT better, it got worse.

"JARED! WHAT THE fuck, son?"

"Fuck these bitches. What are they gonna do?"

"It's just unnecessary, b."

"Let's bounce, man, someone's gonna see this."

At the end of my first semester at Rollins, Jared and Ben came through one night. Jared had too much to drink and bashed out the front window in the middle of a roiling frat party that we'd crashed for the free drinks. Ben and I were drinking in the stairwell when we heard the glass shatter and then saw Jared coming up to us with a silly grin and a fast walk.

We all hustled outside and got about fifty feet down the sidewalk when we turned back to see sixteen frat guys rushing through the door like some kind of clown act at the J. Crew circus. The main dude came out, chest puffed, screaming.

"Which one of you assholes broke that window?"

We didn't trip. The three of us had been through so much shit before, we knew the drill.

"What window?"

"The fucking window that's on the sidewalk now!"

"Yo, man, I don't know what you're talking about."

"Eddie, we know you, man. Which one of your boys broke the window?"

"Son, I have no idea what you're talking about. No one broke any window."

I remember that "Late Registration" was bumpin' through the Chi Psi window. My boy Jacob always played that shit "Two Words" and it was coming through that window like theme music. "We in the streets playa getcha mail / it's only two places you'll end up: either dead or in jail." Sixteen angry frat boys were tightening their semicircle around us, but for some weird-ass reason all I heard was Yeezy until I realized people were still barkin' at me.

"Dude, you go to school here, just tell us which one of these assholes broke the window and it's not a problem."

"Yo, I'm not saying it again. We're walking this way. If y'all have a problem, come with it."

Jared, Ben, and I started to walk off and the frat boys looped around us to form a circle. Sixteen of them punk motherfuckers and not a nann one of them swung on us. Everyone was waiting for someone to throw the first punch and we weren't about to, 'cause we were outnumbered. Then Ben bucked. He broke the line around us and started running down the street.

"Where you going?!"

"He's probably getting the gat, son."

We didn't have a gun. There was no reason. None of us were into shit that deep but the frat boys didn't know. At the time, I thought I was playing it smart, making them think Ben had the ratchet. It worked because a few of them fell back. Jared and I stood our ground still surrounded by the remaining mob of frat guys, who were now crowding us even closer, starting to push us around a little. There was a lot of bullshitting, but we figured that by the time Ben came back with the car, we'd just jump in and be out.

After about five minutes, Ben pulled up in his Mitsubishi Montero. I dived into the passenger seat but Jared stayed on the street.

"Jared, get in the car, man!"

"Naw, fuck that."

"I'ma go get him."

I stayed in the passenger seat while Ben tried to get Jared, but he wouldn't move. Jared was a stubborn motherfucker. He never ran, never backed down, and even though we didn't have a move, he wanted to have it out right there on the street. There was this big juicehead named Keith that came up to Jared—easily three times his size. Real talk, Keith was about six foot three, 225, all muscle, but if they fought, I still would've bet on Jared. It's not about size in a street fight; whoever throws first wins and Jared always threw first. I stayed in the car waiting for Ben to get Jared out of there, but he stayed in Keith's face. After a few minutes, I got out and took the driver's side and honked the horn in Jared's ear but he didn't even turn. I had a feeling this fool was really gonna try to fight sixteen people solo. I was proud of Ben. He was actually making peace that day telling the frat dudes that we'd pay for the window, that Jared was drunk, apologizing for him, trying to get us all out of there without a fight. Right when Ben was about to resolve the situation, though, I saw Kaywan creepin' toward Ben's left side with a tire iron.

"BEN! TURN! TURN!"

By this time people were yelling and screaming on the street, Kanye was at full pitch from the window, and half the school had poured out onto the sidewalk from a house party on the block. *Still nowhere to go.*

"BEEENNNN!!!" Kaywan reared back with the tire iron, aiming at Ben's head. I had no choice. I stepped on the gas.

VRRROOOMMM! BAM!

"What the fuck!"

I drove the Montero into the crowd as Kaywan dived out of the way and hit Keith. Jared and Ben got loose, the other kids ran, but Keith jumped onto the side bumper of the car and tried to punch me through the window.

"You fucking chink!"

I raised the window, but his arm was still in the car. This fool just wouldn't let go. One arm was in the window grabbing at my face and the other grabbed the rail on top of the SUV. In those situations, some people can't see straight. Everything starts to blend together, but I was different. Things always came clear to me. I could see a way out. There were people everywhere, but I had to get Keith off. I stepped on the gas, went toward a spot with no bystanders, spun the car 360, and threw Keith off the car. His ass went tumbling into the street like flaming goat shit.

I turned the whip around to pick up Ben and Jared. Finally, Jared got in the fucking car.

"What the fuck was that, man? I was about to calm that situation!"

"Son, that A-rab was about to whomp you with a tire iron!"

"Just go, man, just go!"

I jetted down Holt Avenue, but before I could make the left out of school grounds we heard jake.

WHHHHRRRRRRR WHRRRRRRR WHRRRRR!

"Step out of your vehicle!"

"Why the fuck is the SWAT team here?"

Three cop cars swerved in front of us with SWAT logos and barricaded the SUV in a triangle. Two squad cars slid in parallel and a third came up the middle facing us head-on. Immediately I put the car in reverse and stepped on it. Before I could back into another street, three more cars blocked us from behind.

"Eddie, stop the car! They got us, man!"

"Naw, I can go up the grass."

"Son, get the fuck out of the car! We're surrounded!"

Ben was right. There was no way out . . .

"Stop the vehicle and step out with your hands in the air!"

"We goin' out like this?"

"We don't have a choice! Fucking stop the car, Eddie!"

I put the car in park, ate the weed in my pocket, and got out.

"Put your hands in the air!"

Everyone sees this scene in movies or hears about it from friends, but the first time you get popped for some real shit is no joke. I knew that I wouldn't face serious charges for the fight in high school, but this was bad. We were drunk, high, driving, and I hit someone with a car. I looked into the lights and for the first time in my life, things started to blur. Usually I was calm and collected, but I knew it was over. I looked into the blue, got stuck in the red. Time's up.

"Get on the ground! Get the fuck on the ground!"

I felt like I was sleepwalking. Everything slowed down. Like the first time you get high and think, This can't be real.

"Get the fuck on the ground!"

"Eddie! Get on the fucking ground, man! They're gonna shoot you!"

I looked up and the cops were in position. Doors out, crouched behind with MP-5s, one dude sitting in the car talking into the intercom.

"This is your last warning! Get on the ground with your hands behind your back!"

It took everything I had to get down. I wasn't ready to go away. For some reason, I knew to get down, I wanted to get down, but I couldn't. I didn't know when I'd be free again. I felt like I was looking at myself from the outside when my hands finally went up slowly, I kneeled in the middle of the street, and lay the fuck down. Jared and Ben were already down so as soon as I hit the deck, the cops rushed us. I couldn't see with my face down but I felt it. Cold steel on the back of my head. There's nothing that can prepare you for that feeling. All the hair on your neck stands up and you feel the chill down your spine to the toes. Cops apply the chokehold, cuff you, and the whole time there's the barrel of an MP-5 on the back of your head. I watched my life flash by me in those sirens. It was surreal. I knew I wasn't going to be in jail forever, but it was definitely gonna fuck my life like Rick James on a couch. As it's all happening, I hear this kid I served yelling from the window of the frat.

"That kid Eddie sells short bags!"

"Check his pockets! I just copped from him this week!"

I didn't respect those kids at all, always knew they had it in them to snitch if things got hot. But they were the least of my worries. Before we knew it, Ben switched sides and started singing on the street.

"I'll tell you anything you want! Eddie always gets me in trouble! I didn't do shit this time!"

"Ben, shut the fuck up!"

"Naw, man, I'm not going down for y'all this time. You guys fucked up this time. I'm not going down."

He lost it. The cops were even shook because Ben was out on front street literally telling cops he'd say anything about Jared and me. He was still on probation for a prior assault charge, but he didn't have to give us up—even if he just said he was a passenger in the car and didn't see what happened, he would have been fine. Within a few minutes, the cops put Ben in a squad car and he was gone.

"Yo, is he for real?"

"I don't know, man. You shouldn't have hit him with the car!"

"And you shouldn't have fuckin' broken the window, man. Are you serious right now?"

"Shut the fuck up. I'm not talkin'."

"Me neither."

Within minutes, the entire school was on the block. Everyone heard the sirens, saw the lights, and there I was with Jared, standing cuffed up on the corner like zoo animals. I knew I was done. When Jared and I finally got to a holding center in Winter Park, Ben was nowhere to be found.

"Where'd you guys take Ben?"

"Oh, your friend's already out."

"Motherfucker . . ."

"Jared, you hear that shit?"

"Yeah . . ."

"We're going to need statements from you two."

"Fine."

First mistake I made was giving the statement. We knew better, but for some reason we just weren't thinking and wrote the damn statements. They took us out one at a time. Jared first, then me.

"You boys know we've never had a call like this at Rollins ever, right?"

"What do you mean?"

"Which one of you had the gun? Or should I say 'gat'?"

"We don't have a gun."

"Somebody has the gun and you're going to tell me who."

"Nobody has a gun, man."

"We got a call from a student saying someone ran to get a 'gat.' So somebody's telling me where the gun is or you're going to Thirty-third."

"Do what you gotta do, but there's no gun."

I found out later that this kid Connelly jumped behind a bush while the whole thing was going down and called the cops when Ben ran to get the car. That's why the SWAT team showed up. The cops thought there was a gun involved, but we never even had one. About three hours later, the cops put us back in a cop car and drove us to the Thirty-third Street Jail.

TWO

12.

NIGHT MARKET

Like Huo Yuanjia in *Fearless* fleeing Tianjin in shame, I was down and out. Not in a good Cam'ron ft. Kanye with the 1970s Heron flow, either. I was down and out facing trial for aggravated assault with a motor vehicle, a third-degree, level six charge with a maximum five-year sentence. Enter the motherland.

I didn't want to go to Taiwan. The last time I went, I was twelve. We stayed at my aunt's crib in the middle of the summer with no AC and there were mosquitos and moldy-smelling clothes hanging everywhere. I got diarrhea eating street food and the Chinese kids looked like Sanrio characters flashing peace fingers and jazz hands. Fortunately, the parents knew better. I'd fallen completely off the tracks and the only trick they had left in their kung-fu manuals was to send the kid home to marinate on things.

The trip was part of a program that officially went by the name of Study Tour, but people called it "Loveboat." The concept was simple from our parents' point of view: go home, see the motherland, and, eventually, get someone from the same tribe pregnant. I wasn't opposed to getting anyone pregnant. But I wasn't sure I wanted to hitch the rest of my life to an island whose only real draws were cheap video games and stinky tofu.

The video games were bootlegged, but the stinky tofu was real: an ugly, smelly tofu that's cured in rotten cabbage. In Taiwan, they take the tofu, fry it, and serve it with garlic oil, vinegar, chili sauce, and *pao tsai*— pickled vegetables, usually carrots, cabbage, and radish. My mom and her friends used to go to a Taiwanese restaurant in D.C. to eat it, but even there they'd only serve it for *xiao ye* (midnight snack) after 11 P.M., when most of the *lao wai* (foreigners) had left, because the smell from the tofu was so funky. This shit-smelling food was my favorite thing about Taiwan. But after a plea deal, I had an opportunity. I could get approval to visit Taiwan, or sit at home on felony probation. So off I went.

I was sleepwalking on my way to Taiwan. That's how I felt when I got to Taoyuan International Airport. For months, I'd dreaded the trip, but then all of a sudden it was on me.

It was the same airport I flew into when I was twelve, but it was different this time. Everywhere I looked, Taiwanese people in suits, in sandals, in tank tops, in Iverson jerseys, with mole-hair growths, without mole-hair growths. No matter where you turned, slanted eyes were watching. The cabdrivers were on that dress shoes and socks flow with shorts waaayyy before Thom Browne! I mean, it definitely doesn't look the same when you have a belly-out tank top and bowl cut, but you get the picture. Like RZA said, "Protons Electrons Always Cause Explosions," and fireworks went off in my head.

WHEN I ARRIVED in Taipei, to the college that hosted the trip, I was late as usual.

"Meester Huang?"

"Yeah, checking in."

"Ay yah! You are very late, sirs!"

"My bad."

"What do you means 'my bad'?"

"Like my fault, my bad. It's all good, can I still check in?"

"No, not good! We thought you weren't coming and gave your room away."

"Yo, I just flew nineteen hours. I'll sleep in a bathroom if I have to."

"Let me check . . ."

The woman at registration went to the office and started speaking to her supervisor in Chinese. Apparently, they'd given my room away to someone who was on standby. I overheard their conversation, but there were two other guys who were late as well and in the same position as me.

"I don't know if you want to do these, but there ees one room on the girls' floor that has a bed availables. There are two other males roommates to be your companion, though, so not awkwards with all the females on floor."

Taiwan, I love you. I felt like King Jaffe Joffer up in the joint. *Please feel free to serve me your most eligible shawties.* I went to the room, saw one bed free, and slept for twelve hours. The next day, I woke up stankin'. All in, it had been about thirty-two hours since my last shower—this for a dude who doesn't go eight days without a shape-up and ten hours without a shower. I mean, baby girl, I make Cool Water smell good. My first day in Taiwan, it was middle school dance party steez; I sprayed on whatever cheap cologne I could find.

I grabbed a towel, put on my Iceberg Muttley flip-flops, and went to the bathroom. In front of the sink was a girl with long black hair in a turquoise American Eagle shirt and shorts, putting in her contacts. Even though she had a finger in one eye, I thought to myself, If the other side looks like this one, just without a finger in the eye, she's pretty damn fly. Despite being from stankonia and only wearing a towel, I figured it'd be OK to say hello.

"Wassup!"

The girl totally bugged out, threw in her other contact lens, and ran out without saying a word.

Despite crashing and burning, I figured I could still enjoy my shower. I walked into the stall and next to the shower was the toilet. Not just any shitter, but a squatter: a hole in the floor with a wastebasket next to it for your shit tickets. You could take a shit, brush your teeth, and wash your dick at the same time if you wanted to. I mean, I respect the creativity, but the last thing I want to do while showering is take a shit or fall in the squatter with a sign next to it that says, "Put dirty papers in can." To complete the décor they had a neon green flyswatter hanging on one side of the window in case you wanted to kill mosquitos while doing all four of the above. I didn't have to work out all summer, I just did the circuit in the shit-shower-swat room.

After going to the "gym," I got back to the room and met my roommates. They were pretty much what I expected. Glasses, Hang Ten gear, goofy T-shirts that said MIT: Made in Taiwan. You know, not God body shit. This was always a funny negotiation for me. On one hand, I had childhood photos of me wearing the same uniform and it cracked me up, but once I decided I didn't want to be the Taiwanese Balki Bartokomous, I made money to buy Nike and 'Lo.

"Hey, I'm Richard. What's your name?"

"Eddie, wassup, man."

"I'm Tim!"

"You Taiwanese, dude?"

To go on the trip, you had to be Taiwanese because the government paid for it. Tim had orange hair, so I figured daddy was a white man.

"Ha, ha, yeah, man, I'm half Taiwanese, dude!"

"Oh, that's what's really good. I was just curious. Yo, y'all know we're on the girls floor, right?"

As I said those words, Richard looked like he was about to puke on his MIT shirt. Even as a nineteen-year-old, he was still working his way through the cootie stage.

"Yeah, it's kinda weird, but I think we'll be OK."

Tim gave me the universal eye-roll for "this dude needs GPS to find his dick." We all got dressed and went down to eat breakfast. I got in the elevator and saw the girl with the contact lenses.

"Hey, weren't you just in the bathroom?"

"I don't know what you're talking about."

"Yo, stop playin', you remember me! What's your name?"

"Ning."

"I'm Eddie!"

We went down to the cafeteria for breakfast: rice porridge, black pickles, dried pork *sung*, fried peanuts, vegetables, tofu. It went on and on.

Porridge is our soup, our grits, our sustenance, so it's pretty much the go-to for breakfast. For the first time, I ate with a bunch of other Taiwanese-Chinese kids my age who knew what the hell they were doing. Even at Chinese school, there were always kids that brought hamburgers, shunned chopsticks, or didn't get down with the funky shit. They were like faux-bootleg–Canal Street Chinamen.

That was one of the things that really annoyed me about growing up Chinese in the States. Even if you wanted to roll with Chinese/Taiwanese kids, there were barely any around and the ones that were around had lost their culture and identity. They barely spoke Chinese, resented Chinese food, and if we got picked on by white people on the basketball court, everyone just looked out for themselves. It wasn't that I wanted people to carry around little red books to affirm their "Chinese-ness," but I just wanted to know there were other people that wanted this community to live on in America. There was one kid who wouldn't eat the thousand-year-old eggs at breakfast and all the other kids started roasting him.

"If you don't get down with the nasty shit, you're not Chinese!"

I was down with the mob, but something left me unsettled. One thing ABCs love to do is compete on "Chinese-ness," i.e., who will eat the most chicken feet, pig intestines, and have the highest SAT scores. I scored high in chicken feet, sneaker game, and pirated goods, but relatively low on the SAT. I had made National Guild Honorable Mention for piano when I was around twelve and promptly quit. My parents had me play tennis and take karate, but ironically, I quit tennis two tournaments short of being ranked in the state of Florida and left karate after getting my brown belt. The family never understood it, but I knew what I was doing. I didn't want to play their stupid Asian Olympics, but I wanted to prove to myself that if I did want to be the stereotypical Chinaman they wanted, I could.*

---

* It may seem contradictory to say I want people to preserve their culture and then reject certain things like the model-minority expectations, a la carte, but there is a fine distinction to be made between stereotypes and actual culture. In my Chinese America, I don't care if you have high SAT scores or use chopsticks. All I want to know is if you are aware of shared problems and issues due to our skin, eyes, and country of origin.

———

AFTER BREAKFAST, WE went to language class. Compared to my parents and older cousins, I didn't speak Chinese that well. But in Study Tour class, I realized that I was actually one of the more fluent speakers, especially with food. I knew the names of everything, but unless it was a food item, I couldn't write it. The teachers thought it was funny and kept calling me the hungry kid: *"Xiao Ming hao ci!"* I couldn't help it: all I thought about was pussy and food. So, after class, I asked Ning out. To eat.

"Yo, you hungry?"

"Not really."

"Let's go to the night market anyway. It'll be fun."

"Isn't there a curfew?"

On "Loveboat," there was always a story about people from the year before either getting pregnant or married, so they instituted a curfew. When we first got there, Tim and I started snooping around the dorm and went to the ground floor. On the back side of the dorm was a window that the guard at the door couldn't see from his position. So we broke the window. Delinquent 101 shit. They really should have made it harder.

The curfew was a curse because Taipei is the best at night. The neon lights go on, the youth come out, and street vendors serve everything from fried squid in a bag to stinky tofu to *oh-a-jian*, an oyster pancake. *Xiao ye* is an event, like reverse brunch. By the time *xiao ye* comes around, you've most likely already eaten all three meals, but in Taipei, around 12 A.M., people start to come back out for late-night food. There are no tablecloths, servers, or even backs on chairs. I learned that a three-star dining room doesn't always equate to three-star food and developing-nation garage stands could get Ferran Adrià any day. The best things I tasted were humble, honest, and served on bright green melamine plates by people wearing sandals and getting high on betel nut.

Ning and I crawled out of the window and made our way through the dark to Shilin Night Market. On the way, we nearly got killed by the crazy Taipei traffic. Scooters are a serious life hazard in Taipei. Wherever you try to go, a scooter is cutting you off. One-seaters had two people on 'em, two-seaters had three, and three-seaters had a family. They were like Mexican vans on two wheels with the top cut off.

Although I tried to play it cool, my first trip to the Shilin Night Market changed me. While most head to the food court segment, I preferred the vendors sprawled down the nearby side streets and alleys. The atmosphere was elevated and electric—neon lights blazed with synthetic colors and the smells from all the cooking overwhelmed me. It was like being in *Eat Drink Man Woman* with smell-o-vision. I can't remember exactly what Ning and I ate at the market or even what we talked about, but I know I was wearing a Charles Woodson Raiders jersey and Ning had on these hilarious platform sandals with multicolored flowers on them.

Ning didn't actually say words a lot of the time; she just made sounds or bobbed her head.

> "EEW."
> "STALE."
> "HU-HUH."
> "ERR."
> *HEAD BOBBLE*
> *NOSE WRINKLE*

It was kind of disturbing at first. She was eighteen and native Taiwanese but came to America when she was four. You'd never know she was born in Taiwan since she grew up in America, but it was there dormant just like it was for me. Ning was unlike any girl I'd ever hung out with. No games, genuinely nice, totally herself all the time, and comfortable with whatever naïveté or ignorance there was about her. She was one of the most self-aware, confident people I knew, but she projected it clothed in insecurity.

In a strange way, even with our goofy clothes, Ning and I fit right in. Everyone in Taiwan is mismatched, outfitted in American-style clothes as interpreted by ardent Pokémon fans. Asians are funny; we can take any-thing and repackage it for your inner eight-year-old. As a kid who grew up with Girbauds and *The Chronic,* it was refreshing to see people just having fun. Hip-hop hadn't had that since Kid 'n Play's "Ain't Gonna Hurt No-body." If my homies from Florida had been around, I would've probably been clowning these night-market anime lovers, but that was the best part. They weren't. And in the absence of their gaze, I allowed myself to en-counter a part of myself I'd lost, shunned, and cast aside years ago. Tony Kushner talks about serpents shedding their skin too early, but I was a different animal. I had to shed my skin in America if I ever wanted to re-claim it on my own terms that summer in Taiwan.

Taiwan got me into food in a way I'd never experienced it before. When I went to Taiwan as a kid, my parents knew where to go, but this time, at the night market, I had to eat my way to my own discoveries. We realized that the way to eat in Taipei was to identify the house special and bounce around the street to complete a meal. All you had to do was look at the customers. Even if a restaurant had twenty items, if their signature was open-ended pot stickers, that's the only thing people ordered. With-out the stall even advertising it, you'd know what to order. The key is not to go too big at one stall and blow your load. Every stall was different, and you could get almost anything in the Shilin Night Market. Taipei is for food nerds what Amsterdam is for hooker connoisseurs.

Every dish has a basic, foundational technique, but after that, it's open for the individual cook's artistic interpretation. By far, the three biggest dishes in Taiwan are minced pork on rice, soup dumplings, and beef noo-dle soup. Minced pork on rice, everyone will tell you, *ah-ma* (grandma) makes best. It's all about childhood preferences. The dish is proletariat home-style chic; updating, modernizing, or remixing it violates the whole idea of minced pork on rice. It's ground pork and diced pork belly stewed with black shiitake mushrooms, five-spice, and rice wine. What distin-guishes one minced pork dish from another is the sweating of the pork. You don't want to brown it. The trick is to sweat the pork so all the mois-ture evaporates, but the flavor stays in the pot. When your soy sauce, rice wine, and water go down, it picks the fond back up and reincorporates the natural juices and flavor that you cooked out of the pork. A lot of them had *Roh gin mien,* which was a childhood favorite of mine. When I got a cold, my mom would take fish paste, pork strips, and carrots and make a boiled dumpling out of them, then serve the dumplings in chicken soup and cabbage with vinegar, white pepper, and cilantro. The technique was a lot like Southern chicken 'n' dumplings.

With soup dumplings, everyone knows the best is Din Tai Fung. So since *ah-ma* wins in minced pork and Din Tai Fung wins on soup dumplings, the only Taiwanese dish where the hood title is really up for grabs is beef noodle soup, the holy-grail-sword-in-the-stone of Taiwanese cuisine. I ate beef noodle soup everywhere. It was the one food item that screwed up our stall ordering strategy. People love the dish so much that even if it isn't a specialty of the house, it gets ordered, on the off chance that you'll discover the next great beef noodle soup at some random stall in the night market. At least that's why we ordered it. I had it at the Grand Hotel—too much soy. At karaoke—not fortified enough with bone. At the college cafeteria—almost not beef noodle soup anymore. At a super-buffet—ehh.

I sometimes wondered why no one restaurant had risen to the challenge and dominated beef noodle soup like Din Tai Fung did soup dumplings or Da Dong does Peking duck. The difference is that beef noodle soup has no bounds. Soup dumplings and Peking duck aren't open to wild reinterpretation because there are strict parameters and fewer components to work with. For beef noodle soup, the only prerequisites are beef, soup, and noodles. Some cooks add tomato, some don't, some use anise, some use cut chilis, some use whole chilis, some like thick noodles, some like it thin. Every year it seems like there's a new beef noodle soup champion. Stalls display their medals and awards, but like Zagat ratings and assholes . . . everybody's got one.

During that trip to Taipei, I had a lot of good but not great beef noodle soups and it was disappointing. I started to examine my mom's version. She always had the perfect balance of tomatoes, scallions, ginger, just enough garlic, chilis, and her secret: peanut butter. Our family loves peanut butter. We whip it together with sesame paste and boiling water to create a brownish gray slurry that we used for body in a lot of our soups and stews.

Nine years later, I went to Taipei Main Station with my dad. They had just opened a new food court, divided into sections. There was the bento box section where vendors sold only bento box favorites like fried pork chops, minced pork on rice, and *tong-a-biko* (Taiwanese sticky rice). They had a section for sweet congees where people specialized in dessert congee, there was the curry district where all the best curries were, but the crown jewel of the food court was the beef noodle soup section. There was an area of roughly a thousand square feet that had six beef noodle soup vendors who had all at one time won Best in Show.

It was like a beef noodle soup ice-cream shop. The vendors each gave tastes of the soup to coax customers. It was insanely competitive: imagine going to a food court that had six burger joints or five fish 'n' chips stalls. I can't imagine anyone thinking it was a good business move to set up shop next to five people selling the same item, but that's the beauty of Taiwanese food. We have very discerning palates and people have an appreciation for nuanced flavors. Every one of those stalls was busy because they each put their own intricate twist on the soup that made them distinct from each other. I tasted every one of the soups and they all stood out in their own way but it's not the way Americans think of "owning a dish." You hear chefs talk frequently about "owning dishes," but it's all about big movements like deconstructing a dish, putting a sauce on top, or entirely changing the presentation. When Taiwanese-Chinese people compete on beef noodle soup and attempt to own the dish, it's all about the two-inch punch. You can't even see what it is they did different; it's the slightest move of the needle that manifests itself in the soup. Perhaps you snuck a few soybeans into your stock to give it more depth and umami. Maybe you flash-fried your beef to cook off the first instead of blanching it. Or, maybe you sautéed some peanuts with your aromatics. Inspired, I continued to work on my own version, using my mom's recipe as the foundation.

HERE ARE MY TEN BEEF NOODLE
SOUP COMMANDMENTS:

---

1.   Throw out the first: always flash-boil your bones and beef to get the "musk" out. I've gone back and forth on this a lot. I would sometimes brown the meat as opposed to boil, but decided in the end that for this soup, you gotta boil. If you brown, it's overpowering. The lesson that beef noodle soup teaches you is restraint. Sometimes less is more if you want all the flavors in the dish to speak to you.

2.   Make sure the oil is medium-high when the aromatics go down and get a slight caramelization. It's a fine line. Too much caramelization and it becomes too heavy, but no caramelization and your stock is weak.

3.   Rice wine can be tricky. Most people like to vaporize it so that all the alcohol is cooked off. I like to leave a little of the alcohol flavor 'cause it tends to cut through the grease a bit.

4.   Absolutely no butter, lard, or duck fat. I've seen people in America try to "kick it up a notch" with animal fats and it ruins the soup. Peanut oil or die.

5.   Don't burn the chilis and peppercorns, not even a little bit. You want the spice and the numbness, but not the smokiness.

6.   After sautéing the chilis/peppercorns, turn off the heat and let them sit in the oil to steep. This is another reason you want to turn the heat off early.

7.   Strain your chilis/peppercorns out of the oil, put them in a muslin bag, and set them aside. Then add ginger/garlic/scallions to the oil in that order. Stage them.

8.   I use tomatoes in my beef noodle soup, but I add them after the soup is finished and everything is strained. I let them hang out in the soup as it sits on the stove over the course of the day. I cut

the tomatoes thin so they give off flavor without having to cook too long and so you can serve them still intact.

9.   Always use either shank or chuck flap. Brisket is too tough. If you want to make it interesting, add pig's foot or oxtail.

10.   Do you. I don't give you measurements with this because I gave you all the ingredients and the technique. The best part about beef noodle soup is that there are no rules. It just has to have beef, noodle, and soup. There are people that do clear broth beef noodle soup. Beef noodle soup with dairy. Beef noodle soup with pig's blood. It would suck if you looked at my recipe and never made your own, 'cause everyone has a beef noodle soup in them. Show it to me.

After the first two weeks on Loveboat, we had "Family Day." We were supposed to go out for the day with our families in Taipei. Most people still had some family in Taipei, but I didn't. While my mom and dad were born in Taiwan, the rest of their families were from mainland China. By the seventies, there was just more opportunity in America than in Taiwan so most of my family left.

In Taiwan, people would always ask about your family heritage since everyone's journey to Taiwan was different. Some were Native Taiwanese, Hakka, some were Japanese-Taiwanese, *Wai Sheng Ren* (Chinese-Taiwanese), etc. And on family day at Loveboat you could expect to tell your family history at least once an hour. Luckily, Ning came to my rescue.

"Hey, what are you doing?"

"Nothing, I'm gonna go play basketball."

"Aww, do you not have family?"

"Naw, not here."

"Ha, ha, orphan boy!"

"Whatever . . ."

"Well, do you wanna come eat with my family?"

"What are you guys eating?"

"Sushi!"

"Really? Sushi in Taiwan? Why would you do that?"

"Whatever, go play basketball, orphan boy . . ."

THE SUSHI SPOT wasn't more than a garage on the street level of an apartment building. Cook downstairs, live upstairs. You walked in and on the right side was the standard blue Japanese curtain with octopus cartoons. Behind the curtains was the kitchen, barely four feet by three feet. Ning's aunt and uncle were really good people. They didn't pry about my family, didn't seem to mind that I was wearing my Orlando Magic jersey backward, and ordered a ton of food. It was par for the course for the Juang family.

The sushi was very cold. In Taiwan, they keep the sushi at a temperature several degrees lower than in Japan or America. Sometimes, you'll even get thin ice chips on the surface of sashimi. The chunks are significantly larger and cut like two-ounce slices of New York strip. Thick, wide, and blocky. I didn't like it. To me, sushi is about mouthfeel and texture. When you serve the fish close to frozen and in bricks, it defeats the purpose.

The sushi sucked but Ning was cool. While other girls were obsessed with dick, going out, cliques, and ladder climbing, she was totally oblivious. Part of it was naïveté, but another part of it was just that she didn't buy into the things people told her were important. She lived in her own cocoon, a cocoon filled with anime, bubble tea, and fantasy novels. I was dismissive at first, but then we started playing Mario Kart and Super Smash Bros., and smanging. It was like returning to some version of me that had gotten lost over the last decade, since I was a kid with my brother Emery, crawling through the house and playing Mortal Kombat at 2 A.M. with the sound off while my mom was asleep. Emery and I'd read comics, watch kung fu flicks, and not give a fuck about this girl or that party or who had beef. I realized that I missed that.

It's not until I'm writing today that I realized why we got along so well. We were both wolves in sheep's clothing. We'd realized early on to "play dumb." I dumbed out destroying everything in my way, but Ning did the opposite, built a pleasure dome and kept to herself. Before I met Ning, it was only in the really hard times that I looked at myself and forced myself to understand who I really was and not get lost in the act. But I didn't have to act around her, I could just be.

Ning also got me back in touch with my identity. While I was out drinking Mad Dog 40/40 and running over frat boys with Mitsubishi Monteros, she went to Chinese school on weekends all the way up until her senior year of high school. Instead of sneaking into bars or clubs, she was going to Bubble Island with her girlfriends. We kept making fun of each other, but as they say, opposites attract. I had become so obsessed with not being a stereotype that half of who I was had gone dormant. But it was also a positive. Instead of following the path most Asian kids do, I struck out on my own. There's nature, there's nurture, and as Harry Potter teaches us, there's who YOU want to be. Every part of me was something I sought out and encountered. And that summer in Taipei, I looked around and saw myself everywhere I went. Pieces of me scattered all over the country like I had lived, died, burned, and been spread throughout the country in a past life. Here I was coming home to find myself again in street stalls, KTV rooms, and bowls of beef noodle soup. All the things instilled in me from a young age by my family and home, rehydrated and brought to life like instant noodles. They never left, they just needed attention.

I REMEMBER SITTING in the Taipei airport the day I left Taiwan. Ning had a flight around the same time so I walked her to her security gate and said goodbye. I wasn't big on goodbyes. I remember she had a giant backpack, shorts, and something orange on, but I wasn't sad. I knew I'd see her again. She already planned to come visit me in Florida when she got back. But I was worried about Taiwan. Who knew when I'd come back? There was a part of me that dreaded going back to Florida. It was like going back to work.

I knew that in a matter of days, I'd be back to the land of slanted-eye or ching-chong jokes. After those months in Taiwan, I started asking myself:

Why? Why the fuck do I have to be Q-Tip cryin' Sucka N!gg@? I was sick of explaining myself, sick of being different, and sick of Florida. I felt something weird and new: I was happy. Reconciled. I learned my lesson from America and didn't want to go back. But in truth, in Taiwan, I was different, too. I had to explain myself to people in Taiwan just like I did in Florida and I realized that if I stayed, I'd have a whole new set of hurdles to face. And I was already buggin' out because I was about to miss the Redskins' second preseason game after Danny Wuerffel set the world on fire in the first one. I was stuck in the middle.

The airport honestly felt more like home to me than either Taiwan or Florida, and I enjoyed every moment. There was fried chicken, beef noodle soup, hamburgers, Coke, *Apple Sidra,* fried rice, and doughnuts. Something for everyone. I guess it's the only place I didn't have to explain anything. Everyone was in-between. The relief of the airport and the opportunity to reflect on my trip helped me realize that I didn't want to blame anyone anymore. Not my parents, not white people, not America. Did I still think there was a lot wrong with the aforementioned? Hell, yeah, but unless I was going to do something about it, I couldn't say shit. So I drank my *Apple Sidra* and shut the fuck up.

13.

ROYAL HUANG

When I came back from Taiwan, I was on a mission. Somehow everything was coming clear, like juices dripping from a turkey timer. I saw that my interests in hip-hop, basketball, food, comedy, and writing were symptoms of a larger interest: finding a place for myself in the world or making one. School helped me give that larger interest more precise names—racial identity, social justice—and I was determined to figure it all out.

I finally felt free. For years, I knew what I wanted to do but felt guilty because I knew my parents wouldn't approve. They wanted me to be a business major, but I knew it wasn't for me. I fought them, I argued, and hated them because so much of my life was stunted due to their wants and desires. Once I understood why, I stopped reacting with anger. They were so cute and delusional trying to come up in the world using the master's tools. Luckily, I got my Audre Lorde on and realized you can't tear down the master's house with the master's tools.

Instead of living my life trying to please them, I started to jux them.

Sometimes being honest isn't good for anyone. I knew I wasn't going to give in to my parents, but I also knew they'd never understand, so I had to be a trickster. I did what I wanted to do, made a plan for myself, and kept them in the dark. I said the things I needed to say so they could sleep at night. Every semester, I'd sign up for one class that I could show them a textbook for, like marketing or business administration. On my own time, I took a ton of classes in different departments: anthropology, sociology, English, Asian studies, film, women's studies, African-American studies, and even theater. I ate the shit up. All of a sudden, I loved school. I didn't even want to get fucked-up anymore. I started to read every book I could get my hands on and joined the school paper to practice writing. I couldn't believe how long I had been kept in the dark but as I opened each book I saw there were other people like me who saw the things I saw. I gave up trying to find friends at college and befriended dead people between the margins. For years, I just didn't know how to express it but reading things like Teresa de Lauretis, Audre Lorde, Booker T. Washington, W.E.B. Du Bois, and Toni Morrison, I got it.

The most important professor in my entire life was Dr. Jennifer Henton. She was a strong black woman from Philly with a voice like Marge Simpson. All the kids at Rollins hated her. No one recommended her classes, everyone said she was difficult, and no one really got good grades in her class. But I looked at the syllabuses for her classes and thought to myself, These are all hit records! Syllabuses became like playlists for me those days. I was just into school and got mad excited thinking about all the new shit I'd learn every semester. The first class I took with her was a film criticism class with a feminist angle. At first I had no idea how I was going to relate since I still called bitches hos and hos bitches, but I signed up anyway. The class was housed in a cottage on campus with a round table in the center of the room. Dr. Henton looked like a cat lady holding an Alcoholics Anonymous session. I knew because I was taking anger management and alcohol/drug abuse classes every week as part of probation.

She was fragile and soft-spoken, but once we got into the course work, I'd never seen a woman go so hard. She changed my entire view of women. Where she saw bias, misogyny, racism, classism, and the like, she pointed it out, and never felt like she needed to curb her opinion for people when she was right. She reinforced a lesson my pops tried to teach me with his hands: NEVER EVER EVER back down if you're right. If you have evaluated all the perspectives, gone around the round table, and come back around with the same opinion, then walk right up to the offending party and tell 'em why you mad. I realized that as wild as I'd been up to that point, I still curbed my opinion ever so slightly because I was surrounded by conservative white people at Rollins.

ONCE WE HAD a debate about emasculated Asian men in Hollywood. Dr. Henton busted out a book called *Screening the Asian Male* and it made total sense, but the idea of the emasculated Asian wasn't new to me. My cousin Allen was the first to point it out to me one day when we were still kids:

"Yo, you notice Asian people never get any pussy in movies? Jet Li rescued Aliyah, no pussy! Chow Yun-Fat saves Mira Sorvino, no pussy. Chris Tucker gets mu-shu, but Jackie Chan? No pussy!"

"Damn, son, you right! Even Long Duk Dong has to ride that stationary bicycle instead of fucking!"

"You see!"

I never thought a professor would back me up, but Dr. Henton literally put the topic onto the syllabus! We talked for hours about how Asian men should be getting pussy in movies and I couldn't have agreed more.

THEN THERE WAS Dr. Maurice O'Sullivan. He was the longtime English chair and if not the most respected, clearly the most pugnacious. He went by "Socky," short for Socrates, and he was definitely the gadfly of Orlando Hall. You see, most professors don't engage. They start conversations, let the kids play, and referee. Dr. O'Sullivan was a different animal. He's the old dude at the YMCA that will dunk on twelve-year-olds just 'cause he can. Every class, this dude knocked me out in the first round. No matter how prepared I was, he tore me apart. If I tried to use something from Shakespeare, he would undercut me by having an equal and opposite quote from another Big Bill work. He always got me because he had a deeper well to draw from. He also had a wit and sense of humor. He was my kryptonite. Bird and Magic, Hakeem and Shaq, Yao and Dwight, Mo and Me. But I went home, thought about what Dr. O'Sullivan said, and came back every day to get my ass kicked. I remember I turned in a satire as a book report once and he said to me, "Eddie, nice try. Tragedy is easy, comedy is hard, you're not funny." I laughed and went back to the lab.

Prof O was from an immigrant family like me. He told me that back in the day, Rollins charged him with teaching African-American literature because he was black Irish. All my arguments, strategies, and opinions were old news to him. Every work I referenced was available to him. I was twenty and he was sixty-plus. He had kids, a lifetime of memories and experiences, how the fuck was I going to beat this dude? Not only was he smart like the other professors, but he had logos, ethos, and pathos. Most professors got the logos and ethos but been in the ivory tower too long to have a handle on pathos. Then I realized . . . I gotta hit this motherfucker the one place he's weak and play his strength against him: age.

One of the most influential texts I read was Emerson's "American Scholar." The one passage that really stuck with me was his line about young men in libraries:

> Meek young men grow up in libraries, believing it their duty to accept the views, which Cicero, which Locke, which Bacon, have given, forgetful that Cicero, Locke, and Bacon were only young men in libraries, when they wrote these books.

That was the answer. You can't idolize and emulate forever. At some point, you gotta cut the cord and go for dolo. I thought of Locke and his idea of tabula rasa. I realized that I needed to build arguments, philosophies, and a style grounded in my era and experiences.

Dr. Henton taught me to fight without hesitation, but Prof O taught me to box. He gave me a lesson on discipline. I remember he called me a shotgun: "You have all this energy and it's unruly, but like a shotgun, you need the barrel to direct the buckshot just enough."

Those professors changed my life. I went from a punk kid that fought without a true understanding of the who, what, when, where, and why to a contrarian with a cause. I'm probably the only student on felony probation that won college awards for women's, African-American, and English studies. I won the Zora Neale Hurston and Barbara Lawrence Alfond Award in 2004. By all accounts, it was the year of the Rotten Banana. I had all them cats quoting Biggie, Lao Tzu, and Nas by the time I was gone.

Finally, after three years of learning, I got my degree but not without a hitch. The last lesson came from Professor Papay. At first, I hated Professor Papay. She kept picking on my grammar. I always had a voice, heart, and now a mind to my writing, but no grammar. Up until my last year in college, I didn't know what semicolons were for so I just didn't use them. Whether it's cooking, basketball, or writing, I was like Latrell Sprewell. If I couldn't go left, I just got really good at going right until someone stopped me. That person was Professor Papay. No matter what I did, I couldn't get passing grades on my papers in her class because my grammar was so bad. If Prof O was my first title fight, Prof Papay was my first title defense, and she came southpaw.

I basically wrote in slang and had all kinds of fucked-up syntax, subject-verb agreement, and run-on sentence issues. While the other professors overlooked my grammar and credited me for my content and perspective, Papay focused on my weaknesses. She made me a deal. I could pass her class and graduate if I went to the writing workshop. It was worse than probation 'cause I cared about my writing, yet here I was walking with my head down into the writing center. I never wanted to admit I didn't know how to speak or write English properly, so I avoided it. For years I figured it was like video games. Some characters don't have any defense or hit points, but they compensate by being really ill in other categories. Luckily, Professor Papay didn't let me slide.

The kids at the center were really cool. My tutor was this girl Emily. She didn't judge me, she liked my writing, and I could ask her anything without being laughed at. We literally had to start with capitalization because I didn't understand what was supposed to be capitalized and what wasn't. Even to this day, I can't spit out the rules, but intuitively I can "feel" what is proper grammar. I remember asking her shit like:

"Yo, so, if semicolons break up complete sentences, why don't we just use periods?"

"Because they are complete sentences, but not separate thoughts."

"Oh, like 'My Melody'?"

"Huh?"

"You know, Rakim: 'I say one rhyme and I order a longer rhyme shorter; a pause, but don't stop the tape recorder.'"

"I guess that's it . . ."

"Word! I get it. Use a semicolon when you want people to think about the shit together, right?"

"Ha, ha, yeah, exactly."

That was my thing. I learned enough from class and books that I wanted to see their thoughts, rules, and concepts at play in the modern art that I related to. No matter how much Shakespeare I read, it wasn't my era. The classics gave me a foundation and skill set, but now it was my turn to write some new shit.

I started applying to English or film schools. I figured, with good grades and two major awards from Rollins, that schools might overlook my felony but it wasn't so. There wasn't one grad school that I got into.

About six months later, I was chillin' at home with my family watching the Pacers play the Pistons at the Palace. With less than a minute left in the fourth quarter, Ben Wallace drove to the bucket and Ron Artest took a hack at him. Wallace wasn't feeling it so he came back hard at Ron and threw him back a good twelve to fifteen feet. As Ron fought to keep his balance, both benches cleared, mayhem ensued, and it was Reggie Miller in a two-piece jawn fencing off Ron Artest from the Pistons. Behind Reggie, Artest lay down on the scorer's table and even put on headphones at one point just to stunt on Wallace. Things started to calm down and you figured the dust would settle, but some fan threw a large soda from right field meant for Artest. Luckily, Reggie was able to keep Artest at the scorer's table, but then more fans threw drinks at the Pacers. Within seconds, Artest ran into the stands with Stephen Jackson and started whompin' the fan that threw the drink. Or at least someone close to the fan that threw the drink.

As Artest and Jackson started walking out of the stands, another Pistons fan ran up on them and took a swing. Artest sidestepped, dodged the punch, and then stuck the dude right in the face. Meanwhile, down on the floor a fan rushed Jermaine O'Neal and he had to defend himself, too. As the whole scene unfolded, my brothers and I got mad hyped. I was always an Artest fan from his St. John's days but I couldn't stand the Pacers. After watching the Pacers dismantle these punk-ass Pistons fans, I was a fan. For years, we've seen fans in Cleveland, Philly, and now Detroit throw shit at players from the stands. Who the fuck else goes to someone's work and thinks it's OK to just make it rain with fountain sodas and beer bottles?

You hear people spit that backward logic, "Athletes make tons of money, we bought tickets and have a right to throw shit!" Bankers make money, too, but I'm not running up into Chase and throwing milk shakes at the homie selling subprime mortgages. If anyone did that and then got the shit beat out of them, there would be no question whose fault it was. But here people threw shit at the Pacers and expected them to just take it. Typical American hypocrisy in action. The incident went a good eight minutes before the first semblance of security showed up.

The next day, David Stern suspended nine Pacers without pay for 146 games and a total of $11 million in lost wages. I understood why the Pacers were suspended, but Stern not only didn't protect his players, he took no responsibility for what ensued and buried his players. It was one of the most disloyal moves I've ever seen in my life. I always hated Stern. From changing the hand-check rules to his legislation of culture to his failure handling Malice at the Palace, Stern has proven to be one of the coldest, most heartless individuals I've ever seen.

I always listened to 740 AM Sports Talk Radio in Orlando. Everyone calling into the station placed blame on Artest, Jackson, and O'Neal, but as you listened to them you could literally hear the racism oozing out of their comments. Using code like "animals," "gorillas," "punks," "no class," "ghetto," "un-American," etc., people tried to tie the incident to a deeper cultural chasm. It was 100 percent horseshit. Look, if it's "hood" to hit someone for throwing a drink in your face, move me to the projects because that's me. I wasn't raised to take a shot in the face and curl up in a ball. I wrote a letter to the *Orlando Sentinel,* making that point.

IT WASN'T ONE of my best works, but what was meant as a letter to the editor became an article on page two of the sports section on November 28, 2004. My dad freaked out. "That's my son! Eddie! You're in the paper!"

Two minutes later he came back with the newspaper and asked, "Eh! Did you get paid for this?"

"Naw, it was just a letter to the editor."

"Ohhh, so you're still not professional?"

Typical. I didn't care, though. Later that day, I got a call from the *Sentinel*. After years of writing my own mock drafts and goofy pick 'em articles in the college newspaper, the editor of the sports section wanted to offer me a job as a beat writer. I couldn't believe it. Six months after college, still on felony probation, I was about to be a beat writer for the local paper. I put on my only suit, got a haircut, did push-ups, and got into my car as fast as I could.

You opened the doors to the *Sentinel* and the first thing you smelled was fresh ink. Huge machines thirty feet long, nine feet tall, with endless sheets of newspaper running in and out. Instantly, I could see how "newspapermen" fell in love with the life, worked over these desks for decades, getting next to nothing in return. Running around Orlando for years without a purpose, I felt like I finally found one. For the last eleven years of my life, my dad and I had read the *Sentinel* every morning despite its conservative bent. He was addicted to the sports section and here I was. It wasn't just me that arrived, it was my father, too.

I was interviewing for a lowly beat writer position covering high school basketball, but we didn't care. The whole family bugged out and it was the most important interview I'd ever have. They led me to a conference room with a contract on the table. It was a standard contract for writers that I scanned quickly and signed. About fifteen minutes later, a big white guy standing six one and roughly 230 pounds came walking in with glasses on. I'll never forget the first words he said.

"Oh, wow, that face . . ."

"My face?"

"I mean . . . your face. You know . . . you look young, that's all."

"Yeah, I know, but you don't put the beat writers' photos in the newspaper, do you?"

"No, but no one is going to talk to you with that face. I'll try to get you some work, but I just don't know how we can make this work."

Just like that, it was over. All because of "that face."

That face . . . What the fuck did he mean by "that face"? I could go on for pages trying to unpack everything he meant by that, but I won't give this cracker the satisfaction. I knew what he meant, my family knew what he meant, and you know what he meant. That was it for me. I wanted power, I wanted respect, and I never ever ever wanted anyone to tell me about my face again.

14

I KNOW A LITTLE BIT

After my interview at the *Orlando Sentinel,* I was forced to face a few realities. Although professors at Rollins gave me a chance and saw through the surface, other people were still going to judge me based strictly on appearance. No matter what I did in Florida, there just wasn't a critical mass of progressive liberals who'd seen more than rednecks on John Deere ride-ons. The only thing I had in common with most people is that I watched the Chappelle show and even then we laughed for different reasons. I decided to do something so no one could ever look down on me again. I went to law school.

I didn't even want to be a lawyer. I had no idea what the law was about, but I did know that when you passed the bar, you got an Esq. at the end of your name. My other options were M.D. or CPA so I went for the J.D. I remember the *Black Album* had come out the year before and Hov's verse kept ringing in my head:

Aren't you sharp as a tack, you some type of lawyer or something?
Or somebody important or somethin'?

People always fucked with me 'cause they assumed I was a quiet Asian that wouldn't say shit or know any better. I spent my life bitin' back, but I was tired. I didn't want to keep proving myself so I figured devote three years to this bullshit degree, to show people I can do something most people couldn't, and be done with it.

You figure getting a professional degree can't possibly put you in a shittier place than you were in previously, but that's a misconception. It's like having kids. In theory they cool, but the motherfuckers will shit on your life mad quick if you're not ready. It's a gamble. If you don't have a scholarship, you spend about $200K for three years' tuition, room, board, and books. Most people take out loans so that's another 7 to 13 percent interest over twenty to thirty years paying it all back. By the time you factor in three years of lost wages, you're just glad New York City got free condoms and 3-1-1.

Stats will show 70 percent job placement after graduation, but they'll count people that got temp, paralegal, or any ancillary work. If you are one of the lucky 15 percent of students that get a big firm job, you have to bill 1,800 hours a year at minimum. If you worked Monday through Friday fifty-two weeks a year with no holidays, that's 6.9 hours a day. It doesn't sound bad until you get to the firm and realize billable hours means actual hours that they can charge to a client. Eighteen hundred doesn't count the hours you spend sitting in Brooks Brothers* waiting for old heads to give you billable work to do. It doesn't count the hours you have to spend at "optional" networking, mentoring, circle-jerking events. It also doesn't count the hours spent avoiding passive-aggressive dickheads who want to compete on everything from doc review to how much starch you have in your shirt. For most first- to third-year associates, you have two days of waiting for every one day of billable work so when you do get it, you're staying till 3 or 4 A.M. to do the best job you can and hope you get more.

By my count, if you finished in the top 15 percent of your class, nailed the interview, made it through the summer associate phase, billed 1,800 hours a year for six to seven years, saved enough to pay off loans, then you

---

* Please believe, your boy never stepped foot in a Brooks Brothers, but that's what people rock.

most likely lost your hair, your friends, and any sense of dignity, happiness, or meaning in your life. On the upside, you probably got really ill at fantasy sports waiting for billable work. I used to give myself haircuts or download porn onto an external drive, and I once told a senior associate that my secretary was lactating when he asked why there was a stain on the memorandum of law I wrote for him. Not only was the J.D. a bad investment, but the law wasn't anything I thought it would be. It wasn't about justice. All those courtrooms with Lady Justice holding scales are just pitching propaganda. If courtrooms had a statue of Justice Scalia with the inscription "Most People Fux Wit Us," that'd be closer to the truth. Not very inspiring.

Here were my choices: I could read cases about sentencing guidelines, work at the Innocence Project fighting against wrongful convictions,* volunteer in Jamaica, Queens, family court and watch families get torn apart because of the legal technicalities, or I could get the fuck out and realize that the Lox were right all along: money, power, and respect drive the world.

I WASN'T MEANT to be an attorney, but I was meant to go to law school. It made me a disciplined thinker, it forced me to think logically not emotionally, and it taught me to respond in an organized manner. Flowery language, Jonathan Swift, and propaganda wouldn't work against attorneys. Their hearts were cold fucking places that "I Have a Dream" wouldn't appeal to. The only way to win in law school was with dead-ass logic. I had no intention of being an attorney, but I was down for another round of mental training.

During Christmas break of my first semester, there was this competition called the Association of the Bar of the City of New York Minority Bar Fellowship. We were all given a set of legal facts and asked to write memorandums of law. Any student who qualified as a "minority" could apply

---

* I ended up doing all those things. My first year, I volunteered at Jamaica, Queens, family court a few times and second year, I got picked to work at the Innocence Project with Vanessa Potkin, who to this day is probably my favorite attorney.

and the school would select students to represent at the city-wide competition. From sixteen schools, about sixty students were selected. After writing the memo, getting high scores, and then participating in competitive interviews, I won one of the fellowships. The prize was a job at a top-100 law firm. The reaction from other students at Cardozo was hilarious. People were so competitive and saw every job someone else got as a job that they lost. I didn't agree and always told people what Cam'ron said: "Can't get paid in a earth this big? You worthless kid!"

As a minority at law school, I was on a lonely-ass island so I joined APALSA. It was the first time I ever joined an Asian club. Within a few months, I remembered exactly why I hated it. Everyone was concerned with jobs, but not what it should mean to be an Asian with a law degree. It was the same drill as always. I thought that I'd be joining a club that would provide opportunities to do pro bono work on legal issues that affected the Asian community, but it was all cursory. Every month, we'd have meetings, invite Asian alumni who worked for firms, family court, legal aid, etc. and they'd talk to us about their jobs and if we were interested in getting similar jobs, they said that we could email them. It sucked chicken feet.

I proposed that we spend money on cultural events or bringing in Asian councilmen/women to speak with us, but they only cared about jobs and an annual ski trip. The whole club was full of pea-brained, slanted-eyed idiots who thought upward mobility meant they could climb a ladder and escape ignorance. I knew better and started going to meetings for the Minority Law Students Association that a black woman, Michelle Andrea Smith, headed up. For some reason I can't explain, black people just understand the quan better than Asians. I know I'm being ignorant and stereotyping, but for real, the BLSA and MLSA always understood from jump when I mentioned how programming should talk about social issues and not just jobs. I ended up organizing a panel that brought Jeru the Damaja and Professor Akilah Folami to speak about the Telecommunications Act of 1996 and its impact on hip-hop, radio, and Internet freedom. I also invited Lawyers of Color to come back and talk to us about office politics. After my first summer as an associate, I had stories about uncomfortable situations where people would say culturally insensitive shit that I would usually womp somebody in the face for.

I played that Dave Chappelle skit "When Keeping It Real Goes Wrong" and talked about how close I got to that moment. Surprisingly, as soon as I opened up about it, everyone had a story about white people talkin' out the side of they mouths at work. We all laughed about it and realized we'll never teach them all at one time, but we had to be patient, bite our tongues, and talk amongst ourselves when shit got bad. My white and Jewish homies always came and supported the events, too, because they understood their own duality. That's what I loved about New York: even white people hated white people. No one wanted the stereotype of an ignorant white dude to represent them and white people policed themselves.

There was also this cat Tommy Wu,* who had the ill Chinaman look with gelled hair combed over, always in a suit with glasses, looking real business all the time. At first look, I wrote Tommy off as just another Asian herb, but I was wrong. I never went out for drinks with Tommy or got to know him outside of school but that was my bad. Every panel I put on, Tommy was there. When I worked at the Innocence Project, Tommy was there. He didn't talk to me much, but he always laughed at my jokes or chimed in when we talked politics, and I started to remark to my boy Peter Shapiro,† "Ay yo, this bull Tommy is 'down.'"

"Took you long enough."

"Ha, ha, come on man, you SEE Tommy, you thought the same thing!"

"You said it, not me!"

"Fine, well I'm sayin' it now, I was wrong."

"I'm sure Tommy will appreciate that."

* Tommy's family still owns Nom Wah Tea Parlor, the oldest dim sum joint in New York. Respect homie.
† Shapiro was my homie that worked at the Innocence Project with me. We kinda kept to ourselves talking Michigan football and hoops. He used to work at *Vibe* and reviewed RZA once, so most people in the industry believe it's Peter he's talking about on "Nutmeg" when he says "Crazy as Shapiro! Multiply myself ten times standin' next to zero."

Tommy was my lesson in not judging a book by its cover. Even in his Asian Mormon missionary get-up, he was down for the cause.

THE MOST IMPORTANT person I met in law school, though, wasn't a professor or mentor, at least not in the legal sense. Captain Jason C. Morgan liked to say that I was his "Ace Boon Coon." Jae was half Jamaican, half Chinese and darker than a pair of chocolate wallos. Every time we went out to eat, he'd ask waitresses the same damn question:

"Excuse me, excuse, but let me axe you a question."

"Yeah?"

"What do I look like to you?"

"Come again?"

"Like, racially, what do I look like?"

"I dunno . . . black?"

"You sure about that?"

"Is this a trick question?"

"Darkness, just order the fucking food, man! You holdin' her up."

"Chinaman, I am not talking to you and I save time ordering food because I ALWAYS get the chicken. So instead of spending her time asking how the burger is prepared or asking for sauce on the side like your bitch ass, I'ma ask this . . . So final answer, black?"

"Yeah . . ."

"Look at my eyes, still black?"

"So you're Asian."

"I told you, Chinaman! She can tell!"

"Man, you fucking forced her into that answer, you crispy motherfucker!"

"Shit, but you still use more tabasco than me, Mr. Eddie Black."

"AHAHAHAHAHAHA, you already know."

Jae was my mans. In my lifetime, he's the only person I ever met that hustles harder than me. Son would have Xboxes, them hundred-game cartridges, clothes, and Nike SBs in the trunk of his car every day. You'd see Jae running in and out of school with boxes of shit trying to sell it to students looking for a deal. Instead of going to class, Jae and I would just blaze and head downtown, to chill at skate and streetwear shops.

Around 2004–2005, streetwear boutiques were popping up everywhere. Shit was ill 'cause every store repped different brands. I remember when cats like Lemar and Dauley came out with graphics that looked like the 1991 Skybox NBA Set with sweaters that had Biggie on 'em saying things like "Spread Love It's the Brooklyn Way." There was Reason, which put out my favorite shirt of all time, they flipped the Ramones tee to say Diplomats: Cam, Jimmy, Juelz, Freeky. Dipset had the mixtape shit on smash. Every month, there was some new Dipset that you had to cop. Sickamore had this cat Tru-Life that dropped "New New York" and G-Unit was going hard with The Game on Black Wall Street tapes. It was probably the best time since the mid-nineties to be in New York as a hip-hop streetwear-head.

Back then, when the culture was still building, people were loyal to stores, brands, and the cause. The style was retro-nineties, loud colors, vector or photographic driven, skinny jeans, selvage denim, lots of Japanese brands, and hip-hop/street culture content. There was also a political aspect to streetwear. Speaking for myself, I was sick of rocking logos for people. When people started printing their own shirts on AAA or American Apparel blanks, we got to rep the culture through the clothing. In the post-9/11 era, a lot of the more powerful messages about individuality, free speech, and what it was to be American manifested themselves in streetwear.

The only major brand we kept rocking was Polo, but most of us were stealing 'Lo. I heard about this crew called the Lo Lifes that would run into department stores fifty or sixty deep and just jack all the 'Lo off the racks. Shit was mad hard. I remember I was at Sutra for Just Blaze's birthday one night when he came in with the Snow Beach pullover and motherfuckers didn't even care if Blaze was spinning, they just bugged over the pullover. If you don't know, peep Raekwon in the "Can It All Be So Simple" video, god got the Snow Beach joint in there and that's how most people remember it. Raekwon is the original 'Lo-head and one of my favorite tracks is when he reps all that mid-nineties style in "Spot Rusherz":

You know the kid with the most doe-getters
And terrors on fat shit clique they rock Lo sweaters

Ironically, life was coming full circle. Here I was chasing Polo that I used to get as hand-me-downs from my pops. It was ill that Raekwon shouted out shit like 'Lo 'cause the people that designed it never expected it to end up in our hands. Didn't no one in the meetings at Polo say, "You know who our 'ideal man' is? You know who it is we're designing for? The Black Lex Luthor."* That's how streetwear flipped fashion on its head. Instead of designing for some six-foot, 150-pound medium man, they were making shit for us. Every brand had a different cut, different "ideal man," and theme. There was fierce competition and people knew not to shark-bite each other. If the Hundreds came out with a paisley hoodie you could self-dye and freak out, someone in New York had to come harder. There was always this bicoastal streetwear competition; Leo from Union said it best: "How does L.A. even have streetwear? They fucking drive!" Union on Spring Street was my favorite shop. It was owned by Maryann, who helped start Supreme, a huge streetwear brand, with her boyfriend, James, back in the day. The two main streets most people hung out on were Lafayette for Supreme or Rivington for Alife, but I always went down Spring 'cause Union was my shit. While Supreme and Alife carried their own lines, Union carried ten to fifteen different independent brands at any moment. They were the first to carry Visvim, BBC, and eventually my brand.

The single biggest driver of streetwear was Nike SB. From 2004 to 2008, Nike SB put out some of the craziest shoes kids had ever seen. The shoes were referential and mirrored what was going on in street art, music, and youth culture. Everyone has theories as to why, but my feeling was that SB was the only division that Nike gave creative license to roam free, do limited runs, and create just to create. They weren't working under extreme oversight like the people doing Jordan, LeBron, or Kobe. The shoes always referenced skate, street culture, hip-hop, and New York. I

---

* One of Raekwon's many aliases.

remember when Supreme would get the newest SBs and everyone in Soho was confused why there were hundreds of kids in snap-backs and Urkel glasses camping out for days in front of the stores. The reason was simple: if you made it into the store with the first wave and got a pair at box price (i.e., retail), you could flip it for five or six times more online.

Jae was smart. Instead of waiting in line, he went on the Nike Skateboarding website and started calling stores in different markets that couldn't move the shoes. Whether it was Wisconsin, North Carolina, or Nevada, Jae set up deals with the stores so that as soon as the cases of SBs came in, he would buy them all at box price. It worked for the stores because they couldn't sell them for more than box price anyway and now they had guaranteed sales. The only catch was that if they got caught, they'd lose their license to sell Nike because the company wasn't down with this kind of sneaker scalping.

Jae taught me his technique but made me agree not to poach his stores. So I went on Nike Skateboarding and started hitting the stores that Jae wasn't already doing business with. I ended up with a couple in Florida because I could talk to the store owners about bullshit we had in common. There was a store in Vermont and a couple of ski shops that happened to have SB accounts, but I needed more shoes so I went international. Jae wouldn't do international because you'd have to pay import taxes. Sometimes if it looked like a commercial package, it'd get stopped in customs but I worked around. We'd have things packed in boxes, no more than eight to twelve pairs in a box, and we made sure people mailed it with the proper labeling so that it was clearly personal. Over three years, we only had one package stopped and we just had to pay a grip to get it out of the post office. I started going on eBay, finding the big SB sellers in China, and g-chatting them. Our best source became this chick that worked in a Chinese chain store called Catalog that had an SB account. She wouldn't tell us her real name, always demanded bank wire, and when we tried to hit on her she said she was a grandma.

Through Grandma, we weren't just getting SBs, she got us Air Max, Jordan, Nike Sportswear, etc., because her store had a quick-strike ac-

count. I ended up with access to any Nike I wanted except Tier 1 drops.*
Once I got the sneakers, I would post them on Craigslist, MySpace, Facebook, etc., and whoever wanted sneakers would hit me. One day in late 2006, I was sitting at Washington Mutual putting $5K in my account to wire over to Grandma. Two kids walked in with the Finish Line Air Max '97s. They seemed like cool kids so I asked them:

"Yo, y'all collect kicks?"

"Yeah, we just got these Finish Lines! Where'd you get those Send Helps, though?"

"I been had them. I got all the SBs, Air Max, Jordans, etc., before they come out."

"Word? Let me find out."

"No homo, I live around the corner if you wanna peep it. Everything is legit. I got receipts from the store and everything."

"No doubt!"

The two kids were Matt and Patrick. They were both from Baruch and had been collecting sneakers for a minute. Neither of them copped that day, but the next week I got a call.

"Yo, is Eddie there?"

"Yeah, it's me."

"Son, it's Patrick and Matt. We had the Finish Lines last week."

"Yeah, I remember you, wassup?"

"We got a order for like twenty sneakers, man, can we come pick up? We got the sizes and everything. All our homies wanna cop."

"Cool, cool, just you two, though. I don't want everyone comin' up in my crib."

"No doubt, my boy Steve wants to come help us carry them, though. Is that cool?"

I still remember the day this dude Steve rolled in. Kid was wearing a Clientele Beanie, Gucci glasses, a Bluetooth, and mad fuckin' cherry ChapStick like he was drinking Kool-Aid and dillz the night before. He was Cantonese, too.

---

* The most rare and exclusive Nikes.

"Son, what kind of style you tryin' to proliferate here, b? You like part cabdriver with the Bluetooth, library with the glasses, you skiin' with the hat, and Hunts Point with the ChapStick. What's really good?"

"Huh, huh, ha, ha, stop playin', man."

Steve had a laugh on five-second delay and didn't care that I clowned him for ten minutes. He just loved sneakers. I kept telling jokes about him to Matt/Patrick and he went through the apartment checking the sneakers to make sure they weren't counterfeit. He was about his business. He'd stop every few minutes to shake his head and laugh, but get right back to the shoes. I kept snappin' on Steve 'cause he had a good sense of humor.

After ten minutes, he says to me: "Yo, are you going to Soled Out this weekend?"

"What the fuck is Soled Out, some cabdriver convention?"

"Naw, asshole, it's a sneaker show this Saturday. My boy Manny runs it, I can get you a table."

"I'm not tryin to go to a sneaker battle, man."

"You would cake though, son. No one is going to have these kicks there. Mork and Mindy haven't even dropped yet and you got twelve pairs."

"Nahhh, I'm good. I'ma just sell these on Craigslist."

That Saturday morning, I get a phone call at 8 A.M. from Jae.

"Yellow fever, wake up!"

"Darkness, stop playin', it's eight A.M., son."

"Yo, I told you I was pickin' you up at nine for Soled Out!"

"Naw, man, I told you I wasn't going to that shit. It's a bunch of twelve-year-old Asians and Dominicans walking around with sneakers on their necks."

"Yellow fever, don't make me run up in your crib and drag your fat ass out."

"Man, I'm five seven and one-sixty, ain't nothin' fat about that. You just skinny 'cause ninjas be eatin' your food on the court, ha, ha."

I hung up the phone and went back to sleep. Thirty minutes later, I heard someone just laying on the horn downstairs. It was Jae in his car so I let him upstairs.

"Goddamn man, why I gotta go to this shit! You got your own sneak-ers."

" 'Cause, you fucking Chinaman. I know that if you don't move these kicks, you gonna borrow money from me and I AM NOT HOLDIN' YOU DOWN THIS TIME!"

"Fine, fine, fine . . ."

That was my problem. I loved sneakers, but I hated hypebeasts. Full disclosure, I did cop the Incredible Hulk Bapes and rocked them with a lime-green sweater and purple shirt so I got caught wide open . . . *once*. I was good at getting all the sneakers, but I was lazy moving them because I didn't like dealing with hypebeasts.

We got to Soled Out in Soho and it was a shit show. People in line had pairs of sneakers tied by the laces hanging from their necks. Others were holding sneakers in the air, some cats came out wearing every piece of streetwear they owned, and there were twelve-year-old kids being chaper-oned by parents at the event. It gave me mental diarrhea, but I laughed a little inside because it reminded me of the time my dad took me to get Penny's autograph at Macy's when the Magic drafted him. Ahhhh, life why u such a contradiction, b?

"Yo, Eddie!"

"Oh, wassup? Steve, right?"

"Yeah! I thought you weren't coming."

"Yeaaah, Darkness made me come."

"Ha, ha, stop frontin', man, you love this shit. You can't act like you don't want to see all these kicks."

"Naw, I like the sneakers, but it's mad bugged out! Son, are you selling laces?"

"Don't start, man! I got sneakers, too. You see these Air Max 90 Homegrowns! They're going for like five hundred a pair."

"Ahhh, my man's selling laces! You got packs of laces, man, that is the most bullshit hustle ever."

That day at Soled Out, Steve helped me man the table and we sold over twenty-eight pairs of shoes. I tried to hit him off, but he wouldn't take any money. He said it was even 'cause he used the table to sell laces, too, but son didn't even make a hundred dollars on laces, so I took him to eat food in Chinatown at Shanghai Cuisine. He lived down the street on Mulberry and Bayard.

He was Cantonese so he didn't eat Shanghainese food all that much. My favorite dish in the joint was the yellow river eels stir-fried with Chinese chives and white pepper. One of the most simple dishes, but the best over rice. You get the gas flavor of the wok on the little eels, aromatic sweetness from the chives, rice wine, and the specks of white pepper to set it off. Steve had never had it before, but he fucked with it. We got some pan-fried buns: *sin jian bao, xiao long bao,* and lion's head meatballs. It was way too much food for two people, but cash had a habit of burning fucking holes in pockets so there it went.

We got to talking and Steve started asking me how I got my sneakers, how the business worked, etc. I was a little suspicious so I didn't reveal too much. Jae taught me how to hustle because he'd already known me for a year and knew I was 100. Steve was definitely a straight-up dude, but you know the kid is cautious. I could see potential, though. Steve loved sneakers, knew hypebeasts, and was good with money. The whole day we sold sneakers, I would always rely on my memory and figure out how much I made by remembering what I brought, what was left, and then see if it matched up with my money. It wasn't efficient, but I was just quick. Steve wrote down everything we sold, the price, the person's email/contact info, and tracked it on a notepad. I didn't want to close the door on him before I gave him a chance to show and prove. At the crib, I still had six pairs of Mork and Mindy SBs so I told Steve:

"A'ight, why don't we go dutch on these six. I got them so you give me half the bread for them and sell 'em. My job is to get the kicks, your job is to sell 'em. We both put up half and split the profits."

"Word is bond!"

Steve has been my best friend ever since. I got money with him, ate with him, broke bread with him, and I hollered at girls with him. He was my twin. Steve spoke Cantonese, I spoke Mandarin, but we had the same values, similar family stories, and eventually we both lived in Chinatown. For a while, I stopped going to law school and just hustled with Steve every day. Anything I needed, he had my back and never asked questions. I remember Steve loved Mobb Deep and always quoted *Shook Ones,* "Watch my fronts, I got your back." Like Zabb Judah said about Don King, "That man is my sunshine."

That winter I was visiting my uncle for his sixtieth birthday in Phoenix when I walked by a newsstand. Out front was *Newsweek* magazine with a light-skinned brother on the cover and the caption "The Race Is On." I didn't know who Obama was so I picked up the magazine and read through it. He seemed like a cool dude, young, and quoted Hov. I went home on the Internet and saw his speech at the DNC. He was a little more moderate than I liked, but he actually had the balls to oppose the war in Iraq, talked about how we needed an energy revolution, and understood how to communicate with people in the new millennium. He was interesting to me, but I wasn't sold yet.

As a kid born on March 1, 1982, I grew up in the excess of the Brat Pack–Madonna–Joe Montana–Michael Jackson eighties and the NWA–MJ–Nirvana–World Wide Web nineties, and we saw the residual battles from seminal cases like *Roe v. Wade* or *Regents of the University of California v. Bakke.* The issues I remember were global warming, gun control, music file sharing, cocaine versus crack sentencing guidelines, C. Delores Tucker versus Hip-Hop, affirmative action, abortion, and *United States v. Microsoft.* Besides the Rodney King incident and the 1992 L.A. riots, there really wasn't anything that warranted stopping the Knicks' game besides O.J. That is, until 9/11.

I remember that day. I was sitting in a chair waiting for social problems class to start. The professor was late and none of us knew what was going on. We didn't have smartphones yet and I didn't text. We looked out the window and some classes were letting out randomly. People would walk up to the window screaming, "They took down the towers!" Before we could follow up, they were running down the street. People didn't know what to do so we turned on the TV and there it was, over and over.

People reacted with hate and fear and then community by wearing American flag shirts, bandannas, crying, huddling, lost, and senseless. They packed the gymnasium to talk about how they felt. A lot of students were from New York so I understood their pain. For them, it was personal. But for me, it was surreal. I didn't take it personally: I'd never subscribed to America. I never felt included in this country. To this day, someone tells me to go back to China at least three times a year and *I live in downtown New York.*

Americans. Americans. AMERICANS. They've called me chink. They've treated me like the Other. They laughed at my food, they laughed at my family, they laughed at my culture, they wouldn't give me a proper interview because of my *face.* Americans. They did that. When 9/11 happened, I was an observer. I mourned for the victims and felt for the people as individuals, but this wasn't my fight. It wasn't the victims' fight, either, though. They were caught in the middle as always. The little people suffer for the crimes of few. This fight wasn't between the people that flew the planes and the people in the towers. We all got played by politics we had nothing to do with.

In the aftermath of 9/11, if you tuned in to television stations and watched the debates over the war in Iraq, no one had the backbone to point out the obvious. America, Inc. was running out of gas. We'd squeezed everything we could out of the rest of the world with our foreign policy. The answer was not to go into Iraq. It should have been to look at ourselves, look at our own crumbling policies, and economic mishaps. We should have lowered the debt, regulated the banks, prevented the oncoming mortgage crisis, and reevaluated our foreign policy, but we didn't. We played on the fear of innocent Americans and spent our resources on a nameless, faceless war that tore apart Iraq, emptied our war chest, and left us with an American infrastructure screaming for help. We didn't look at ourselves until it was too late. We spent our money on an arms race against ourself, fought an unnecessary war, and neglected the problems we had on this side of the water's edge.

Yet, in the middle of this mess was Obama. Coming out of the darkest period in American politics since the Cuban Missile Crisis, there he was saying the war was wrong. As I read more about Obama and followed his rise, I saw a man that had his own moral compass. He knew what he felt was right and had no problem saying it. For the first time in my life, there was a presidential candidate that I related to on a cultural, political, and personal level. Obama was, is, and will forever be my homeboy.

That day, along with the *Newsweek* magazine, the new Jordan V Fire Reds dropped in stores. It was the must-have gift of Christmas 2006. Then it hit me: if Obama was going to win, he had to win the youth vote by a landslide. What better way to promote Obama and the youth vote than through streetwear? Additionally, streetwear touched the hood. Usually, the hood didn't vote. I was a college grad in law school and so was Jae, but we had that ol' ignant mentality where we didn't think politics affected us. No one cared about us anyway. Why the fuck would we stand in line to vote without a guarantee that we were getting something out of it? Shit, standing in line for sneakers, you know exactly what's gonna happen. Nike is gonna take your money and send you home crispy. Deal. Obama was the first dude that we saw and said, "You know what, this dude isn't gonna fuck me. He gonna do what he said. I trust him." As much as I like his policies, I have to be honest, that's all it was for us at the end of the day. He was a *face* we could trust. And to hypebeasts, skaters, and hip-hop kids, they probably trusted the owners of local shops more than the talking heads on TV. Our shirts became the Street CNN: Cotton News Network.

I got a pair of Fire Red Vs and didn't cop anything to match because I made my own shirts that Christmas. My idea was to make a T-shirt jersey in the style of Michael Jordan's rookie jersey from 1986. Red with black and white script "Chicago 08" on the front and "Obama 08" on the back. Ning was studying graphic design so she mocked it up, we sent it to a printer, and started our T-shirt company: Bergdorf Hoodman. I realized that if I wanted to see change in the world, I need to make dollars first. Law school was the last nail in the coffin. The experience left me even more cynical than I came in. Everyone was a crook, but I didn't see anything wrong with it anymore. I understood. We live in an adversarial world. The economy, our politics, and the judicial system are all adversarial. If you want your voice to be heard, you have to fight. There's no other way around it. You can't expect people to seek you out; if you know you're right and you have the answers, then it's your duty to tell the world.

Look at Obama. He knew he was right, had a message, and used the channels he had to get it out. Hillary had the big donors, but Obama knew his advantages and played them just like I played Professor O'Sullivan. He made the 2008 presidential race a young man's game for the first time since Kennedy. I didn't have money to donate, but I had an idea so I started dropping off T-shirts to places like Union, Elite Boardshop, Palace 5ive, Union LA, and Digital Gravel. At the time, it was still January 2007 and Obama hadn't even declared his candidacy yet. I was ahead of the curve, but my gut just told me he was going to declare and win. A lot of stores didn't want to carry Obama shirts because they were political, but I broke it down to them.

"Son, think about it. Who shops here? Have you ever seen a Republican with some Izod shit on in here?"

"No, but mad people still like Hillary!"

"Yeah, people like Hillary, but they aren't your customers! Black, Asian, Spanish people shop here and your white customers skate. Every single one of the motherfuckers is voting Obama! Think about it. You're preaching to the choir."

In March of 2007, I got a call from the biggest supporter Hoodman would ever have: Nima Nabavi. At the time, Nima was the godfather of online streetwear. Before all the other Internet retailers, Nima was doing it right. He went to grad school at NYU and he started Digital Gravel to sell street art, streetwear, music, and basically anything related to hip-hop or street culture in general. He was the only other person I met in streetwear who understood its power beyond a five-year blip on the fashion radar and wanted to use it to promote the things he believed in. He never took ads on his site, he supported artists even if it didn't make money, and he was blatantly political in the email blasts he sent out to sell product. To this day, a lot of the integrity we have at Baohaus comes from watching the way Nima carried himself and his business.

Nima also carried Obey, Shepherd Fairey's brand, but even Shepherd wouldn't make Obama tees until late into Obama's campaign. I had been doing it since January '07 because I wasn't some pussy that was scared about what people would think of my opinions. I knew Obama was the right dude for the job and I did everything I could to get behind it. That's the way it should be. Nima bought up every single Obama T-shirt in my apartment after our phone call. The day he put them up, everything sold out in three hours.

Within three months, we had nineteen stores carrying our shirts and I donated 10 percent of each shirt to the campaign. Not 10 percent of profits, straight up 10 percent off the top. No bullshit after proceeds or 1 percent business. I wasn't making that much money anyway, so the point was to get this motherfucker elected and we did. There were people like me in every neighborhood doing the damn thing for Obeezy. Five dollars here, a hundred dollars there, don't smoke that this week and donate the dub kid! It was happening everywhere. We all had a part in it and when Obama got elected, I told myself, Today, you're an American motherfucker.

15.

HYPEBEASTS

In 2009, I graduated from law school in the midst of a recession that killed streetwear. Kids with disposable income for the latest kicks were thinning out. Before the recession, I assumed I wouldn't have to take the job as an associate at a law firm, but when the streetwear bubble burst, I had no other option. Ning, Steve, and I continued designing Hoodman, but most of our retailers started closing up shop and there was nowhere to sell our goods. Nima and Digital Gravel remained our biggest supporter, but even he was having trouble once Karmaloop.com co-opted the movement.

For the first time in my life, I played it smart: I took the job as a lawyer, walked through the doors of a giant midtown office building, and took the seat in my office next to Major Abshed. Major Abshed became my best friend at the firm. He was an international associate from Saudi Arabia who'd gone to Cornell before taking the job as a first-year associate. When he started he was gracious, accommodating, but also fearful. He didn't know how Americans at work would receive him. We'd both been snake-bit before. You go to law school and figure you're being exposed to the crème de la crème of American society, people with money, education, and experience. Yet, somehow, some way they never learn how to treat people.

Working in a law firm was not for me. Major Abshed and I would get high and go to Yemen Cafe in Brooklyn after work. Right off Atlantic near Court Street, it's the best Middle Eastern food in New York. They're known for one dish: yaneez. You sit down, they bring you an iceberg lettuce salad in a wooden bowl like you're eating red sauce Italian, but it comes with a spicy relish instead of dressing. Light, spicy, fragrant, and acidic, it was the best iceberg salad I've ever had. Simple, humble, satisfying. They follow that up with a bowl of clear soup made of lamb bones. The opposite of the salad, the soup is deep, complex, balanced, and mysterious. You can't quite identify the spices because none of them is too pronounced. If you asked me what the spices were, I honestly couldn't tell you. The spices are just there to quell the gamy flavor of lamb so that you can drink the stock and take in the flavor of its marrow. Once you finish your soup, they bring you a plate of roasted lamb.

One day you get neck, another it's shoulder, some days it's chops or shank. The restaurant will give its regulars the shoulder, but I would always ask for neck. I liked to get between the bones and pick the meat out. It is hands down the best dish of lamb I've ever had. Every day, they roast the lamb with Arabic seven-spice, perhaps some lemon zest and extra paprika. The lamb is covered in foil and comes out dripping with juices. Tender, succulent, but not flabby. The lamb has just enough structure while still giving easily to the tap of your fork. Everything comes with Afghani bread, rice, and *salta,* which is a stew made of carrots, onions, okra, and potato that you throw over the rice. To finish, you get cardamom tea. When you're ready, you get up, leave twenty-two dollars, and walk out knowing that you've just spent the best twenty-two dollars in New York City at that moment.

While other associates competed on billable work trying to climb the ladder, I got high and took Major Abshed around the city. When I promoted parties, a sideline that grew out of my streetwear hustle, I'd bring Major Abshed. I'd give him new music; he'd take me to Middle Eastern restaurants. And, of course, we watched basketball. The NBA really is an international game. I've never met someone from abroad that gave a shit about the NFL, or could even decipher it, but they all love the NBA. As an undergrad at Boston University, Major Abshed became a Celtics fan. In 2008, the C's were on top of the world so he never missed a game. It kind of drove me crazy listening to him go on and on about Pierce, KG, and Jesus Shuttlesworth, but I let him have his shine. Major Abshed smoked so much weed watching basketball that I started to buy ounces and split it with him.

THE ONLY INSPIRATION in my life at that time was Hoodman. I tried to re-suscitate the business but it was no use. I should have known it was going to happen. As a kid, I'd seen hip-hop lose its voice and edge when Puffy came through with the shiny suits and Master P started pushing plastic jewel cases. When Eminem came along it was a wrap.* There is a point where everything that meant something to us goes to die at two-for-one Ladies Night.

The same thing happened with streetwear. It became too accessible and the customer base changed. Instead of being a culture created and sold to heads who actually lived in New York, Los Angeles, or the Bay, it became something people consumed on the Internet. Instead of buying the shirts for what they stood for—transgressive, satirical, do-it-yourself democratic street culture—people co-opted it as the style du jour. They rocked it 'cause it was hot, colorful, and played on Friday night. That was it. The people that copped Hoodman switched from hypebeasts and downtown kids to Jersey bros who went to Libation or Spitzers. I was sud-denly dying for the hypebeasts to come back. Originally, I hated the hype-beasts because they never understood the "whys." Why is this design dope? What does this message mean? Where does this allusion or lyric come from? Most of them didn't know, they just read blogs or saw others

---

* For the record, I love Eminem. He was as real as you can be. It's just inevitable that when he came on the scene, top-forty format radio stations started playing his songs and other hip-hop. Before Eminem, only things like "Gangster's Paradise" or *Bulworth* theme songs got play on the Z100s of the world.

wearing certain styles and copied them. They'd always go for the shiniest pieces and the most hyped sneakers, never really paying attention to the more subtle and nuanced designs. Everyone can appreciate Chris Paul or Deron Williams, but what about the Andre Millers* of the world? When I first started following streetwear I was a sucker for the flossy joints, too, but over time I understood it and really appreciated it on a level beyond seeing it as just "style." Streetwear was the product of a greater downtown New York culture and consciousness that pervaded our lives. Downtown New York is a movement and, for a time, streetwear was its uniform.

Despite the fact that hypebeasts worshipped the culture because it gave them an identity, at least they followed the narrative. Like jam band groupies or roadies, having hypebeasts was better than not having supporters at all. I remember hanging out at Union seeing the same kids coming in, unfolding shirts, picking the shittiest, most expensive pieces off the rack while all of us kept from laughing. But at the end of the day, you need the hypebeasts because they drive the culture forward and allow you to keep creating. You just can't bet your culture on their consumption because their loyalty is fleeting.

It wasn't that my brand changed; the critical mass for the culture dispersed. Part of that was because of the way distribution changed with the introduction of Internet retailers into the scene. The retailers—most notably Karmaloop—put the physical stores out of business and the culture lost its gatekeepers, the ones who kept standards high and poseurs out. At every boutique, even if it was owned by some old head, he'd have a kid that helped him with buying that'd tell him "yeah this" or "naw that." Karmaloop, on the other hand, would carry only the big-name, played out, stigmatic brands that set the original style for the culture, but not the smaller brands that were actually moving it forward. For every John Cusack *America's Sweethearts* blockbuster, you need a *Grosse Pointe Blank* or *Better Off Dead*.

Karmaloop had more buying power than any physical store. They'd purchase your entire stock for the season, locking you into exclusivity, and

---

* "I'm Killa, you Andre Miller, got a basic game." —Cam'ron

then undercut all the physical retailers. Nima, on the other hand, would buy your shirts like they were weed. Gimme forty-eight shirts, here's the money, enjoy. No strings attached, no sendbacks, just paper. Shortsighted kids didn't understand that we voted with our dollars. Instead of supporting the brick-and-mortar stores that started the culture, they would try things on at stores and then cop online. Once the brick-and-mortar stores dried up, Karmaloop squeezed designers by cutting deals and making unsold merchandise returnable. This arrangement buried brands because they'd spend mad bread just to produce the order and then took an L when things didn't sell. Designers were idiots: they became creditors for this piece-of-shit company that ate the entire culture whole.

Watching what happened to our culture, I told myself I'd never let it happen to me. It's too important. Sometimes you need to borrow some of the master's tools to survive. I remembered a quote from *Catcher in the Rye*: "The mark of the immature man is that he wants to die nobly for a cause, while the mark of the mature man is that he wants to live humbly for one." I mean, two things I'm not and that's perfect or humble. Somewhere between Nima and Salinger, there I was, a kid that wanted to stunt for a cause.

With Hoodman on the slide, I started selling weed again. Although I made good money at the law firm, I knew it wouldn't last and tried to stack as much paper as I could. I got the work from some people in Crown Heights that had a grow house in Queens. To lower my personal costs, I moved from Chinatown–Little Italy to Fort Greene and lived in one of the row houses on South Oxford and Atlantic. The houses were nice, but a thousand dollars a month less than what I was paying in the city. After work, I'd hang out with the people in the park and play ball on weekends.

There was this ill spot called Cake Man Raven. Everyone knew him for red velvet cake and people from outside the neighborhood lined up to cop a slice, but I stayed on the pineapple or coconut jawn. Through the cake shop, I met the other people in the neighborhood that hustled out of a town house on South Oxford and Fulton owned by these twins. The twins were twenty-year-old kids who grew up in Fort Greene with their mom in a three-story brownstone that became a million-dollar property when the neighborhood gentrified, but they treated it like a trap house. I told them to clean it up, stop hustling, and sell the joint if they needed bread, but they didn't listen. The house was full of roaches, empty Henny bottles, and blunt trash everywhere. These kids didn't even have a garbage can so blunt guts just got thrown on the ground like peanut shells at Five Guys.

To this day, Fort Greene is my favorite neighborhood in any of the five boroughs. I met a lot of creatives like Damian Bulluck, who was early at Fader; Kelvin Coffey, who edited XXL; and Jay Lew, who was one of the illest photographers in New York. Dustin Ross lived down the block and started Studio Booth. Right on top of an African clothing store called Moshood was my boy Jesse Hofrichter, who'd gone to Cardozo and worked at a big firm but produced music and rapped in his spare time. All of us in Fort Greene were just doing our thing, maintaining any way we could. But Fort Greene wasn't Williamsburg. The creatives weren't twenty-year-olds from Nebraska who came because they grew up shopping at Urban Outfitters and wanted to live on the Bedford stop. Fort Greene was and is a real neighborhood. The neighborhood still had a strong black community and I thought that any time there's a Seventh-day Adventist Church in the neighborhood, you can only gentrify it so much. Loved that church. But I was wrong. Even our barbershop, Changing Faces, got phased out; cot damn shame you can't even get a decent cut on Fulton St. anymore.

I DIDN'T FIT in any category, to be honest. I worked at a big firm, played ball after work, and hustled with the kids in the park late night. This Dominican cat Richie lived across the park from me and should have played D-1 ball but never filled out his papers. Instead he was the manager at Target but knew he could do better. Reluctantly, I hustled with him. That was always a predicament for me. I pitched, but it was short term. I never got too hot and I did it for insurance money. These kids looked at it as a career. I took Richie on the train one day to sign up for a JUCO that he could play ball at, but he changed his mind last minute and we just ended up going to Harlem to meet a new connect in the Taft Houses. No matter how talented Richie was or how much shit he talked about what he could do, deep down he just didn't believe it'd happen. He was living day to day: you talk about your dreams, you boast about your talent, and you cop the Foamposites the day they come out because life is simply a collection of small victories. I didn't want to go out like that.

MEANWHILE, THE RECESSION was working its way from the zoom airsoles to white-shoe law firms. On the day we were laid off, Major Abshed and I got stupid high at the crib. At first, Major Abshed's sense of responsibility had kicked in and he worried about how he would pay bills, but he quickly realized that he could go home and regroup. And I realized something, too. It was the first day of my life. I was born again. My money wouldn't last forever, but I had six months to set the rest of my life in motion.

That night, I wrote down six things.

1. Quarterback the Redskins
2. Play for the Knicks
3. Do stand-up comedy
4. Write screenplays
5. Continue working on Hoodman
6. Own a restaurant

Those were the six things I wanted to do with my life. Clearly, quarterbacking the Redskins or playing for the Knicks weren't options, but surprisingly, three through six were. There was something powerful about that, too. I was relieved that the things I needed to do were possible. In a way, I was proud of myself. The aspirations I had for my life weren't things that I needed anyone for. The goals weren't tied to how I looked, who I knew, or what others thought about me. Every single one of them had to do with some sort of physical or creative expression that was within myself: football, basketball, comedy, writing, designing, and food.

That week, I got to work and signed up for a "bringer show" at the Laugh Lounge on Essex Street. The promoters of the show were some weird B&T Jersey fools that dressed like Ellen Degeneres. I had to start somewhere, y'all . . . I had five days before the show so I started writing. I didn't need to watch too much stand-up because I'd already been watching my whole life. My favorites were always Richard Pryor, Eddie Murphy, Chris Rock, Rodney Dangerfield, and Mitch Hedberg. I noticed that as a comic, you don't go up there and cover every aspect of your character. You pick out the most interesting/hilarious facet of yourself and turn that shit up to a hunned. After thinking about it for a few days, I realized there were a few sides to me so I made another list.

1. The smelly Chinese kid who didn't think he was good enough.
2. The kid who thought life was unfair and determined to come up on some Malcolm-X-read-books-and-flip-the-script-on-'em shit.
3. The cynical nihilist who thinks it's all bullshit and the only thing left to do is get paper.

After laying it all out, I played psychologist. I figured the persona that would hit hardest onstage and create the best humor would be #3, the cynical nihilist who just wants to get paid. I called myself Magic Dong Huang and started telling jokes about the Hmong Deer Hunter and Binghamton Shooter. I called them delivery boys gone wild and explained how it was actually good for Asian-American identity. The humor came from the ridiculousness of some fool named Magic Dong Huang telling people that it was a good look for Asians to strike fear into the hearts of Americans since all they let us fuck with at this point was Hello Kitty and Yu-Gi-Oh. My only goal as a comedian was to stomp the life out of the model-minority myth and present a side of me to audiences that crushed their expectations of what it was to be Asian-American.

I talked about how Bin Laden could get more money if he exploited fat-assed Arabic women like Kim Kardashian for his videos. One of the lines was: "Ay yo, Bin Laden, let me tell you about this video shit, son. You got dudes with brown bags on their heads and your boys all standin' around with AKs! Shit is extra 'mo! You know what you need, son? MOTHERFUCKIN' CADILLACS. Cadillacs and fat-ass Arabic girls like Kim Kardashian, face down, ass up, that's how you make a fuckin' video, b."

The subversive joke was that I wanted people to understand how "negative stereotypes" that stigmatized black culture could be used to empower Asian and Arabic people who had been considered model-minority types and vice versa. Our identities in America were polar opposites and by "trading places" we could see how ridiculous it all was. I always felt as if America took half the good traits of a person and impressed them on Asians and the other half on black people, since clearly, no person of color could be a well-rounded, intelligent, confident individual that served him- or herself. Asian men must be emasculated, Asian women must be exotic, black men must be dick-slinging thugs, and black women must be single moms. People think it's funny, but the stereotypes have the power to become self-fulfilling prophecies if we aren't aware.

My favorite set was called Rotten Banana. I talked about being picked on by white people as a kid and how my parents thought kung fu was the answer. I went through a series of jokes creating scenarios that white people could make fun of me for, like my mom sewing "Hollister" onto the back of my kung fu pants so I had something to wear at the beach. I talked about how Asian shawties had flat asses 'cause they were all drinkin' soy milk. "How the fuck you gonna grow a bubble without whole milk, boo?" After cycling through observations of Asian America, I discovered something. "White people weren't scared of kung fu, but you know what they were scared of? Black people!" I remember the first time I told the joke, this dred in the back of the room stands up with his drink in the air and screams, "THEY'LL FEAR US!" The whole room went buc wild and I dropped Jada's line: "I'm in the hood like Chinese wings!" At the core, the set wasn't about black, yellow, or white, but bullying. It applied to any and everyone who was ever picked on and felt like they were the Other.

Not surprisingly, Asians were put off by my sets. By this point of my life, I was used to it. Some of us understand how powerful self-deprecation is, but others want no part of it. The Asians who organized events and experienced the bamboo ceiling would always encourage me to come back and perform in Chinatown, but I hated seeing those crunchy-ass Asian women turn sour every time I told the soy milk joke. I ended up doing a lot of urban shows at places like Latin Quarter and Laugh Lounge. My boy Imagine would introduce me as Duck Sauce and the hood loved it so we flipped the script. I would tell Chinese food jokes and started making and bringing fried rice and chicken wings during the cocktail hour before shows. People loved it and a manager that was helping me at the time suggested that I get an appearance on Food Network since they were always casting on Craigslist.

So one night in the spring of 2009, I went on Craigslist to find a casting for Food Network. There were tons of them every week and this week's was for *Ultimate Recipe Showdown*. All I had to do was submit a bio and a party food recipe. Since all I did was sell tree I had a lot of time on my hands to work this shit. The next day, I got high with Richie and went to Whole Foods baked out of my face. Besides soup dumplings, my favorite dish was Mao's red cooked pork but I always liked beef more than pork, especially oxtail. I would have done oxtail, but it's not the type of thing that makes good party food. Sniffing around the display case, I saw a bunch of different cuts that I never tried to cook at home. For most people, you go back to the same cuts of meat you grew up eating. Richie and the other Dominicans I knew liked blade steak and flank steak. My family stuck to oxtail and shank but served cuts from the rib and loin at our steakhouse. We knew what customers wanted, but we never ate it at home. For my recipe, I decided to experiment with different cuts. I knew that I wanted something flavorful with good texture for a braise. I always liked the look of skirt steak rolled up in the display case on a piece of butcher paper with texture more similar to skate than beef. I had skirt at Mexican joints and Sammy's Roumanian, but never cooked it myself. I was curious about it so I asked the dude at the counter for three pounds of skirt and took it home to red cook.

Going online, I found out that the meat had a liver-y essence, since it was the diaphragm of the cow, so it would be interesting in a braise. Red cooking was always debated in my family. My mom and her family were from the north so they'd do a braise that started by throwing out the first. The pork was always flash-boiled until gray, leaving behind bubbles of gray blood in the pot. After it was blanched, they'd rinse the pork and let it rest. The water got tossed, the pot got wiped, and then the pork got browned with rock candy and aromatics. It was also their custom to not use chilis or peppercorns when making red cooked pork shoulder. My dad's side did Mao's style red cooked pork since they were from Hunan. They would cook the first by searing the pork and preferred using pork belly over shank or shoulder. When the pork was reintroduced in a braise, it'd be accompanied by chilis, peppercorns, and garlic. I seared a couple of skirt steaks with just salt so I could taste the essence without anything masking its natural flavor. I could tell immediately that it wouldn't play with the green onions that we usually used in red cooking, so I decided to use white onions. The meat also had a nice flavor if you got a good high heat sear that left a char, so I decided to cook the first by browning as opposed to blanching.

I used the chilis, peppercorns, garlic, ginger, and white onions. As I smelled the skirt steak sautéed with the aromatics, I realized that I had to neutralize the liver-y quality with something. Digging around the pantry, I pulled out a bottle of Moutai, China's finest grain alcohol, aka *bai joh*. No one cooked with this shit because it tasted like flaming Kim Jong Il's asshole, but I had fucked around with Moutai before and knew that if you ignited it, the sorghum in it took on a sharp sweetness that would be perfect. A lot of people red cook with dates, but I wanted something different and knew the Moutai would work. I put in about five ounces of Moutai and ignited it with a lighter. Instantly, it enveloped the skirt steak in sharp vapors that finished with a hint of pineapple. I also hit it with some fermented sweet rice sauce that had a more rounded sweetness and nose while still being alcohol based.

The skirt steak needed a good ninety minutes to break down and finish so I added some soy sauce, rock candy, and water, turned down the heat, and let it simmer. I turned on my TV to watch the Knicks game and hit the Roor. After about thirty minutes of watching Nate Robinson and Jamal

Crawford throw the ball out of bounds, I passed out. I was totally knocked out when I smelled something burning. It took me about five minutes to realize the burning skirt steak was in my kitchen and not a fucking dream. I bounced up, ran to the stove, turned it off, and threw a quarter-cup of cold water into the pot just so it stopped cooking. Luckily, the entire sauce hadn't caramelized yet. I pulled out a big chunk of skirt steak and peeled off the charred crust. Underneath this crusty, dark, fossil-looking piece of skirt steak was ill, tender, dark pink pieces of sweet, savory, aromatic skirt steak. I knew from that first burnt piece of skirt steak that I had a hit record.

I tell people all the time. Whether it's a girl, a skirt steak, or a record, you know in the first five seconds if it's a hit. That first time I ate red cooked skirt steak, I was blazed out of my face, the smoke alarm was going off, and all I smelled was burning sugar, but that first bite was the eye of the storm. It was complex, layered, and hit every note that you could ask for in a piece of braised beef. I had some short-grain sushi rice in the rice cooker, sautéed some onions with soy, sugar, and scallions, and ate them over rice with the skirt steak. That night, I wrote up the recipe and sent it into the Food Network. I didn't even think about it 'cause I already knew.

About two months later, I was rollin' around the Costco in Sunset Park with my boy Stephane. As I reached into a giant bottle of Cheese Puffs, my phone rang. It was Ning.

"Oh, my gaaawwwd!!!"

"What?"

"Food Network called!!!"

"Oh, word? Why they call you?"

" 'Cause they tried to call you like ten million times and you didn't pick up so they called your 'emergency contact'!"

"For real? Hol' up."

I checked my phone and she was right. Somehow I had five missed calls. Oh well.

"Damn, Steph, did you hear my phone ring?"

"Yeah, but you never pick it up."

"True story."

"What'd they say, Ning?"

"They said they narrowed it down to six people and four of you will make it to the finals!"

"Ay yo, Steph, they got coconut Ciroc at Costco? We got to celebrate."

"DIDDY LIQUOR!"

16

THEY DON'T LOVE ME, THEY JUST LOVE MY TIGER STYLE

I knew from the first moment I walked into the Food Network studios at 75 Ninth Avenue that the shit was gonna be cornholio. The show I got cast for was *Ultimate Recipe Showdown,* which took four home cooks from a national pool of more than thirteen thousand contestants to compete in various categories. Our category was "party food." Initially, my recipe was for Chairman Mao's red cooked skirt steak over rice, but the network asked for something handheld. I didn't get it and said that rice usually goes in a bowl. I mean, that's pretty fucking handheld, but they didn't go for it. So . . . I did what every culture does when Americans can't understand something: I put it on bread. From *banh-mi* to *baos* to arepas to Jamaican beef patties, it takes a little coco bread to make the medicine go down. Barack, I told you to put the health-care bill on some Red Lobster cheddar biscuits, dun!

In the green room was Thalia Patillo, who was from the Bronx. She worked as a newscaster and was gonna make empanadas. There was this dude Dave, wearing a bright yellow aloha shirt that made him look like Jon Bon Jovi, and lastly, Karate Grandma. The casting director somehow found this old woman from Wisconsin who was a second-degree black belt and made ill crostinis. You could tell from jump that we weren't picked solely for food, but because we represented different demographics and a "clash of civilizations" could unfold. That is one of the more interesting things about food TV. It's very difficult to separate race, culture, and food. Yet the network doesn't want to approach it in any sort of intelligent or meaningful way. They just want to infuse race into the conversation with food, code words, and friendly faces of color.

Thalia had big dreams of opening some sort of empanada catering business. Karate Grandma was a competitive cook and went around the nation doing things like *Ultimate Recipe Showdown,* and Dave was a music producer who wanted some cash for studio equipment. Me? I was using the appearance to build my reel for comedy appearances so my intention was to blow the thing up. When I went in for the interviews, they kept asking, "Are you excited to meet Guy Fieri?" I remember telling them, "Do I look like I'm excited to meet some fake tan backwards-sunglasses-wearing asshole with frosted tips?" When it was time for the competition, I was already a few drinks deep, taking shots of the Moutai that I was supposed to cook with. If I won, I won, but I just wanted to have a good time and throw the show off. I hated television, I only watched HBO.

About fifteen minutes into the competition, my skirt steak was braising and I had to piss like a motherfucker so I left the set and went to the bathroom. I didn't think it was that big a deal but apparently it was "crazy" to go to the bathroom since this "super-intense" cooking competition was going on. The thing that bothered me the most about food TV was that they were trying so hard to create drama. Reality TV never worked for me because it was all manufactured story, drama, and hype. To this day, the only reality show that I've ever enjoyed watching was *ego trip's The (White) Rapper Show.* They basically parodied the entire industry of reality television and stunted on white people for a season; it was my dream come true watching that shit unfold. Not only was the concept bulletproof, but your boi boi MC Search hosted it, with random appearances by Prince Paul. For heads, there wasn't a better reality show.

At *Ultimate Recipe Showdown,* you could tell the action was already scripted.* During the interviews, they kept asking me how I felt about Dave cooking Asian food, since his dish was wontons in some sort of fucked-up kitchen sink peanut sauce. I could tell there was a *Last Samurai* story line brewing and Dave was being set up to take me down. I didn't care because *of course that's what they were doing.* They asked me on the show what I thought and I responded, "To be honest, it's really bad Asian fusion, but some people like that." Not only did I get away with it, but people were laughing their asses off.

That's the confidence that New York gave me. There was finally a city that appreciated what I had to say and the honesty with which I said it. When I would speak my mind like that in Orlando, people would literally call me "racist." I wasn't, though. Chinese or not, seeing food or any cultural artifact bastardized just pissed me and most New Yorkers off. In my mind, America's culinary scene was premature with the whole fusion jump-off. Most Americans don't even understand the differences between Shanghainese, Hunanese, Sichuanese, or Cantonese food. Even in New York, where these cuisines are readily available, people are just now starting to understand and identify the nuances. A lot of chefs are in a hurry to profit off of appropriated versions of ethnic food without any respect, recognition, or understanding of where these flavors come from. There's a double standard, too. When my dad had a steakhouse, everyone questioned whether a Chinese person was qualified to open a steakhouse. We had to have white people front like the chef and owners. It was not OK for my dad to sell steak, but white people cooking Asian get more attention than the people in Chinatown who actually know what the fuck they're doing.†

---

* It is my opinion that the show followed a narrative that eventually affected the outcome of the show. It is not a fact.

† White people think it's unfair I give them a hard time for cooking OUR food or even having the audacity to say it's OUR food, but it's bullshit. You know what's really unfair? Not getting a job at the *Orlando Sentinel* 'cause of my FACE. Not getting the same opportunity for the same job for the same pay for the same work because of this FACE. That said, there are people like Andy Ricker cooking Thai or Michael White cooking Italian who do the cuisine proud. They love, live, and breathe the shit. They aren't fucking around with the food, they respect what it is, and they don't talk about "elevating," "changing," or "reinterpreting." They understand it's good as is. More on that later.

(Note to Reader: as you read the next three pages, go on Spotify and play that motherfuckin' Gershwin *Rhapsody in Blue*. That's the only thing that should be in your head right now.)

What I liked about New York was that food took priority. For immigrant families, food drives your daily life, holidays, vacations, everything. You put in work just to maintain your food culture and eat the things you would back home. In most American cities, dinner is an afterthought. In Orlando, my friends and I would almost never eat before heading out. We'd get high, watch sports, and wait till 11 P.M. to wild. New York was different: dinner was the event. Everyone fights for the 9:30 P.M. seating, the 11:30 cabs before the changeover, and beating the door before midnight if you're not on the list. People follow the big fall openings, wait hours for café seating in the spring, or buy out their favorite courtyard in the summer. Even in the winter, people are taking car services from TriBeCa to East Harlem for a table at Patsy's on First Avenue in ten-degree weather. There are your cornball Yelpers, bloggers, and photo takers, but most of us are into it as a culture and foundation of the city. Restaurants are gateways into New York's neighborhoods. You may never go to the Heights if you don't cop haze, but Malecon may be the hook that gets John from accounting on the A train. Somehow, food has become a social equalizer. There's no way you're getting John into Le Baron and there's no way you're letting John drag you to Turtle Bay after work, but dinner is something you can agree on. Peter Luger's, steak for five, Canadian bacon, tomato salad, hash browns, no one use the fucking steak sauce—who can't love that?

In New York, everyone's a historian: we know what used to be on what block, who replaced it, and how the neighborhood has changed since Shopsin's moved from the West Village to the Essex Market. People protest closings, fines, violations, and fight for their restaurants. But most important, New Yorkers know their food. I remember the day Frankie's 17 on Clinton took the pepperoncini with olive-oil-packed tuna off the menu. It was 11 P.M on a Sunday night, an hour before close.

"Frankie's 17, how may I help you?"

"Yeah, I want to make a delivery order."

"Lemme get your address?"

"One-oh-two Norfolk Street, apartment seventeen."

"Oh, hey, how's it going?"

"Wassup?"

"What can I get for you?"

"Same shit: cavatelli with red sauce, broccoli rabe on the side, pepper-oncini with tuna."

"Ohhh, we took the pepperoncini off the menu."

"What?"

"We don't do the pepperoncini anymore."

"How do you not do the pepperoncini anymore? Nobody told me about this shit."

"Ha, ha, they just took it off, I'm sorry!"

"No, for real, I don't think you understand, I NEED that pepperon-cini. I order it every time I blaze. Like, is there someone we can talk to, to like fix this."

"Ha, ha, Eddie, I'm sorry, we love you, but it's just not on the menu anymore."

"Uggggggggghhhhhh."

This happens every time a menu or ingredient changes. When I opened Baohaus, one day we switched purveyors for red sugar and cus-tomers noticed. I never thought anyone but myself or Evan would care, but people complained. I didn't want to switch, but our old purveyor just ran out of stock. I liked how we all took ownership in the city, its culture, and its food. We still argue all the time about soup dumplings. Tourists and cornballs love Joe's Shanghai, but everyone knows it's Nan Xiang Xiao Long Bao holding down Flushing. Just like we argue whether Riley should have pulled Starks in Game 7, we'll go on and on about how great the lox and whitefish are at Russ & Daughters, but how undeserving their bagels are. The biggest travesty in downtown New York is that you have to buy your lox at R&D then take the train up to Ess-a-Bagel to put to-gether a proper lox, caper, red onion, cream cheese, on sesame or salt bagel. We wish 2nd Ave Deli was still on Second Avenue, we worry about the old man's health at Di Fara Pizza, and we still don't understand how people can go to Szechuan Gourmet and order from the American Chinese menu while we get busy with the chili leek intestine casserole and a Diet Coke.

But despite the misfires, overhyped openings, and super-restaurants that mar the landscape, New York is the best eating city not named Tokyo or Taipei, and we owe it to people Fresh Off the Boat. From the old chick selling churros on the Sunset Park D train to the stray cat crawling over the counter at Fort Greene's Farmer in the Deli to Peter Luger's in Williamsburg to Great N.Y. Noodletown on Bowery to Shopsin's on Essex to Baohaus on Fourteenth to La Taza de Oro on Ninth Avenue to Sapporo on Forty-ninth to the golden elevator at Kuruma Zushi to Lechonera in Harlem to SriPraPhai in Woodside to Mario's on Arthur Avenue, it's an army of first- and second-generation immigrants that feed this city. I love the Knicks, I fux with Fool's Gold parties, and I stay coppin' kicks, but living in New York, it became clear to me what I loved the most was the thing I loved all along: food.

By the time we reached the midpoint in the competition, it hit me like Woody at the end of *Manhattan*. Was it too late? Did I fuck up? I needed that girl! At that point, I wasn't even paying attention to the competition. It was more fun fucking with the audience, but something woke me up. After the scores for the first round came out, Dave was in the lead, I was second, Grandma was third, and Thalia was fourth. As I walked into the test kitchen, I heard the staff chefs and cooks mumbling to each other.

"This is such bullshit. His wontons sucked."

"For real, did you try Eddie's baos?"

"Are you kidding? I made rice to eat it on."

"It's better on rice?"

"It's Chinese food; of course it's better on rice."

I wish I knew the Asian woman's name, but she was a Food Network chef who came up to me before the second round and said to me, "Hey. Don't worry about the competition. This thing never works out the way it should."

"Ha, ha, yeah. I figured Dave gonna be the last samurai standing, like Tom Cruise and shit."

"That's so fucked-up but true. You know how it is . . . television. But seriously, everyone in the kitchen ate the skirt steak and it's phenomenal. Where'd you learn to cook?"

"My mom."

"Well, we see a lot of people come through here and you're good."

"Thanks."

In the end, I lost the competition, but won the crowd. After we finished taping, people kept coming up wanting to try the skirt steak. Thalia's family was mad cool and said they were even hoping I would win. Thalia herself was gracious, wished me the best, and everyone encouraged me to cook professionally. The last one to come by was magenta Guy Fieri himself.

"Hey, bro. You kicked ass today, man."

"Thanks, Guy."

"No, for real. Look, this is TV. Don't pay attention to it. You got the chops. Don't give up."

"Give up on what?"

"Cooking, dude! Go for it."*

Anytime I went to restaurants, I would pick on what could be improved, write notes, and practice at home. Cooking was something that I loved to do on my own. I didn't agree with people on their interpretations, their favorites, or their preferences and didn't care because my tastes were mine. That's the thing I really loved about food. I couldn't build my own Jordan Vs, I couldn't draft for the Redskins, but I could make my own food. Nothing stood between me and the flavors I craved. The only thing that kept me from cooking professionally was the feeling that people wouldn't understand my food. I saw idiots ordering lo mein for most of my adult life at Cantonese restaurants that made amazing seafood pan-fried noodles. I didn't want to be those motherfuckers' Captain Kirk.

---

* And despite the fact that Tony Bourdain and I both think Guy Fieri looks like a rodeo clown, I have to say, he played a part in encouraging me to do this. I can't cosign Tex-Mex sushi or wearing your sunglasses backward, but one time . . . he got it right. So, as I say this with a trashcan under my head in case vomit involuntarily spews out of my eyes, "Thank you, Guy Fieri."

I remember at Cardozo, there was this kid Barry Goldstein who thought he knew everything about Chinese food because he lived in China for a year or two after college. When I ate hot pot, I always mixed sa cha sauce with sesame paste, garlic oil, a raw egg, and a teaspoon of soy. Barry said to me once, "That's not how you eat hot pot! That's some new-age Taiwanese thing. In Beijing, you don't mix the sauces."

"Son, I'll say this the nicest way I can. I'm Chinese and you're an idiot."

Barry had a false sense of confidence. He had been impressing his white friends for years with his "knowledge" of Chinese food and figured he could school me, but it was a joke. One of his friends at dinner that night mixed his sauces and said to the table, "You know, it's pretty good when you mix it, Barry." For the most part, people who have grown up eating a food their entire lives love learning new techniques or variations within the same pantry. My mom's beef noodle soup takes on a new ingredient every three to five years, and hot pot seems to find a new protein every season. I'm confident in my taste because it's been refined over thirty years of eating the same dishes hundreds of times. The problem with expats is that they never get to say shit in China. When they're over there, they are like dogs being led around from restaurant to restaurant by locals trying to take them for a ride. They may taste one or two variations of a dish and form opinions based on that cursory knowledge, hanging on every word like it's the holy grail. When the expat gets home, he's in such a rush to impress false maxims on any fool who will listen. People who don't understand something need poles to grasp, but those who truly love and understand something through experience don't need those training wheels. Food is that way for me. There's a difference between bastardizing an item and giving it the room to breathe, grow, and change with the times. When Chinese people cook Chinese food or Jamaicans cook Jamaican, there's no question what's going on. Just make it taste good. When foreigners cook our food, they want to infuse their identity into the dish, they have a need to be part of the story and take it over. For some reason, Americans simply can't understand why this bothers us. "I just want to tell my story?!? I loved my vacation to Burma! What's wrong with that?" It's imperialism at work in a sauté pan. You already have everything, do you really really, really need a Burmese hood pass, too? Can we live?

Writers ask me: "So, should Americans be allowed to cook ethnic food they didn't grow up with?"

I reply by asking: Are you interested in this food because it's a gimmick you can apply to French or New-American food to separate yourself from others? Or, will you educate your customers on where that flavor came from? Will you give credit where it's due or will you allow the media to prop you up as the next Marco Polo taking spices from the Barbarians Beyond the Wall and "refining" them? The most infuriating thing is the idea that ethnic food isn't already good enough because it goddamn is. We were fine before you came to visit and we'll be fine after. If you like our food, great, but don't come tell me you're gonna clean it up, refine it, or elevate it because it's not necessary or possible. We don't need fucking food missionaries to cleanse our palates. What we need are opportunities outside kitchens and cubicles. #Sing #Clap #ItsMe*

COOKING WAS A hobby but the whole Food Network experience threw me for a loop. Literally, the day before, I thought I'd be spending the next nine years of my life going across America, telling the same jokes at clubs every night. I loved stand-up, but admittedly, I was bored. Writing sets and performing was a lot of fun, but to really get good, you had to tell the same jokes every night in different clubs. Some nights you'd do three shows in different parts of the city. By the time transportation was paid for, you went home with a hundred dollars and a hangover. I thought to myself, What is it I really want to do? That list I made wasn't a good list at all. It was an empty list of jobs. They were vehicles that could get me places, but where was it that I actually wanted to go?

After we finished taping, Emery, my dad, and my mom took me to eat

* Ten points if you know where that's from . . .

at Kunjip in Koreatown. In the winter, I craved their *kalbi tang*. The whole family was really proud of me because throughout the taping, I never misrepresented our food, I spoke out about shitty Asian fusion, and I didn't play into the network's agenda. A lot of audience members went up to my parents throughout the day and told them they really appreciated someone who knew what they were talking about regarding Chinese food and wasn't shy about calling others out.

It became clear what I wanted to do. My entire life, I'd been looking at it all wrong. First it was football, then it was basketball, then it was comedy, and movies and restaurants, but what brought it all together? Why was it that I was on the verge of tears when AI lost to Kobe? Why was it that I related to Eddie Murphy's ice cream joke? What was it about *Do the Right Thing* that made me watch it three times a year? Race. Race. Race.

My entire life, the single most interesting thing to me is race in America. How something so stupid as skin or eyes or stinky Chinese lunch has such an impact on a person's identity, their mental state, and the possibility of their happiness. It was race. It was race. It was race. Apologies to Frank Sinatra, but I've been called a "ch!gg@r," a puppet, a pauper, a pirate, a pawn, and a chink; that's life. I am obsessed with what it means to be Chinese, think the idea of America is cool, but at the end of the day wish the world had no lines. Like Michael Ondaatje writes, "All I ever wanted was a world without maps." *The English Patient* is full of knowledge:

> We die containing a richness of lovers and tribes, tastes we have swallowed, bodies we have plunged into and swum up as if rivers of wisdom, characters we have climbed into as if trees, fears we have hidden in as if caves.
>
> I wish for all this to be marked on my body when I am dead. I believe in such cartography—to be marked by nature, not just to label ourselves on a map like the names of rich men and women on buildings. We are communal histories, communal books. We are not owned or monogamous in our taste or experience.

You have tattoos and others have piercings, but for me, there's nothing that says more about me than the food I choose to carry every single day. As a kid trying to maintain my identity in America, my Chinese was passable, my history was shaky, but I could taste something one time and make it myself at home. When everything else fell apart and I didn't know who I was, food brought me back and here I was again.

I was twenty-seven, just laid-off, looking for a new career, fresh off the set of a shitty competition show with a bowl of *kalbi tang* staring me in the face. The answer was clear. Eddie Huang was going to open a restaurant. Of course, my family didn't get it.

"Eddie! You don't want to be a chef. Look how little Chef Andy at Cattleman's makes?"

"Mom, it doesn't matter. I made money at the law firm and it sucked."

"You need to use your law degree. You can't let that go. You spent all that time!"

"It's a sunk cost, Dad. I'm not going to throw any more time and money just because I've already wasted so much."

Emery wanted the best for me, he knew my food was good, but he was scared. He was never the one in the family who would take risks so he sided with my parents. I didn't care, though. I would be thirty in three years and I felt a lot of my life had been wasted trying to please my parents or do what Chinese people were supposed to do in this country. I was done. Ironically enough, the one place that America allows Chinese people to do their thing is the kitchen. Just like Jewish people became bankers because that was the only thing Christians let them do, a lot of Chinese people ended up in laundries, delis, and kitchens because that's what was available. From Rothsteins to Huangs to Todd Anthony Shaw, the outsider's credo is get in where you fit in, fool.

AS A FIRST-TIME restaurant owner, I wanted it all. It's like the first time you smash. You wanna try every position on shawty before she changes her mind or you run out of bullets. My entire life, I was that dude. I hated editing my writing, I hated following rules, I hated accepting realities, but that year in Fort Greene really changed my perspective. I was humbled.

For six months, every two days, I woke up, got the work from Crown Heights, and either took a train to Grand Concourse and the Taft Houses, or gave Richie the work to do the drops. By 2 P.M. I was done so I played ball with Ben Griesinger, Jesse Hofrichter, and Rafael Martinez aka the Prince of Brooklyn. All four of us were unemployed so we hit the court at 2 P.M. like clockwork. We called it UBL: Unemployment Basketball League. It was a cold fucking winter that year.

All four of us were hit hard by the recession. Jesse and I had money saved, but Raf was fresh out of law school with no job. I remember one day Raf came to UBL mad excited.

"The Prince is feelin' good today, son."

"Oh, word? What's really good?"

"I was on Craigslist this morning and yo, Brooklyn Industries is hiring a manager!"

"For real? That's wassup. Need that paper. They hiring multiple managers or just one?"

"Ay yo, this is my listing, man! If they need two I let you know but you can't shark-bite my Craigslist ad."

We were that HONGRY. Grown-ass men fighting over who could apply to Brooklyn Industries first. Every day, we all hit Craigslist, message boards, looking for any leads on jobs. I was the least motivated, 'cause I was still gettin' money, but I knew it was short term. Either the comedy shit had to pop off or I'd need a straight job by this time next year.

Every day we met up, played ball, but talked about what we would do with our lives. Grown men waiting to exhale. We all had the same struggle. It was very clear in our heads what each of us wanted out of life, but there were some gaps in the path between here and there. Jesse was the most neurotic. He'd come up with an idea, we'd support the idea, and then he'd shoot his own idea down. It became clear really quickly that Jesse just liked to argue. You could never come to a conclusion or plan of action with Jesse because as soon as he said he'd go right, he'd go left, which would be a dope crossover move on the court, but the funny thing was, when this guy played ball he'd stand on the baseline and wait to shoot fifteen-footers! I loved Jesse and he always held me down, but he was definitely on some Woody Allen Mental Doppelganger steez.

Ben, on the other hand, knew exactly what he wanted to do. He was a temp schoolteacher trying to get into grad school. It was a tense time waiting for his grad school applications to go through, but he knew it was a matter of time.

Raf wanted to work in music. Since college, Raf wrote at places like *Prefix Mag* about concerts, albums, and hip-hop in general. He knew more about music than anyone I'd ever met even though he made some of the worst playlists I've ever seen, littered with random Top-40 hits he was a sucker for. He couldn't make a playlist without a minimum of three Pitbull songs. Raf went to law school thinking it'd help his career in music, but he realized quickly it was the wrong move. Seeing how little music attorneys got paid and how quickly managers, agents, and labels took off, he felt like he bought a ticket to a B-grade hustle. I told Raf if that's how he felt he should just go to shows, hang with artists, and sign talent, but he didn't think he had the contacts yet so he stuck with the legal grind. He liked making fun of other people's hustles. For instance, there's always that raggedy-ass manager that somehow put the hooks in a good artist, threw him on a few mixtapes, but doesn't have the skills to take it to the next level. Happens all the time and we all laugh, but I'd tell Raf: you can't be clowning people who are actually doing things if you aren't even trying. As a reasonable man and the Prince of BK, he got it. That's what I liked about Raf. He was a grown-ass man. If you pinned something on him that was true, he wouldn't flinch, he wouldn't squirm, he'd own up and fix it. I always respected that about the Prince.

But once I knew I was opening a restaurant, the sky broke and everything was clear. It was the most exciting time of my life. The freedom felt good. It was the first time I can remember waking up every day and not feeling like I owed somebody some shit. All my life, I'd wake up to my parents fighting or my mom yelling at me to grow up faster. It never stopped. Then, when I went to college, I stayed in trouble. I remember the year I got charged, I just woke up every day thinking my life was over. Every interview or application I filled out, there was that convicted-felon box to check that never went away. It's a fleeting moment, but those first ten minutes of the morning when you're barely conscious are the worst. You wake up to this fog of fear, confusion, and uncertainty. I swear even now I wake up some days not knowing who I am or where I'm at. In law school, I woke up every day knowing money was going down the drain for a degree I wanted no part of. And even if I passed the bar exam, I might not pass the character fitness test because of my past. For three years, I kept thinking, "I may not even get that piece of paper I wanted!"

I was constantly thinking about how to get out. Those years between twenty-four and twenty-seven, when you start to realize things don't always break the way they're supposed to, are sobering. When you're eighteen, you're hustlin', you got friends producing, DJ'ing, in bands, all the girls look like someone in the movies, you figure everyone is gonna blow up like soda and water. Shit is just fun. But you hit twenty-four, half your friends are strung out, some are in jail, some got herpes, everyone got HPV twice, and you realize, yeah, we're in a movie: *Requiem for a Dream.*

For a while Hoodman held me down. It was the outlet I needed for my creativity. I got a taste of what it was like to own your own business, create new accounts, market a product, etc. If it weren't for Hoodman, I probably would have taken a straight job. You have the balls to take risks when you're young because you don't see all the barriers. You just see a way to win. The problem with Hoodman is that I made the classic first-time-director mistake. I tried to serve too many masters. It never works. I wanted the restaurant to represent everything about me, but I refused to make the same mistakes twice.

A week after the taping of *URS,* I started a blog. I was always an idiot with brainstorming so the first name that came in my head I registered on Blogspot. Five minutes later I realized the name was terrible, but I couldn't change it, so I just used a domain with the shitty name www.thepopchef. blogspot.com and made the title of the blog "Fresh Off the Boat," which was more my steez. From jump, the blog was ridiculous. The fifth post I ever put up was of a dude with a ski mask robbing a bank with this text:

So, after cooking, I went to go get a loan. That is me above. Things went well until they asked me for some information:

LLC, TAX ID, ETC . . .

For all you aspiring entrepoorneurs out there, leave the gun, bring the Tax ID.

They said that to get a loan, I needed to do these things:

REGISTER THE BUSINESS

GET LLC

GET TAX ID

ESTABLISH CHECKING ACCT

PUT IN APP FOR BIZ LOAN

LOOK AT OUR PAY STUBS

LOOK AT OUR TAXES

Chase was cool, though. Once I took off the mask, they sat down, told me that they could actually do the LLC and tax ID registration for me. So that was dope. Will let you guys know how it goes with the loan application.

This was the sixth post, titled Reader Questions. I didn't actually have any readers at that point, so I made up questions and answered them myself.

I love reader questions. Almost as much as I love getting really blazed using my volcano vaporizer and eating gummies . . . but not quite. OD'ing on gummies is still my favorite thing to do in life. It's just not so fun when your teeth are rotting and your breath is stanking 'cause you fell asleep eating a pound of gummies watching *Martin Yan's China. Martin Yan's China* is the best way to brush up on your Chingrish. Phrases like, "This is the fashion" or "Rook how beaurifo my kung pao panda rook on dees rotus reef" *are great for get togethers during the moon festival!*

Anyway, reader questions . . .

"Where is the restaurant going to be?" Either NYC or Boston. Looking in both places right now, specifically East Village south of 13th, north of Houston, in NYC, and Brighton/Brookline in Boston.

"Is this a Chinese restaurant?" Well, I am a Chinaman, there will be a few Chinaman items, but no, it is not a "Chinese restaurant." But like they say, "You can take a Chinaman out the paddies, but he will still put MSG in all your food."

I didn't know where the blog or the restaurant was headed, but I was having fun and honestly that's all that mattered. I wanted to keep that mindset and energy that I'd had just chillin' in Fort Greene playing ball and hustling every day. I never wanted to find myself in a situation again where I was doing things because someone told me I was supposed to. From the ground up, I was going to detox my identity of any and everything that someone else put there without my blessing.

I knew that I couldn't afford a big space in Manhattan so I started my search for spaces in Brooklyn: Fort Greene and Bedford-Stuyvesant. A lot of people still thought of Bed-Stuy as "Do or Die." I kicked it out there, hung out at Pratt after playing ball, and went to house parties in the fragrant old brownstones with scrolling stonework on the façades. To me, it was dope, even though I realized that if you had a restaurant in Bed-Stuy, you weren't going to draw customers from outside Bed-Stuy. That was OK with me. The concepts that worked in Bed-Stuy were neighborhood restaurants or grab-'n'-go, casual-seating type joints, which fit what I was trying to do.

What I wanted to open was Baohaus, a restaurant that specialized in Taiwanese *gua bao*. I hardly ate bread, because I liked rice, but I knew that in America, rice would never usurp bread as the starch of choice. Growing up, I never really liked *char siu bao*, but it was always the number-one item among *gwai lo*. The big white buns—*baos*—filled with barbecued pork—*char sui*—were familiar and translated well to Americans. I figured baos would be the perfect bridge. They were an obscure, traditional, ambulatory Taiwanese dish with characteristics that Americans would understand. The bread gave people enough of a pole to hang on to and allowed me to put whatever I wanted between those lily-white baos. Plus, it was kinda cool making baos since Grandpa originally made his living selling mantou, which uses the same dough as a bao, just shaped differently.

I really liked the Baohaus concept, but began to feel that it wouldn't take off in Bed-Stuy. Everyone I talked to in the neighborhood felt like it was something I'd really be fighting an uphill battle to introduce. I had assumed all along that I couldn't afford spaces in Manhattan, but with my search in Brooklyn running dry, I went to the Lower East Side.

I always liked the LES—when I moved from Orlando to New York, my first apartment was on Orchard Street on the LES, above the Arivel furs store across from Reed Space in 2005. I walked around all day looking at spaces, but all my appointments were dead ends. Brokers would list spaces on one block, but they were never where they said they were, nor were they the square footage they said. Everything was too big. Around 6 P.M., I finished all my appointments and walked down toward Alife to check out sneakers. Out of the corner of my eye, I saw a sign in Chinese on Rivington Street hanging over this subterranean space next to the graffiti mural by Schiller's that people always took photos of. I peeked into the space and it was perfect. Roughly four hundred square feet, full of random lowboys and freezers, and this dope exposed brick. I called the number, left a message, took a photo, and waited to hear back.

The next day, the landlord called back. The address was 137 Rivington Street, the rent was $2,900, and they were looking for good credit, three months' security, and 4 percent rent increases. My credit sucked because I had had to rack up debt to get through law school and I was still paying loans. Once I got my credit score to the Realtor, he wanted six months of security. It was bullshit. No one needed six months of security on top of a good-guy guarantee but this landlord was a fucking asshole. Landlords in New York are generally the scum of the earth. They're beneficiaries of the worst kind of nepotism, eating off the good business decisions of their parents. They have no compassion because they've never had to work for shit or know how it feels to need a fucking break. There's no incentive for them to rent to someone who gets the neighborhood and wants to bring something of substance. Every one of them would love to be the landlord for Spitzer's or Starbucks. They want neighborhoods like the LES to gentrify, sell out, and attract dollars from big chains. After weeks of negotiating and trying to get a loan from Chase, I gave in and put up roughly five months' rent in security that totaled over $17,000 which left me with $13,000 for everything else.

17

WORLD STAR

I wanted Baohaus to be a place the neighborhood embraced. Not a bullshit coffee shop that says it's for the neighborhood but kicks people out or doesn't let them use Wi-Fi if they don't buy anything. I remember those years in high school where we got in trouble smoking in parking lots outside the 7-Eleven because we had nowhere to go. Most of the time, we got busted 'cause the register dude called the cops. As a kid, I remember always wanting to hang out at comic book or sports card shops. Then it became record shops and basketball courts and as I got older spots like Union. But there was never a restaurant that I would just wake up and go kick it at as a kid. Besides McDonald's, Wendy's, or Chick-fil-A, restaurants were for old people. I wanted Baohaus to be a youth culture restaurant that the neighborhood could post up at. Not moms and dads and nine-to-fivers, but the kids across the street, the freelancers, the unemployed, and the people that hung in the neighborhood because they'd scammed their way into rent-controlled apartments. At the core of Baohaus would be this truth: no one would kick you out, call the cops, or serve you shitty 7-Eleven pressed Cubans.

Most restaurateurs you talk to, the food comes first. It really didn't with me. Food was never the issue. My food was, is, and always will be ill. New York was full of restaurants with good food, but few with a mind. You read the dining section in the *Times* and it's the stepchild of the style section. People forget how powerful the *culture* of a restaurant is. Food is what's on the plate, but dining extends beyond it. When you go to Taiwan or China, you don't go to soulless super-restaurants with high ceilings and filet mignon. You go to the Dan-Dan Noodle Stand that your dad grew up at. I wanted the atmosphere at Baohaus to be everything that the Dan-Dan Noodle Stand was to my dad as a teenage Taiwanese street kid, but the food was for my mom. We argue, we fight, but at the end of the day, her moves are the only ones I've ever stolen in the kitchen. I always cook for my own palate but every single thing is derivative of the flavors and techniques she instilled in me. People talk about "family restaurants," but Baohaus really is. The funny part is, my family wanted nothing to do with it.

A week before opening, I went home to see my family and everyone had long faces. No one could believe I was throwing away my degree to sell Chinese-Taiwanese fast-food. It made no sense to them. I couldn't understand.

"Dad, you ALWAYS talked about that Dan-Dan Noodle Shop! You own a restaurant! Why is it such a big deal when I want to own one?"

"Because you're not ready! You don't know what you're doing. And, and . . . you spend all this money on this degree to stand behind fryer? You crazy! What have happened!"

That weekend, we didn't even really talk. We just walked by each other waiting for it to be over. Evan didn't believe in the idea, either, but he was a really special kid. Anytime someone in the family got outcast, Evan would befriend them. He was the only one in the family who got along with everyone. I didn't always get along with Emery, my mom didn't get along with my dad, and vice versa, but Evan got along with everyone. I remember in high school when my dad dropped Evan off for the first day of his senior year, Administrator Lott stopped him.

"Mr. Huang!"

"Hey, what's up, Mr. Lott? I am surprised to see you first day. My kids can't be in trouble before it starts, right?"

"Ha, ha, ha, no, no one is in trouble, Mr. Huang. I just wanted to tell you something."

"What is it?"

"Well . . . Eddie? Eddie was bad. Emery was mean, but Evan? Evan is an angel!"

We never stopped laughing at Evan for being called an angel, but it was true. He is the nicest person anyone will ever meet. Like the rest of us, he got arrested for bringing a knife to school and hit a kid in the head with a hockey stick when the kid called Evan a chink. He's still a Huang. But he's the best we got.

I was keeping to myself and gave up convincing my parents, but Evan went out of his way to talk to me about the concept, asked me questions about Baohaus, and really got in my head. I remember him telling me: "I think Mom and Dad are right, but you're pretty set on doing this so I'll do it with you."

That's the type of loyalty, family, and love that you really only see in films. It's not supposed to be real. Literal translation of what Evan told me: "I think you are going to fail and it's a bad move, but I'll ride with you and go down together if that's what has to happen."

My parents were pissed when Evan told them he was going to come help me. It was bad enough that I was going all-in; they didn't want me dragging Evan along, too.

"Eddie! You can't do this. You convince everyone, but don't ruin your brother's life! He has to go to school."

"Mom, no one is ruining anyone's life. He goes to UCF. That degree is worth less than a coupon for free McRibs."

"What the fuck is McRib? Don't change subject!"

"Yeah! You are sneaky, convincing Evan. You know what you should do? You should go work for David Chang!"

That's what really set me off. David Chang is the chef who unwittingly popularized a bastardized version of Taiwanese gua bao. He tells the story of how he created the Momofuku pork bun in his book *Momofuku*.

It came about because he'd eat at Oriental Garden in Chinatown. It's a great Cantonese restaurant that Chinese people go to for weddings and birthdays because it's expensive, but some chefs go to on the regular because, well, they can. Chang would go there and get the "Peking duck." This story is ludicrous on a number of levels. You have this "chef" ordering Peking duck at a Cantonese restaurant that serves the duck in gua bao. Peking duck is served in pancakes, not baos, for a number of reasons. You eat the skin in the pancake so that you get the texture of the skin, the body of the hoisin, the sharpness of scallions, and the thin starch from pancakes. Then you eat the actual meat solo to taste the flavor and make soup with the bones. Any official Peking duck restaurant does it that way. I'm all for innovation, cereal milk, and the evolution of a dish, but it needs to be intended. Serving "Peking" duck in baos is just plain lazy.

Chang asked the chef where to get the baos because he had an idea. He wanted to serve roasted pork belly in the baos. It's a great idea that blew up and gained Chang notoriety as *the man* in New York. To this day, publications like *New York* magazine still credit Chang for introducing New York to the gua bao. I was mad, but I respected the hustle. The only way to get even was to set up shop myself. I thank David. Just like he came up on gua bao, I jumped off his success and brought the title home. A Taiwanese kid makes the best gua bao in New York just like it should be.* "It's my island!"—crazy dude in *Braveheart*.

The bao became a vehicle for me to speak about everything from Brianna Love to Long Duk Dong. One of the most important things I did when opening Baohaus was that I told people I wasn't a chef. Food isn't the first thing I've done and it won't be the last. Baohaus wasn't a restaurant, it was an idea. An idea that couldn't be understood with the language and vocabulary of traditional restaurants. Although I did not set out to tell my entire life story through the restaurant, I did. What saved me was that I had the confidence this time around to know what stories I didn't want to tell. And those stories were anyone else's but mine. I realized the problem with Hoodman wasn't that I tried to do me, it was that I tried to do everyone else, too. Once we had a hit with my Obama and "I Shoot Hipsters" tees, I listened to too many other people. We looked into "develop-

* *New York* magazine 2010 Best Bun, *New York Times* flawless $25 and Under Review, and nine out of ten Asians with taste buds and an IQ over 80 like us better.

ing a line" and growing the way other brands did when we should have just stuck to our guns. With Baohaus, we stayed true to ourselves and that's how Rivington was won.

We opened with only five items: Chairman Bao, Haus Bao, Uncle Jesse, Boiled Peanuts, and Bao Fries with Sesame Sauce. That was it. I didn't want a vegetarian item, but when we did a tasting of the menu at my South Oxford row-house apartment, I realized Jesse couldn't eat anything so I made him a fried tofu bao with sweet chili and sesame paste. Everyone knows Uncle Jesse from *Full House,* but the inspiration was actually Jesse Hofrichter. The boiled peanuts were a Southern thing that my friend Tyler dropped on me a couple of weeks before opening. My grandpa loved boiled peanuts and fried chicken so it was the perfect item to bring us full circle.

That's how everything went at Baohaus. Nothing was inspired by famous chefs, farms, or trends in food. It was the manifestation of my friends, family, and memories. I knew we'd kill it, because there's nothing more powerful. We weren't cerebral cooks inspired by Harold McGee. When we opened, there wasn't even a budget for staff. All the money was spent on equipment and the first week of food. There was three hundred dollars left and if we didn't break even the first week, we were done. Since I was a Yeshiva grad and it was an LES restaurant, it was only fitting that we opened on Christmas Eve 2009: Chinese food in a Jewish neighborhood on Christmas Eve. Our "staff" was composed of Steven Lau, Simon Tung, George Zhao, Ning Juang, Evan Huang, Stephane Adam, and myself. No one besides Evan and myself had ever worked in a restaurant, but that was the squad we opened with.

It's a funny feeling. The lights go on, the door opens, and for a few hours, no one comes in. All day, there was this one girl, Lia Bulong, who kept asking when we'd open. Since we were still setting everything up, we had no idea so we kept telling her "in an hour or so." She lived down the street on Clinton so she kept checking in.

"Guys! Lemme know when you open, I want to be the first customer!"

"OK, OK, like one more hour and this pork will be done."

"Uggghhh, that's what you've been saying for three hours!"

Of course, when we finally open, Lia is nowhere to be found. You may ask, "Why the fuck didn't you just take her phone number and call?" That's a good question: we didn't have money for a phone. The first customer walked in about fifteen minutes after we opened and everyone jumped her with menus like a bunch of orphans in China trying to braid your hair. As everyone played twenty-one questions, I excitedly made the first bao. I can't remember what it was, I can't remember if we charged her, but I'll never forget the moment. I don't think anyone has ever enjoyed watching someone eat a five-inch sandwich as much as the seven of us smiling at this one Russian chick coming over from Alife. As she left, in busted Lia.

"What the fuck, dudes? Was she the first customer?"

"Ha, ha, ha, yeah, our bad!"

"Ughhh, you guys are the worst!"

Lia was hilarious and has been a customer and friend ever since. That's how it started at Baohaus. Once Lia came in, this girl Sue came in who'd actually gone to high school with me. A few hours later, Warren's dad called me on my cellphone because he saw on Facebook that we opened the shop and he just happened to be in the city for Christmas with Warren's brothers. What are the fucking odds? You open shop Christmas Eve in the LES and your childhood best friend's family is in the neighborhood with no notice? We made $260 the first day and we thought it was the greatest thing ever. Today, we make that in an hour.

After drinking, smoking, and cleaning up the shop, it was 3 A.M., so we didn't open for Christmas. By that time, food writers in the neighborhood were posting things. We didn't know it but Lia actually worked for Serious Eats and Eater, two big foodie websites. Rebecca Marx of *The Village Voice* also came incognito and they had an article up about our opening that same day, but the next day, of course, we weren't open. So we just tweeted that we were tired and didn't want to go to work, which was the truth. Christmas is for the NBA in our house. On the twenty-sixth, we opened up a couple of hours late and a good number of people came in to try our baos. Without us saying anything, everyone was comparing it to Momofuku, which we wanted to happen. The difference was that we braised our pork. Although Chang is Korean-American, his technique is French. Even *bo ssam,* a Korean pork belly dish, uses steamed pork belly. Asians don't use the oven for anything but holding Jordans.

I WAS SICK of immigrants not getting the credit they deserved. I was sick of the Jean-Georges of the world making a killing on our ingredients and flavors because we were too stupid to package it the right way. I was sick of seeing other Asian kids like myself walking to school with their heads down. I was sick of seeing them picking snow peas in the dining room after school and I was sick of not having a voice in America. The only Asian that I ever saw speak up for us was Miss Info on Hot 97 after the morning crew played a song making fun of the tsunami in Japan. My main objective with Baohaus was to become a voice for Asian Americans.* Whether you accept it or not, when you're a visible Asian you have a torch to carry because we simply don't have any other representation. About three weeks after opening, we were the number-one hot restaurant in New York on Yelp. I think Yelp is doo-doo, but it drove a lot of customers to the shop. Day after day, we kept running out of food by 9 P.M. We made more and more each day, but I was the only one that knew how to make the recipes and I simply didn't have the time or equipment to braise more than thirty pounds of pork and beef each day. I'd show up at 8 A.M., work till midnight, clean up till 2 A.M., and take the train back to Brooklyn. If I got home before three I was lucky. We finally realized that the smart thing to do would be to close for an entire day, take a break, get bigger pots and pans, and hire some employees. We wanted to make sure the people we hired fit the idea of Baohaus so we decided to use nontraditional ads that weeded people out for us. The first post we ever put up was titled:

Baohaus Hiring Multi-Tasking Nice People Who
Listen to Ghostface

* Important distinction. Note that I say "a voice" not "the voice." I don't speak for all Asian Americans, I speak for a few rotten bananas like me.

Surprisingly, we got an avalanche of resumes with subject lines like:

"I FUX WITH GHOSTFACE"

"I love multi-tasking AND Ghostface"

"RE: Baohaus hiring Ghostface listeners Tony Starks Pretty Toney n all of that . . ."

Our first hire was Asa Stella, an ex–Whole Foods cashier, bar mitzvah DJ, and Philly kid. He was exactly what we were looking for. Kid came in with fucked-up Adidas high-tops, random Japanese baseball jerseys from thrift shops, and a Phillies cap. We hired him on the spot. The second hire, and to this day my favorite Baohaus employee of all time, was Kate Francis. This was her cover letter:

Hello,

I am writing in response to your Craigslist ad posted on February 4th. My name is Kate and I'm a recent art history graduate from NYU. I also have a degree in Shaolin shadow-boxing aka I can go back and forth on the Wu and Killa Cam in his best years (IMO the pink-fur wearing image I saw on your blog ~ the time of Purple Haze). I live nearby on the LES and although I don't have experience in food service, I do love food in a very genuine, this tastes good and I like it way. I think Baohaus looks delicious. Pork is always great, and I'm stoked to see some Niman Ranch meat on the menu.

Since that ad, we've had others like these:

Are you the same one cryin' for that Billie Jean Jacket?

Date: 2010-10-18, 1:57PM EDT
Replay to: job-ftdzv-2012577118@craigslist.org

Cream still stack it
If the fiends still crack it

You the same one cryin' for that Billie Jean jacket?

If you like stackin' cream and fux wit Billie Jean, Baohaus is hiring.

137 Rivington St. Reply by email with resume. thanks.

Baohaus Hiring People Who Like Pyrex and Cavalli Furs (Lower East Side)

Date: 2010-04-06, 2:35PM EDT
Replay to: job-ftdzv-2012577118@craigslist.org

OK, we get it, yeah you, too...... I know, I know, yeah you, too ...
We ain't looking for Mr. Me Too ... We like people who like breakin' down
belly into buns and sell 'em like gobstoppers. Line resume in the belly of the
email. No attachments. Research Baohaus so you know what you are getting
into. No bum shit.

Strickly for My Astronauts (Lower East Side)

Date: 2010-12-10. 1:06PM EST
Reply to: job-Tdrien-2105691231@craigslist.org

Are you futuristic like puffy vests and moon boots? Do you like rollin' like a
big shot? Chevy tuned up like a NASCAR pit stop? Ice cream, Ice cream,
Ice cream paint job.

If you are cooler than a polar bear's toenails and want money stacks bigger
than mail order brides, Baohaus is for you. We are hiring. Holla back. 137
Rivington St. Include resume in the body of the email. Part of being an astro-
naut is that you get shit done and show up on time, so, if you want puffy vests
without putting in work, you should probably stand alone, gettin' dome from
a thick chick in sandals. #choncletas

To this day, my favorite ad was the one titled "Wanna Play Nintendo
with Caesar-Leo? Pick up the phone, deliver baos to your home." From
the overwhelming responses to the ads, it was becoming abundantly clear

that we were right all along. Despite my parents, other people's parents, and an industry of copycats, there was a genuine workforce and customer base that grew up on the ethos of golden-era hip-hop and wanted to do something positive in an honest, real, socially progressive way. We were a generation of people that listened to Ghostface, tried to impeach the president, and wanted all-natural, hormone- and antibiotic-free pork. Among the biggest influences on Baohaus were *Food, Inc.* and the Bauhaus school of design itself. I chose the name Baohaus because my favorite movement in architecture and design was Bauhaus. It stuck with me 'cause shit was simple, clean, masculine, and conscious. It wasn't aesthetically driven design; there was a mind to it, just like our Baohaus. We didn't have the money to design shit like Bauhaus, but just out of brokenness, the shit was undoubtedly simple if not clean.

Food, Inc. is one of the best documentaries ever made and really drove the ingredients at Baohaus. Food bloggers sometimes write that we're "Alice Waters disciples," but I ain't never ate her food. All I know is that she annoys the living shit out of the big homie, Tony Bourdain. We aren't "locavore chefs" or "farm to table" assholes trying to charge you a premium because we got ramps from some dickhead in a pickup truck. The reason we use all natural, hormone-free, antibiotic-free Berkshire pork belly, beef, and chicken is that it's the right thing to do. There are a lot of independent farms in the game and with restaurants like Baohaus and the aforementioned locavore joints, the food system is changing. I don't believe you need to shout out the farm, the name of the chicken, or all that other bullshit on the menu because it should simply be the standard that we serve all-natural meat. I hope that one day it will be economically feasible that we serve free-range chicken and grass-fed beef, but until customers vote with their dollars and support business models that can afford to use those ingredients, we can't. Customers feel like it's the restaurant's job to do these things, but it's a two-way street; as customers, we're enablers. Without us, it doesn't matter if the chef's heart is in the right place. Someone has to support the vision.

One of the biggest challenges we faced came from cheap-ass Taiwanese people. I remember one chick came up to me and said, "You know, these baos are a lot more expensive than Taiwan. In Taipei, they are much bigger and cost less than a dollar!"

"Well, why don't you buy a nine-hundred-dollar plane ticket and go buy yourself a one-dollar bao."

I had the ill flashback working at Baohaus. It was like Chinese school all over again with the small-minded, conservative Asians that couldn't understand shit if it wasn't in an SAT prep packet.

Evan, Asa, Kate, and I made a few decisions. Instead of appeasing customers or playing into their bullshit, we consulted Bill Cosby, who famously said, "I don't know the key to success, but the key to failure is trying to please everyone." We refused to carry hot sauce in the restaurant because it fucked up the flavor. We stuck to using all-natural meat and kept our prices right where they were. If people told us their grandmothers made it better, we'd tell them to set up shop across the street. At one point, people kept going on Yelp to complain about the no-hot-sauce policy and gave us one star for not accommodating customers. I decided one night to go online and respond by parodying the user and rating my "hot dick."

The comment: "OMFG, I fucking hate Baohaus and their hot sauce policy, but when I complained the owner hit me in the face with a hot dick. That shit was so delicious. 5 stars!"

That became the model for the Baohaus style of service: the Anti–Danny Meyer.

Music was also a huge part of the Baohaus experience. All of us made playlists, and numerous employees were either DJs, rappers, producers, or former street team kids. We almost never hired experienced cooks, because the goal was to create a team of artists who just happened to work at Baohaus while pursuing other dreams. It was a revolving door, but I wanted it that way. I hated growing up working at places like Boston Market that expected you to treat the job like it was your life. I'm cleaning chicken butts, motherfucker, this ain't a lifestyle, this is a cot damn problem! I wanted people to want more for themselves; I wasn't delusional and expected people to move on. If someone wanted to be a career cook, that was cool with me, too. I'd teach them what I knew, give them more responsibility, and they could stay as long as they liked. We've hired, fired, and reconciled, but over two years, we've tried our best to make the Haus a fun place to work.

That was another thing the neighborhood seemed to like. Late one night in the summer of 2010, Tyler, Jesse, myself, and some shawties from South Street Seaport stumbled into Baohaus around 10 P.M. on a Thursday. Usually, we waited till midnight to blaze, but we were so twisted, we posted up on the right side and just lit up. I remember this couple eating baos across from us who couldn't fucking believe it, but once we passed, they were down, too.

People started rolling up and it ended up two or three blunts being passed around. Downtown, a lot of people are up on papers, but Tyler and I being from the field, we really fucked with Phillies, shit got stank. As customers started walking in, we just told them, "We blazing so you can either get down or get it to go." Within minutes, the restaurant filled up and we had to lock the door. Mad people were out partying 'cause it was the summer and everyone tried to get in 'cause we had a glass storefront all hot-boxed. People took photos and by then it was a done deal. Baohaus was unlike any restaurant anyone had ever seen. We came in the game like NWA busting through the "I Have a Dream" banner and never listened to the haters. We don't wear chef coats, we wear Nikes, and Dipset is the anthem.

At the end of February, about two months after opening, we started getting reviews from every paper: *The Village Voice,* Serious Eats (what up, Joe DiStefano?), *Time Out,* etc. Shit was on and when *New York* magazine dropped their Best Cheap Eats issue, we won Best Bun 2010. In the battle for pork buns, Baohaus took it. The restaurant started getting really packed those days with lines fifteen or twenty deep on random Monday and Tuesday nights. Just when we thought things couldn't get better, they did.

In the first two weeks we opened, this white guy named Ahrin had come into the restaurant. One of my favorite customers all-time, he proved my assumptions about ex-pats wrong and it made me happy. This dude spent a lifetime traveling all across China, loved the food, culture, but most important, he understood that the people themselves were cultural artifacts. The last hundred years were the worst in Chinese history and Ahrin had met a lot of people who still remembered the pain despite all the growth and change currently happening. He spoke good conversational Chinese and we talked for at least an hour about food in Beijing. A while after Ahrin got there, his wife joined with their newborn. I didn't catch her name at the time, but they ordered everything on the menu. I sent them an order of Beijing Vinegar Peanuts on the house, but they insisted on paying. His wife was really nice, but ended up breastfeeding in the restaurant and didn't talk as much. I figure by this point, Baohaus has seen it all from breastfeeding to hot-boxing to freebasing out of a Mountain Dew can. You want it we got it. I didn't think anything of their visit beyond what it was: a nice family coming in for lunch and some milk.

A month later, we got a call. It was *The New York Times*. They were sending down a photographer because we were being featured in their $25 and Under column. We couldn't believe it. I didn't know what Serious Eats, *Time Out,* or Eater was at the time, but I knew what the motherfucking *New York Times* was. I made sure to have my "T-Bone Steak Cheese Eggs and Welsh's Grape" shirt cleaned, pressed, got a skin to one-and-a-half fade, and threw on my Jordan V Fire Reds. How many times you gonna be in the *Times,* right? If this was the first and last, I was goin' out in J-Vs no doubt. All red everythang, just like Mao. The day the review came out, I realized it was Ahrin and his wife, Ligaya, all along! To this day, that $25 and Under review has been our biggest moment. You can go online and see the article now. Ning is chewing food, Steve is in a scully, and Simon has glasses on. The review came out February 22, eight days after Chinese New Year 2010. We shut the shop down early, drank some Moutai, and called my parents.

"Dad! We're in *The New York Times*!"

"New York what?"

"The *Times,* Dad! It's the biggest newspaper in the world."

"It's not the biggest!"

"Whatever, maybe it's not the biggest, but it's pretty big. Just get *The New York Times* tomorrow, Dad. It's gonna be good."

Evan and I woke up late for work on the twenty-third like a bunch of assholes. We rolled up to 137 and there was already a line outside. Luckily, I had made the braise the night before so once it got heated up, we were ready to go.* Usually we just had two people on each shift, but it was a shitshow. The line just kept getting longer and longer. We called everyone in: Asa, Simon, Kate, any of our friends who were unemployed. It was all hands. At one point the line wrapped around the block thirty-some people deep. From 11 A.M. to 3 P.M., we had the whole block full, and around 3:30 P.M. it finally died down. I was still making baos for the customers in the shop, Evan was organizing receipts, and Kate was mopping up by the fridge. It was the craziest shift any of us had ever worked. People had taken Town Cars from work to eat baos and head back to Midtown, Brooklyn, Chelsea, etc. I'll never forget it. Kate leaned against the fridge. Blond hair flying everywhere, mop in hand, then turned to Evan and me. I had no idea what she had to say, but everything kinda stopped for a second.

"Guys! You realize what just happened?"

"What?"

She smiled at us with this funny look, nose wrinkled, freckles on front street, and said the nicest thing I've ever heard come out of a white woman's mouth.

"You fucking made it!"

Kate was right. Five days from my twenty-eighth birthday, I made it my way.

I told my parents the story, but they just shook me off like they always did. Even on that day, nothing impressed them and it hurt. I started to feel like I'd never make them happy, but I let it go. I had done everything I could. I found myself. I rehabilitated myself. I took every bit of Taiwanese-Chinese culture I'd mustered in twenty-seven years, three hundred and sixty days, and threw it into four hundred square feet of Lower East Side basement. It wasn't a palace, it wasn't even a dim sum parlor, but it was the best I could do and it made me happy even if my parents didn't get it. I realized that night that Cosby's line about pleasing people didn't just apply to strangers, but family, too. You only owe them so much and as

* For the record, braises are best done the night before and eaten the next day.

Asian Americans we have to break away at some point. For a lot of our parents, the World is not enough, but sometimes the *World Journal* is . . .

About two months after the *New York Times* article came out, I got a call from my mom at around 11 P.M. on a Wednesday night.

"EDDDIIIIEEEE! It's your mom!"

"Ha, ha, hey Mom! What's up?"

"What's up! Ha, ha, ha!!!"

"Mom, are you drunk?"

"I'm drunk!"

"What's going on!?!?! When'd you start drinking?"

"Your father opened EVERY bottle of wine and champagne in the house tonight!"

"Why, what happened?"

Dead silence . . .

"What? You don't know?"

"No, what happened? You won the lottery?"

"No, you dumb ass! You're in the *WORLD JOURNAL*!"*

———

MY PARENTS WERE Fresh Off the Boat, I'm a chinkstronaut, and my kids will be on spaceships. I didn't allow America to sell me in a box with presets and neither should you. Take the things from America that speak to you, that excite you, that inspire you, and be the Americans we all want to know; then cook it up and sell it back to them for $28.99. Cue Funk Flex to drop bombs on this. All my peoples from the boat, let 'em know: WEOUTCHEA.

* The *World Journal* is the preeminent newspaper for overseas Chinese people. It is distributed all around the world in Chinese groceries or bookstores and it's how most overseas Chinese people get their news. It's a linchpin of our communities.

ACKNOWLEDGMENTS

First, second, third, fourth, fifth, sixth, seventh, and eighth: I owe everything to my parents, Jessica and Louis Huang. They gave everything for me and my brothers. You can retire now, Dad, we done did it. Mom, stop smoking cigarettes, they cause cancer.

Lao Lao, Lao Ye, Nai Nai, Ye Ye, I still talk to you all the time. Thank you for protecting me and always reminding me to do the right thing even if it's more difficult. I see you.

In chronological order, all the Chink's men . . . and women, of course.

Emery, you were always my a a-like until you decided to stop wearing carpenter shants. Bring it back. This Jay Chou hair cut and tight shirt thing is not wuts really good. It's also very suspect that you have friends who are Scientologists, ha ha ha. Can't it be like back in the day? You know you want to hit Poseidon, eat Zuzu's burritos, listen to Master P, and wear beef 'n' brocs with shants to Chan's. I still remember that day you wore them with shorts laced up to Dad's big event at Chan's just to bug him out.

But, even if you decide to be a Scientologist wearing Armani Exchange the rest of your life, I support you in everything you do. Best memory I have of us is still that day Mom told you not to let the other kids in the basement take your food, so you squeezed the banana so hard that it was all over your hands when she came to pick you up. I'll always let you have the blue dinosaur, love you, brother.

Evan, I'm glad I still live with you, but let's make a deal. I'll stop peeing on the seat if you stop giving five stars to shitty movies on Netflix, because it keeps recommending that I watch *Rio* and *Madagascar*. Do you just search for movies with motherfucking George Lopez toucans and shit? Even though you like animated films with tropical animals, we can both agree that *Angry Boys* is the greatest shit America won't let us watch. Don't forget to always stay focused, finish strong, and expect everything that can go wrong to go wrong. Be prepared, don't half step, you have to want it more than the next guy or he'll eat your lunch, kid. It's a jungle out there. Baohaus Spaceships coming 2013, let's go!

The Vano family: Mr. Vano, Mrs. Vano, Joey, Carl, thanks for all the Vienna Sausage.

The Neilson family: you know I don't believe in God, but if there is a big homie in the sky, she/he got you! All praise be to Mrs. Trista Neilson. You were my second mom and we'll always remember you. Warren, Logan, Stewart, Justin, Mr. Neilson, thank you.

Romaen, Austin, Justin, Jared = A-Team WHAT.

Ning-Hsin Juang, you changed my life. I'd never be who I am if I didn't meet you. From living in a four-hundred-square-foot alcove studio with boxes of T-shirts and sneakers to watching me run sour out of our row house apartment, you were always there doing the nose wrinkle. . . . When you get scared, close your eyes and tell yourself that VICTORY IS IN YOUR CLUTCHES. You can do anything you want, boo. I believe in you. Also, don't let Gizmo eat her own poop; she'll never break through the Alpo ceiling doing hood shit like that. P.S. If Rasheed Wallace didn't wear Air Force 1 bricks, he would have been better than Tim Duncan.

Doug Mother-Fucking Van Sickle, you crazy wooden-shoe-wearing asshole, I couldn't put any of our college stories in this book, but no one needs to hear about you tossing toy cop golf carts or sunburning yourself to death like Kramer. Thank you for always holding me down even when everyone told you I had mental SARS. Love you like I've never loved a white man before, pause.

Steven Lau, you taught me what it is to be a real friend. When I was dead broke, you paid my rent, gave me $ for dollar dumplings, and never said a word when I started buying Jordans instead of paying you back for eight months. Take that Bluetooth off and wipe your lips, god. I'd shout out your shawty, but you gonna love a new one in three months cause you love being in love, motherfucker, CLOSE YOUR LEGS, B!!! Ha, ha, ha.

Rafael Martinez IS THE PRINCE OF BROOKLYN. GOON SQUAD.

Roberto Martinez is the hardest preemie baby in the streets.

Jon Marks is a slave name; I ride for Koncept Sparkz!!! Send gummy bears from Germany or you're dead to me. Manischewitz and Iced Vodka = Grape Mad Dog.

Stephane Adam, thank you for getting me through law school and saving Gizmo's life.

Jesse Hofrichter is Woody Allen's mental doppelganger. His brain is a dog trying to eat its own tail, but Uncle Jesse is a lovable lovable creature that the world needs. Peace, love, and jazzmatazz dun. UBL for life.

Kenzo Digital, you the most powerful ninja in the universe I know! Sometimes I feel like you got the infinity gauntlet or some shit, b. This book doesn't happen without you pushing me to always do me regardless what these parasites think. It's been surreal meeting someone that has a mission in life like we do. Can't stop, won't stop. I'ma BUST YOUR ASS in 2K13 when it comes out!!! You can't stop that Monta Ellis flow. I don't even like Japanese people, but I love you kid!!! Jordan 11s look good on this chinkstronaut, thanks, homie.

Mary HK Choi, shouts to our singular brain.

Follow @heyphilchang.

Master David Laven, you pretty fucking Indian.

Eddy Moretti, let's ride on these punks trying to feed the kids soma. Eat good, smoke good, read good. #Vice

Marc Gerald, you are my sunshine!!! It makes me happy every time I see you with your Chinese flash cards. Glad you are learning the greatest language in the world and continuing the Chinese-Jewish narrative that makes the world a better place ha, ha, ha. You believed in me when others didn't, you defend me when they try to co-opt me, and you support all my crazy endeavors. I've never seen you as an agent because you're family. First of many . . .

Julie Grau, ha, ha, ha . . . <<<I'll send one every day the rest of my life if that's really what you want ;). Even though Jackson never got me those Yeezy 2s, he'll always be a celebrity at Baohaus. Tell Junot, I GOT HIM, ha, ha, ha.

Cindy Spiegel, thanks for making this all come true. Hopefully, my five-hour edit sessions next door with Chris didn't drive you crazy. I RIDE FOR SPIEGEL AND GRAU.

Dr. O'Sullivan, I'm gonna git you sucka.

Dr. Jones, thank you for teaching me that communication is not about berating people, it's about listening, learning, and THEN convincing. . . .

Dr. Boles . . . bitch, please. Eat those chocolates, hold that umbrella, start that fire, Hitchcock life. *Royal Tenenbaums*: two thumbs up. *Memento*: four Siamese thumbs down. Wait, do Siamese twins have four thumbs? I don't think so, but you get the point.

Dr. Henton, STAY MAD! Just kidding, but not really. You gave me the confidence to speak my mind 100 percent, and I'll never forget it. Much love as always. You're the best in my book. Always.

Charlie, I love how you clean up all the messes I create with such precision, but you really need to start chipping in on the pizza parties at The Door. Poor Peter is never going to get his superhero condom company off the ground paying for pizza.

Caroline, stay Italian. Love the denim vest, love the hair, love the shoes. Look good, smell good, eat good. We gonna look really good in private spaceships this year. Keep doing it, boo.

Michella, sorry I mispronounced your name for five months, but thank you for putting every Knick game in my calendar.

Josh and Amir, the Lakers suck, but y'all are ok.

Lastly, Chris Jackson. What more can I say? You pushed me to dig deep and talk about things that were uncomfortable, ignited revelations that took thirty years to uncover, and never judged me. You are living proof that we need more voices of color not only in publishing, but America. You're more than that, though. . . . Your sentiments transcend color and I benefited from your ability to see things objectively at the core. Going over pages, you never let me off the hook with cop-outs just 'cause they sounded good. Others used to let me bamboozle them, but with you it was game recognize game. You'd already seen my tricks. Like Bruce Lee shadow boxing his image in the mirror, you forced me to see myself and break through the plaster mask.

You are exactly what I needed and never had. You didn't get caught in the show and shot me through the heart when I tried to slip away. It took twenty-nine years to meet someone who wanted to go to war every single day between the margins, and we did it with a singular mind. It takes a village to shoot the fair one and you were my village on this track. Rotten bananas forever.

EDDIE HUANG is the proprietor of Baohaus.

He lives and works in New York.